Buildings of the Scottish Countryside

Buildings of the Scottish Countryside

Robert J. Naismith
for The Countryside Commission for Scotland

London
Victor Gollancz Ltd
in association with
Peter Crawley
1989

To Sir Frank Mears

First published in Great Britain 1985
by Victor Gollancz Ltd,
14 Henrietta Street, London WC2E 8QJ

First published in Gollancz Paperbacks 1989

British Library Cataloguing in Publication Data
Naismith, Robert J.
   Buildings of the Scottish countryside
   1. Scotland. Rural regions. Vernacular
   buildings. Architectural features
   I. Title
   720′.9411

   ISBN 0-575-04520-5

Designed by Harold Bartram
Filmset and printed in Great Britain
by BAS Printers Limited, Over Wallop, Hampshire

Contents

Illustrations

Photographs

1   Croft near Braemar, Auchallater   PSC
2   Cromarty   PSC
3   Strathy Point, Sutherland
4   Stromness, Orkney
5   Coldstream, Berwickshire   PSC
6   Auchindrain, Argyll   NMR AG 390
7   Burn of Cambus, Perthshire
8   Finigand Farm, Glenshee, Perthshire   PSC
9   Stair Inn, Ayrshire
10   Huxter, Shetland
11   Torthorwald, Dumfriesshire   PSC
12   Coldstream, Berwickshire   PSC
13   Dunblane, Perthshire   PSC
14   Achamore, Gigha, Argyll
15   Begbie Farm, East Lothian
16   Pittenweem, Fife   PSC
17   Kirbister Mill, Orkney   RSM
18   Dunblane, Perthshire   PSC
19   Dirleton, East Lothian   PSC
20   Biggar, Lanarkshire   PSC
21   Findochty, Banffshire
22   Gatehouse of Fleet, Kirkcudbrightshire   PSC
23   Ullapool, Ross and Cromarty   PSC
24   Milton, Ross and Cromarty
25   New Deer, Aberdeenshire   PSC
26   Monymusk, Aberdeenshire   PSC
27   Torrovaich, Caithness
28   Delgaty Castle Farm, Aberdeenshire
29   Dairsie, Fife   PSC
30   Aberdour, Fife
31   East Saltoun, East Lothian
32   Ascog, Bute
33   Port William, Wigtownshire
34   Burnside, Nairn
35   Callands Farm, Peebles
36   Dunblane, Perthshire   PSC
37   Toberonochy, Luing Island
38   Eaglesham, Renfrewshire   PSC
39   Hopeman, Moray
40   Eaglesham, Renfrewshire   PSC
41   Biggar, Lanarkshire   PSC
42   Pittenweem, Fife   PSC
43   Glachavoil, Argyll
44   Berriedale, Caithness   RSM
45   Nethershield, Ayrshire
46   The Holme, Kirkcudbrightshire

47 Freswick, Caithness
48 Ballindalloch, Banffshire
49 Inverquhomery, Aberdeenshire
50 Mouswald Grange, Dumfriesshire   PSC
51 Strathpeffer, Ross and Cromarty   PSC
52 Gatehouse of Fleet, Kirkcudbrightshire   PSC
53 Sanquhar, Dumfriesshire
54 Oban, Harris
55 Boleside, Selkirkshire
56 Wigtown   PSC
57 Insch, Aberdeenshire
58 Cairnryan, Wigtownshire
59 Gatehouse of Fleet, Kirkcudbrightshire   PSC
60 Dirleton, East Lothian   PSC
61 Sordale, Caithness
62 Eaglesham, Renfrewshire   PSC
63 Kirkcudbright   PSC
64 Pittenweem, Fife   PSC
65 Dirleton, East Lothian   PSC
66 Eaglesham, Renfrewshire   PSC
67 Bridgend, Argyll
68 Stonefold Farm, Berwickshire
69 Highfield Farm, West Dunbartonshire
    (West of Loch Lomond)
70 Marybank, Ross and Cromarty   PSC
71 Moffat, Dumfriesshire   PSC
72 Gatehouse of Fleet, Kirkcudbrightshire   PSC
73 Crumblands, Midlothian
74 Earlston, Berwickshire
75 Lennel, Berwickshire
76 Old Philipstoun, West Lothian
77 Barns, Peebleshire
78 Melrose, Roxburghshire
79 Gattonside, Roxburghshire
80 Melrose, Roxburghshire
81 Newstead, Roxburghshire
82 Union Place, Moffat, Dumfriesshire   PSC
83 Ecclefechan, Dumfriesshire
84 Billies, Kirkcudbrightshire
85 Dalrymple, Ayrshire
86 Fenwick, Ayrshire
87 Cairnwhin Farm, Ayrshire
88 Skeoch Farm, Tarbolton, Ayrshire
89 New Mains, Lanarkshire
90 Biggar, Lanarkshire   PSC
91 Bowling, Dunbartonshire
92 Thorntonhall, Lanarkshire
93 Bankfoot, Renfrewshire

Key to photographs

NMR – National Monuments Record
RSM – Robert Scott Morton
PSC – Peter Crawley
All other photographs were taken by the staff of Sir Frank Mears & Partners

Foreword

The duties of the Countryside Commission for Scotland are to protect the amenity of the nation's fine landscapes and to assist people to enjoy the countryside for recreation. How does architecture come into this picture? As an organisation we are not concerned with buildings for their own sake, but they affect the amenity of the countryside and so we seek to ensure high standards of design, the aim being that each building should be as good as its surroundings. This is a question of harmony and the proper fit of parts, and the builders of old seem to have known the secret of this art.

This book is an attempt to make people more aware of the enduring qualities of the legacy left by these rural builders. Those of us who are fortunate enough to live in the countryside know the charm of this heritage, which pleases the eye and tells the story of Man's imprint on the natural environment. The Commission believes that these often undervalued buildings should be protected and that there is a need for careful husbandry of a unique national resource.

In his foreword to the first edition my predecessor, Sir David Nickson, explained the reasons for the Commission's sponsorship of it. He expressed his confidence that the author had struck the right balance between information of use and interest to architects, planners and builders, and that which would interest the lay reader. How successfully this was achieved has been illustrated by the demand for the book and by the decision to publish this paperback edition.

It is my view that the three most important issues facing all who are concerned with the conservation and development of Scotland's countryside in the foreseeable future are: firstly, a strategic approach to all rural land use; secondly, a revitalisation of rural communities; and, thirdly and most importantly, improved design. To consider properly all three we must learn from and draw on past experience. To this end the content and wider availability of this book will make an essential contribution. I commend it and wish it all success.

J. Roger Carr
Chairman
Countryside Commission for Scotland
Perth, 1989

Author's acknowledgements

This publication was made possible by the initiative of the Countryside Commission for Scotland and the support of its Director, John Foster, and his staff, especially Jan Magnus Fladmark, Assistant Director, who tirelessly applied his considerable abilities at every stage of the survey and in the production of this book, providing a writing collaboration through which it became a reality.

The author also acknowledges the loyal support of the Partners and staff of Sir Frank Mears and Partners, particularly the professional skills and diligence of Douglas Read, Margaret Macdonald, Anne McKay and Jeanette Saunders. The analytical abilities of staff of the Planning Data Management Service at the University of Edinburgh who dealt with the formidable statistical tasks, were indispensable, as was the advice of Mr. Robert Scott Morton on farm buildings. Dr. Brunskill kindly read the text and made valuable recommendations.

The photographs selected from the collection produced by the staff of Sir Frank Mears and Partners have been supplemented by prints from Robert Scott Morton and the National Monuments Record as well as a number of impressive examples taken by Peter Crawley, many of which show the buildings in their setting.

Maps II and III are reproduced from the 1901–1923 Ordnance Survey.

The line drawings are by the author, except for the first six which were the work of members of his staff and include the drawing on page 23 from *Royal Valley* by the late Fenton Wyness, reproduced by the kind permission of the author's Trustees.

Thanks are due for the tolerant understanding of 23,500 or so owners and occupiers who permitted the surveying of their properties. Lastly, but above all else, tribute is accorded to the masons, joiners, slaters, plasterers and blacksmiths who, with little reward other than the satisfaction of work well done, made these buildings for the lasting satisfaction of the generations who have followed.

Robert J. Naismith
Edinburgh, 1984

Introduction

There are many aspects to the rapidly developing interest in the buildings of the countryside and small towns of Britain and of many other parts of the world. For some the interest is mainly pictorial, the cottages and farmhouses, barns and windmills being seen as incidents in the landscape, contrasting with the works of nature, giving point and focus to the other works of man. For others, the interest is mainly historical, these same buildings representing historical evidence which, with documents and aural collections, help the historian to understand as well as to explain the ways in which town and countryside have developed. For yet others the interest is archaeological, geographical or cultural generally. The buildings have often been held to define and represent national, regional or local character.

Studies of these minor or vernacular buildings have been made at the parish or county levels and even one or two at the national level but so far they have generally had an archaeological, historical or geographical basis. None has attempted to establish architectural character. Like a rainbow or a will o' the wisp which can be seen and recognised but defined only in terms of physics or optics, architectural character is easy to see, difficult to define and more difficult to capture and re-create. The components of architectural character are based quite obviously to a large extent on the plan and cross-section of a building, determined in turn by the intended use for which it was designed. But the character comes equally from wall and roofing materials, from the architectural details of doorways, windows, chimney stacks and so on, and from the proportions of plan and cross-section which are reflected in the outward appearance of the building and especially in its main elevation. The architects of the present day make good proportions the aim in their designs and we have no reason to doubt that their predecessors, whether practising under such a style or not, were any less sensitive.

Buildings of the Scottish Countryside is based on systematic fieldwork systematically analysed. The survey on which the book was based was a sample survey taking the buildings as they are, not selecting (as in official 'listing') those which appear to be of special architectural or historical importance. The analysis was one which used the impartial computer to extract and map the results as they emerged at equal density all over Scotland, unaffected by social or economic bias.

The survey was based on external observation of the buildings with a limited time available for the surveyors at the more than 23,000 sites visited. Comparable work in other parts of Britain and in other rather sparsely settled Northern countries meant that the possibilities and limitations of survey by this means were appreciated. More detailed work by scholars in the study of Scottish buildings meant that the appropriate questions were asked by way of visual questionnaire. Although observations were facilitated and standardised in the survey

1. Croft near Braemar, Auchallater

procedure, archaeological study was impracticable and some unanticipated questions may have been raised as the survey proceeded. But in the circumstances of the building revolution which occurred throughout Scotland during the eighteenth and nineteenth centuries this sort of study was rewarding to an extent which would have been much more difficult to attain in England and Wales, where building revolutions were both more frequent and less comprehensive.

The results of the survey and analysis demonstrated the Scottish national character in buildings of the small towns and countryside through proportions, architectural details and constructional materials. The method of collecting field information and the analytical technique have enabled the author to establish the simple proportional rules observed by the designers in producing the elevations of their buildings. The method and technique have made it possible to isolate certain of the architectural details – those of dormer windows for example – which are so significant in these simple buildings. The variety of detailed constructional materials in a country so predominantly of stone and slate has been revealed through the survey. The technique of analysis has made it possible to establish from the survey a dozen or so 'character zones' on the mainland of Scotland with a few more in the island groups. Here national characteristics have been modified to produce the sub-regional or local variations, numerous in areas of relatively dense settlement, few in the highland and island areas of more sparse settlement. The result is a systematic guide to local style such as has not been produced in quite this way for any other part of the British Isles.

The result will benefit all who are interested in the Scottish countryside. Architects will understand to an extent not possible before in what context they are proposing to build. Academics, whether historians or geographers, folk students or students of recent archaeology will have a new context in which to set their work. But above all those who know and love the Scottish countryside whether as residents or visitors will be able the better to understand what they appreciate and one hopes that with greater understanding will come even greater appreciation.

R. W. Brunskill
August 1984

1 The survey and other sources

In 1979 the Countryside Commission for Scotland decided to initiate and sponsor one of the most detailed surveys of traditional building ever made in any country. Its scope was to range over the whole of the Scottish countryside. The object was to seek out the national character of this tradition and to reveal the local characteristics which lie embedded within.

Most of the buildings covered by the survey were built between 1750 and 1914. About one-quarter were dispersed rather than gathered in villages and hamlets. In most other European countries villages had been developed from early times, fostering conditions for local varieties of styles and character to take root around tightly built communities. Such circumstances produced the beautiful historic villages of England which seem to possess characteristics that are readily recognisable as being uniquely local. Although the eighteenth-century renaissance brought many new towns and villages to the Scottish countryside, the older tradition of isolated single buildings or small groups has endured to this day. Thus it is not so easy to assess Scottish country building by walking down village streets, as can be done in parts of England, where all the buildings are laid out conveniently like pictures in a gallery.

Full assimilation of the varieties of building character in the Scottish countryside has been difficult to achieve until recently because of this isolation and wide distribution. Now the availability of new techniques of data handling and analysis has made the task easier. Just as modern science has afforded new views and aspects of the earth and planets, so computer methods have enabled a truer and wider vision of regional variations in building tradition to be obtained than was previously possible – as well as enabling the view to be trained into sharp focus on any particular aspect of the subject in close detail. However, the survey was not made so much in anticipation of finding unknown buildings as in an endeavour to study buildings in both a comprehensive and an individual sense – in short to discover basic characteristics as well as the extent of regional variety.

23,500 small buildings taken at random in a ratio of about 1:10 were examined, recorded and photographed. Large buildings, mansion houses and churches were excluded. The end of the period under investigation was set at 1914 because most buildings up to that time had been the product of local designers employing local materials. Buildings erected after this were less influenced by local tradition because of new building methods and because they were governed to a much greater extent by centrally-evolved controls of design which tended to result in suburban rather than rural architecture. So this volume, like the survey, concentrates on houses, farms, village schools, mills, village halls, inns, gatehouses, shops and other small-scale rural buildings.

All of Scotland except a few of the more inaccessible islands was embraced in the survey, and burghs and towns up to a population of about 2,200 were included for investigation. The study was entirely concerned with external appearance and accordingly this book does not deal with aspects of internal layout and decoration.

The discoveries set out in this volume have been derived from the inexorable procedures of the computer. It has sifted and digested vast numbers of coded items and brought forth a profusion of maps and statistics. The book does not attempt to exhibit these productions which are preserved elsewhere for study by experts.* The computer has not made any value judgements or entered into literary composition. For these the author and editorial advisers accept all responsibility.

In the preparation of this book, the writer has drawn on many related texts previously published. These are listed in the bibliography, but special mention of some key sources may be useful to the reader as well as serving the author's desire to acknowledge the help and inspiration derived from the work of others who have ploughed the same furrows before him.

The books by Sir John Stirling-Maxwell, in 1937, and by John Dunbar, in 1966, still stand as the most comprehensive general texts on Scottish architecture. Although their books are concerned with the full spectrum of building types, including the grand monuments so well recorded, they both deal with domestic-type rural buildings in some detail. Ronald Brunskill is one of the leading writers on vernacular buildings in Britain but, among those in Scotland who have specialised in this field of study, Alexander Fenton and Bruce Walker stand out because of their valuable contributions. In particular, their joint book *The Rural Architecture of Scotland*, is indispensable for serious students as is Robert Scott Morton's *Traditional Farm Architecture in Scotland*. The activities of the Scottish Vernacular Buildings Working Group have been instrumental in the production of a series of authoritative publications on the study and recording of rural building traditions. On a broader canvas, the historical background is covered by the papers published in *The Making of the Scottish Countryside*, edited by M. L. Parry and T. R. Slater. Finally, those wishing to delve into more detailed study of what follows in the next chapter, will of course turn to Christopher Smout's classic: *A History of the Scottish People 1560–1830*.

*The field records of the survey and copies of the computer print out from the analysis are incorporated in the collection of the National Monuments Record which is held by the Royal Commission on the Ancient and Historical Monuments of Scotland.

The background

2   The changes after 1750

Buildings are more than a response to the needs of shelter for living, work and leisure. Their design has an extra factor reflecting the essence of contemporary experience and aspiration. In this compound, the past as much as the aims for the future, become inescapably mixed. In order to appreciate building as architecture, an understanding of the background of the times which produced it is necessary. The buildings dealt with in this book are mostly products of the stimulating age in eighteenth- and nineteenth-century Scotland when every aspect of human affairs was being subjected to vigorous intellectual application and imaginative reappraisal. This urge energised the minds of all sections of the community and in every part of the land. It was a time when ploughmen became poets, and poor scholars, philosophers. While Scots of international standing were receiving world acclaim for their architectural design, rural builders were in their own independent way producing the architecture of the Scottish countryside. In the matter of style, the architecture was of a consistency in its attention to proportion and craftsmanship to leave a heritage still worthy of care and attention.

The making of any style springs from intellectual forces. National style emerges when a whole people is inspired and motivated by the same aims in taste and artistic sensibility. In order to understand the style of any period it is necessary to appreciate, along with the practical considerations, the dominating causes and the preceding conditions which these causes set out to change. The re-building in Scotland's countryside happens to be a subject that can be submitted to such examination with the reward of learning how a small nation can transform in every way the material, social and artistic life of its people. In terms of practical value, comprehension of this past achievement could guide builders in the present towards the promotion of a new Scottish style of the future.

The influence of the burghs and towns
Before the Industrial Revolution, most Scottish burghs and the countryside were joined in social and commercial dependence. Only in the late nineteenth century did the process of independence of industrial development introduce the sharp divisions between town and country attitudes. The rebuilding of the country burghs began for practical as well as social reasons in the late seventeenth century. Many towns introduced new styles and techniques, some of which were soon reflected in the rebuilding of farms, cottages and manses in the surrounding countryside. The first wave of new villages, small towns and town extensions soon fired the energy and imagination of landowners and townsmen alike, and this early awakening can be regarded as the beginning of unifying ideas acting between small towns and the countryside.

The architecture of country buildings after the mid-eighteenth century was

2. Cromarty

as rich and abundant as the new agriculture which accompanied it. Both events changed the face of the countryside. Before this Scotland had mostly concentrated its architectural genius on town and city building and in the tower houses. The majority of country people were left to survive in primitive structures of clay or rough stone walls, windowless and roofed with timbers straight from the tree and covered with thatch (3). The emerging style, however, was influenced as much by the older buildings in the cities, burghs and the countryside as by the new ideas which were refashioning it.

The dominance of the Scottish burghs in commerce obliged the countryman to sell his products at their markets and so the older buildings in the high streets and market places would be widely known. It happens that prior to the new building in the countryside, conditions in the burghs were exercising the minds of the authorities. Evidence exists to show that various burghs had become aware of the desirability of improving the condition of buildings within their boundaries. It started with orders to have the older decaying buildings removed. Stirling passed an order in 1671 that all ruinous houses were to be taken down and destroyed. In 1692 Ayr recorded that there were 140 'waste' houses and 'several ruinous'. Brechin, as late as 1762, issued a prohibition on retaining houses with thatch and wood chimney vents. New houses were to have slated or tiled roofs and stone chimney vents. Defoe, with sarcastic wit, described Dysart in Fife in 1724 as 'A town in the full perfection of decay'. In the late seventeenth century, Glasgow was making grants for the rebuilding of houses in broached stonework or ashlar.

The authorities were concerned with the continuation of the former custom of building in timber and especially of roofing in thatch. The extent of the

3. *Above right* Strathy Point, Sutherland

4. *Right* Stromness, Orkney

Fife's thatched buildings make up new field project

BY DAWN RENTON
dawn.renton@press.co.uk
Twitter: @ffpDawn

Fife's historic, traditional thatched buildings have been recorded for the very first time as part of a unique field work project.

They feature in the report, 'A Survey of Thatched Buildings in Scotland', a full-colour photographic survey of every thatched building across the country – which includes 17 in the Kingdom.

This new resource helps to build a full picture of this important part of Scotland's vernacular built heritage.

As well as containing locations, photographs and information on the type of thatch, the different techniques and

its condition, it also offers an insight into the building itself, with details and stories from the owners or occupiers being featured in a number of the records.

This initiative, the first of its kind, is a partnership between The Society for the Protection of Ancient Buildings (SPAB), who carried out the survey, and Historic Environment Scotland, who grant funded the project.

Colin Tennant, head of technical education and training at Historic Environment Scotland, said: "Thatched buildings are an iconic part of our heritage – and Scotland's wider historic environment – particularly in some of our rural areas.

"They form a unique part of our diverse built heritage and culture, providing a real

insight into the craft skills and traditional practices of our past."

Matthew Slocombe, director of the Society for the Protection of Ancient Buildings, added: "These buildings are quintessentially Scottish and their historic value is immense.

"Yet perhaps because they are humble working structures or perhaps because of the very way they were built – lying low to protect and shield their former occupants – we have allowed them to slowly vanish from the radar.

"This survey will pay an important part in helping to safeguard and understand these valuable and iconic buildings."

Thatch was the first roofing material used in Scotland, and the country has one of the most diverse ranges

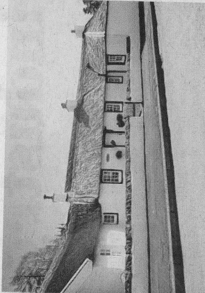

Collessie's Wee Hoose features in the survey.

of thatching materials and techniques found in Europe.

It is hoped that the findings from the survey will help contribute towards a better understanding of thatch traditions, its survival and protection, whilst

promoting the craft skills involved in the process and overall helping to inform the future of thatched building conservation in Scotland.

The survey can be found at www.historicenvironment.scot.

7.10.2016

tality get a taste e industry

time jobs.

As well as gaining insights into the wide range of career opportunities offered by the hospitality, leisure and tourism industries the young people built on their enterprise skills by getting experience of creating and making their own mocktails and hands-on experience of being a choco-latier.

The event included ice-cream demonstrations, pitching their skills against one another in a housekeeping challenge, as well as marketing and public relations to name a few of the challenges.

Pamela Stevenson, lead officer of Fife Council's eco-nomic development team, said: "Taste the Industry is a

"Through the Culture of Enterprise, we've been able to create opportunities for young people to build on their enterprise skills and gain in-sights into the world of work. These programmes build on strengthening work being down to support the Devel-oping the Young Workforce agenda."

Karen Manders, depute head teacher at Bell Baxter, said: "The Taste the Industry event held at Bell Baxter today was a wonderful piece of col-laborative working which has opened up the eyes of young-sters from both Bell Baxter High School and Waid Acad-emy to all aspects of the hos-pitality industry.

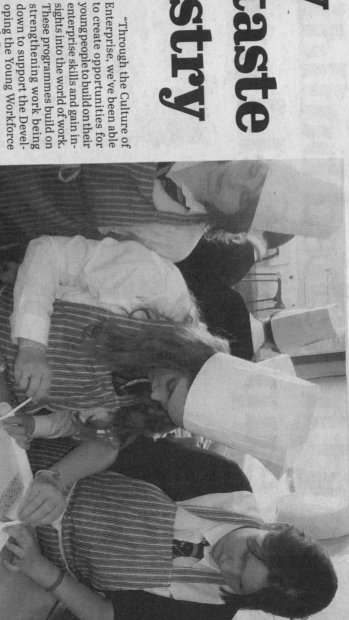

School pupils put their enterprise skills to the test.

youngsters whilst developing tomorrows workforce."

Stephanie Wade, director of Tennent's Training Acad-emy, added: "I've worked in the hospitality industry since I was at school. It's a great way

rewarding fast paced career.

"There are a whole host of opportunities on offer in every corner of the world, from jobs in tropical beach resorts in the world's most remote islands, to high flying (and paying) ex-ecutive director or closing every

out of a determination to change the perceptions of our industry and it starts with young people, right here in Scotland.

"Scotland has growing tourism industry and em-ployers need new talent to

use of timber framing in town houses in seventeenth-century Scotland has not yet been fully investigated. The prevalence of thatch, however, is well documented. In the seventeenth century there were many houses in Inverness built of drystane walls and turf supporting low thatch roofs. The same town at that time also had some houses described as 'miserable hovels covered with turf and a bottomless tuber basket in the roof for a chimney'. By the end of the eighteenth century, there still existed thatched houses in the suburbs. Rutherglen's last thatched house remained until 1837. Even Dunfermline, where slate had been used for roofs from the late fifteenth century, possessed in the eighteenth century houses partially of timber, heath and 'furze' roofs. Brechin got rid of its last thatched house in 1810. The danger of thatch was spectacularly demonstrated when, in 1624, Dunfermline was nearly totally

5. Coldstream, Berwickshire

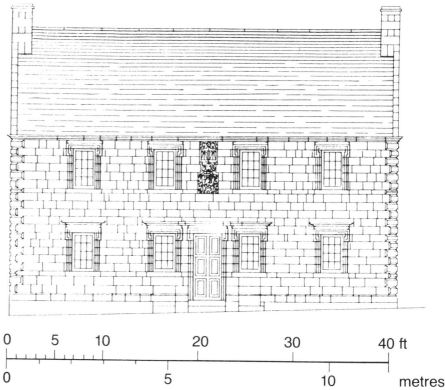

destroyed by a fire started by a boy shooting a pistol at the roof of a thatched house. Only a few slated houses escaped.

The awakening of a more expectant mood in burgh building also moved the authorities in the eighteenth century towards more than the protection of buildings from fire. People began to disapprove of the style of building. Rightly or not, the streets of Montrose in 1760 were criticised because the houses were 'in that bad style of building with the gable ends to the street'. This observation is revealing because it betrays a departure from the traditional northern European style of considerable antiquity (4) to placing the broad facade to the street as favoured in the south since the renaissance.

When Dunfermline in 1752 planned a new street, the council claimed that with houses on both sides it would be a great ornament to the town. In 1734, Montrose had adopted a proposal to demolish the middle row of buildings running up the centre of High Street. The council took this decision 'for beautifying the town'. In 1684, when Milne proposed the building in Edinburgh of the court bearing his name, he claimed it might prove to the 'decorment of the town'. In recent times we have proposed demolition only for the needs of 'development'.

The conditions and events in the burghs which led up to the earliest rebuilding in the countryside began in the mid-eighteenth century and they may be summarised as follows:

(1)   many of the burghs still contained the older style of buildings with thatched roof and with timber or stone and turf walls;

(2)   the hazard of fire had prompted authorities to make orders prohibiting the use of thatch and sometimes other materials such as turf and timber in new building or for rebuilding;

(3)   the beginning of the eighteenth century witnessed a new attitude to the design and appearance of buildings; and

(4)   the new styles adopted did not follow the traditional style of street architecture which had evolved since mediaeval times, in the form of gable ends placed towards the street.

A precursor to the new style was built by the late seventeenth-century architect, Tobias Bauchop, for his own house in Alloa (d.1). The classical approach in his work was displayed in this house, which must have looked very modern when built in 1695, and the countryside buildings of fifty years on had a close affinity with it. Unfortunately, this building was not given a grant by the appropriate bodies about twenty years ago when prompt attention could have been of great service in its preservation, but had to await almost to the point of demolition before substantial aid became necessary to save it.

The great Georgian building schemes in Edinburgh started at Brown Square and, later in 1766, at George Square. Other towns also started new town building in the late eighteenth century, such as Stonehaven, Perth and Stirling. The significant point about these new-style building activities is the fact that they were concurrent with the start of the rebuilding in the countryside. The spirit that drove on the townsman was the same as that which impelled the countryman. The driving force which created the new urban buildings was also producing the new agriculture, the new philosophy, the great school of Scottish painters, the poetry, the novels, the advances in medicine, science and industry. The builders of the new countryside were certainly not merely the camp followers of the pioneers of the resplendent urban facades. No doubt, there was as much movement of craftsmen between town and country then as there is today. There were certainly some cases of notable architects, who were engaged in the new towns also advising on country estate and rural building. Nevertheless, the whole building enterprise was part of one single movement wherein, in building terms neither country nor town came second.

Countryside buildings before the mid-eighteenth century, apart from

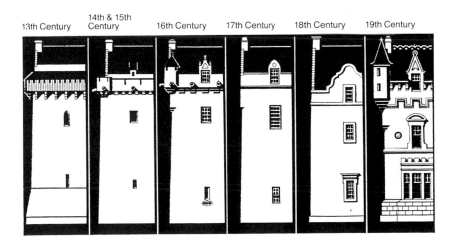

13th Century   14th & 15th Century   16th Century   17th Century   18th Century   19th Century

d1. Tobias Bauchop's house

d2. The evolution of the Scottish tower house (after F. Wyness)

churches, consisted generally of the laird's tower house, the farms and small houses. The country people in the eighteenth century had hard before them, in most parts of Scotland, examples of the tower house (d.2). The areas where these were least found, were on the mainland in Inverness-shire and in parts of Ross-shire. Some had been in existence then only a little more than a century but others were of a much older foundation. These houses showed how stone could be built and how it would last. Some of the tower houses were also altered and added to during the eighteenth century. Their chief characteristic was strength and solidity, but they had other features which could not be easily cast from the mind. They were invariably built in stone and sometimes harled. The grandest had pitched roofs of thick stone slabs but many were slated. Chimneys were prominent and dormer windows frequently seen. The principal windows were vertical and built with rybats. Door openings tended to be wide and low. Gables were usual. Screen walls, where they had been introduced, possessed large arch-topped gateways. The masons of these great towers often built with square ashlar, but in areas where local stone was unsuitable they adopted the techniques of rubble construction. The French influence could be seen in turrets and tall conical roofs.

When the country builders came to build the farms and small houses in the mid-eighteenth century, nearly every domestic feature of these tower houses was borrowed but put together to meet the needs of domesticity rather than of defence. These tall houses were richly and uniquely Scottish. By repeating much of their detail, the buildings of the countryside, erected in the late eighteenth and nineteenth centuries, kept to an unmistakable national tradition while reforming the architecture into a new style without any loss of either. In this, the countryside differed from the towns and cities. The grand facades of the new exteriors in the large urban centres broke with tradition to such an extent that the older national style was virtually submerged in the continental styles based on Roman architecture. Pevsner declared that he could see nothing Scottish in the New Town of Edinburgh and that it would look equally at home in London. He certainly could not have been taken round to the backs of the grand crescents and streets to see the rubble walls, the projecting round-ended rooms and the irregular fenestration, nor could he have considered the near turnpike style of internal staircases.

As described and illustrated by Colin McWilliam in *Scottish Townscape*, the towns of Scotland did possess stone buildings in the traditional style prior to 1750. If they did not serve as models for the later periods of town building, they may nevertheless have influenced country building. Despite the many references to the simple primitive form of much of the urban housing, contemporary records also cite examples of stone building. Fynes Moryson at the end of the sixteenth century remarked on the stone houses in Edinburgh's High Street and, by the middle of the seventeenth century, Franck reported the houses in Dunblane to be of stone. Montrose came in for special mention for the quality of its stone houses in the mid-seventeenth century: 'Good houses all of stone'. By the eighteenth century, all Kirkcudbright's houses were said to be of stone 'but not all after the manner of England' (**63**). Their style was Scottish to an Englishman's eye. Although not abundant, the stone buildings in the cities and towns were of sufficient number to indicate the basis of a national Scottish style.

The countryside before and after 1750

Although Scotland did have some established villages prior to the eighteenth century, rural settlements were more commonly smaller units such as clachans or 'ferme touns' comprising families working the land in joint tenancies, large single tenant farmers with cottars and hired labour, or communities of small 'feu-ferme' proprietors. Indeed such groupings probably seldom extended very far socially and economically beyond their primary agricultural functions. Thus seventeenth-century travellers remarked on the relative absence of villages, even in East Lothian where evidence suggests that they existed in earlier centuries.

The small farms and buildings in the countryside before the resurgence of rural building in the mid-eighteenth century had all the defects and characteristics of the small houses in towns of earlier times. By the end of the eighteenth century when the new houses were replacing the old hovels, the reports of the widespread wretchedness of country building were being received from every county. The rate of progress of improvement in agriculture and building diminished with the distance away from Central Scotland. In 1814, Orkney still had farm buildings 'meanly executed and irregularly arranged . . . husbandry at the best is but imperfectly conducted'. Shetland was similar and the offices were described as in general 'despicable'. At the end of the eighteenth century agriculture in one island was described as 'at best slovenly and often preposterous'.

The Highland houses and farms at the end of the eighteenth century were equally very poor. Three quotations from those times will serve to give an insight into the conditions with which new building and agriculture had to cope in the Highlands, the first relating to Kiltearn.

'Among the 385 houses in the parish, there are not forty in which a person accustomed to a decent accommodation would choose to lodge a single night . . . The greatest number are built of earth, and are usually razed to the ground once in five or seven years when they are added to the dunghill. Indeed, they cannot afford to build them of better materials, not even with clay and stone.' *First Statistical Account*, 1791.

'The dwellings of cottagers are not worse than those of the native farmers. The same roof covers men, women, children, cattle, dogs, pigs, poultry, etc.' *General View of the Agriculture of Ross and Cromarty*, 1810.

'It must afford great pleasure to every lover of his country, to observe the neat cottages that are erecting in several parts of the country; but it will be long ere the people will learn the comforts of cleanliness and the use of chimneys. In many places where these have been constructed, the people do not use them, but prefer breaking a hole in the roof of the house, and lighting their fire on the floor. Smoke they say keeps them warm.' *ibid*

The buildings of the small northern farms at the beginning of the nineteenth century may have been very basic but had survived as a type for hundreds of years. Richard Hakluyt in 1577 said of the Orcadians that 'their houses are very simply builded with pebble stone, without any chimneys; the fire being made in the midst thereof'. The family occupied one side and the cattle the other: 'very beastly and rudely in respect of civilisation'. In contrast, the improvements which had commenced in the Lothians by the mid-eighteenth

century were such that by 1805 it was possible to report that the farm buildings were generally 'two storeys containing upon the ground floor, parlour, nursery, kitchen, larder, milk house, laundry, etc. and in the upper floor four rooms'.

By the beginning of the eighteenth century, although the houses of the country aristocracy and lairds were in course of being changed into formal country mansions, the old inadequate habitations of the farm workers persisted even in lowland areas. There were some larger houses occupied by the richer farmers and country merchants like the brewer or the miller. These would have been two storeys in height, built up with stone walls and covered with thatch, and they generally had a sitting room with a fireplace. The lower floors of such houses had two glazed windows, while the upper floors had two bedrooms and a closet. The majority of houses, however, had a single room 6 metres by 4·5 metres (20 feet by 15 feet); some were as small as 3·6 metres (12 feet) square. Occasionally there was also a small barn. Windows had no glass because of its prohibitive cost in Scotland at that time, and a wooden shutter was the next best cover to the window apertures for protection from the weather. Readers interested in rural living conditions at this time will find much relevant detail in Alexander Fenton's *Scottish Country Life*.

6. *Top right* Auchindrain, Argyll

7. *Above right* Burn of Cambus, Perthshire

The new approach to agriculture
The agricultural changes, introducing new crops such as the potato across Scotland, began between 1750 and 1780. Winter feed crops such as turnip called

for a new form of management and farms had to be enclosed and boundaries built for larger fields. The farmers needed more labour for preparation, for singling and for harvesting. The old order of 'ferme touns' and community farming had to go. The whole process of enlarging the number of farm workers, building new farm buildings and increasing stock was then set in motion. It was made possible because small tenant farmers with insecure tenure had no rights to resist the changeover to larger units and field patterns suited to the new methods. The opportunity for financial gain was there in the backward agriculture of Scotland and it was vigorously seized. So the old picture of struggling labourers and impoverished cultivation was erased and the new vision of prosperity made real. The results are still there to be seen and the buildings are the subject of this study. Practically nothing survived of the old 'ferme touns' and Auchindrain township in Argyll, now a museum, is the only place in Scotland where one may still get a picture of what this older farm life was like (6). Families were turned out from work and home wherever new farms were established. Yet this relentless process seems to have been accomplished without friction except in the Highlands, where stubborn attachment by crofters to the land was met and overcome by the implacable owners exercising their rights with indifference to sentiment and human misery to the extent that the heritage of bitterness still lives on.

In the richer areas, large farms were established and farm labourers' cottages were more numerous. These farms belong to the Lothians, Berwickshire, and

8. Finigand Farm, Glenshee, Perthshire

27 *The changes after 1750*

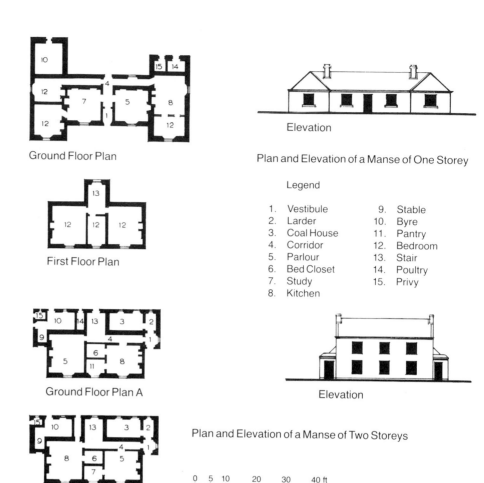

Ground Floor Plan

Plan and Elevation of a Manse of One Storey

Elevation

First Floor Plan

Legend

1.	Vestibule	9.	Stable
2.	Larder	10.	Byre
3.	Coal House	11.	Pantry
4.	Corridor	12.	Bedroom
5.	Parlour	13.	Stair
6.	Bed Closet	14.	Poultry
7.	Study	15.	Privy
8.	Kitchen		

Ground Floor Plan A

Elevation

Plan and Elevation of a Manse of Two Storeys

Ground Floor Plan B

parts of Roxburgh, Fife, Perthshire (**7**), Angus, Aberdeenshire and Moray. The smaller farms to be established belonged to the dairying areas and the hill lands (**8**). The crofts in the Islands and the west were less affected by the new agriculture and changes in croft houses came much later.

Influences of the church and the estates

Improvements were also being introduced from another quarter. A very clear idea of the style of new manses demanded at this period may be formed from the specifications and plans then set down. In the early eighteenth century it was decided that specific entitlements should be afforded to parish ministers in respect of land holding or glebe and manses. This enlightened policy was formed to induce men of learning and culture to accept charges in the country to serve rural populations remote from centres of teaching.

Manses from certain West Highland parishes were to consist of a 1½-storey building with overall internal dimensions of 12m × 4·5m (40ft × 15ft) and 3·6m (12ft) to the wallhead. The manse was to be gabled and furnished with a loft.

Three rooms were to be placed on each floor, the stair to be centrally positioned, and the door to be located on the south side of the building. It was specified that the roofs were to be covered with turf and bracken. The orientations of rooms were also laid down as follows:

kitchen and byre to south and east,
stable and barn to the south and west, and
a yard 12m × 18m (40ft × 60ft), being placed between the two wings.

The garden at the back on the north side of the house, was reserved for kale, corn and herbs. These clearly defined requirements established a form of building, which became in the general arrangement of the house itself, a frequently adopted form in the late eighteenth and nineteenth centuries. Illustrations of the other types of manses of the eighteenth century are given in diagram 3. They are of interest in showing that both the one and two-storey versions which were also being built, gave a pattern that could be followed for other less commodious houses of the period.

The larger estates also promoted new building. Examination of official records and estate archives brought to light much information about the building activity on the estates during the period under review. Sometimes the owners worked with local tradesmen in preparing designs, occasionally using local architects, but notable architects of the day were frequently engaged by some estates for carrying out more important projects. As a consequence of this their attention was turned to the design of minor ancillary buildings, such as inns or lodges, and thus the new stylistic ideas spread from the main centres and took root in the countryside (**46**).

d3. Plans of early nineteenth-century manses

9. *Below left* Stair Inn, Ayrshire

10. *Below right* Huxter, Shetland

The antecedents of the new style of building

As has been indicated, the older types of farm and domestic buildings over most of Scotland largely disappeared during the period of rebuilding. Only in the remote areas and in the Islands did any of the older buildings remain, especially if the walls had been stone built (**11**). The speed of change was so fast as to invite the notion that evolution in building, having hardly moved

since mediaeval times, was abruptly sundered and revolution imposed. Despite the thoroughness of the process of destruction and rebuilding, the influence of the past was not altogether obliterated. The older buildings were long and narrow in plan, were divided internally by light partitions, and there was only one storey. The roofs were covered in turfs and heather or thatching, although the supply of straw was short in many parts of the country. Few farm houses would be slated, and chimneys were often absent and open hearths with an aperture in the thatch for venting the smoke had to suffice. The walls were built irregularly and only approximately parallel. Windows, if provided, were small and sometimes unglazed. Where the frontages ran along sloping ground, the wallhead would slope also, and corners were only roughly angled (**10**). There were no steps at the front door. Some of these characteristics appear to have been carried foward into the new buildings. The survey established how the single-storey house was still preferred in the rebuilding over much of the country. That $1\frac{1}{2}$ and 2-storey houses were also erected only emphasises that the retention of the one-storey house was the result of deliberate choice. The custom of the long narrow plan shapes continued, although the country builders could have built to a square type of plan if they had so desired, for square-plan buildings of nearly nine to ten metres deep were not uncommon in the towns. They could have built 2-storey square-planned houses as was done in other European countries, but the older form was preferred so that in this respect the direct line of evolution prevailed. The new houses, especially in the north, often adhered to the older types of front doors with the greater widths first used for the passage of animals as well as the occupant and his family.

The survey also showed that adding of steps up to the front door of a house was only reluctantly adopted in stages over a period of about a hundred years. The burgh houses in contrast made front door steps almost a fetish. Up the important flight of steps, the owner and his guests had to go, to enter the town house. Downstairs in the semi-basements went the lower orders symbolically kept in their proper place. Basements were a rarity in the countryside and only found in a few of the smaller towns (**12**).

The affinity of country people with the land on which they live contrasts with urban living where citizens and their immediate interests are well removed from the countryside. Tenement flats have long been accepted in Scottish towns and the owners of Georgian town houses had their public rooms set high above their gardens. The sublime in this attitude of thought was reached by that great stylist of the twentieth century, the French architect Le Corbusier, who paradoxically saw himself as an anti-stylist. He divorced his blocks of flats completely from the land and set them on 'pilotis' up in the air beside his rarefied philosophy.

The main antecedents of the construction, form and details of the new Scottish country houses of the mid-eighteenth century and later may be summarised as follows:

(a) the form may have descended from the older farms and country cottages;

(b) the construction methods derived from the traditional use of stone and lime or clay which had been employed in Scottish buildings for centuries, along with the pitched timber roofs covered by slates and tiles; and

11. *Right* Torthorwald,
Dumfriesshire

12. *Below* Coldstream,
Berwickshire

31   *The changes after 1750*

(c)   many details were borrowed from the tower houses and the stone buildings in the burghs built prior to 1750, e.g. dormers, vertical windows and end gables.

The form of courtyard in large farms (**15**) with arched gateways and balanced facades followed an older tradition of connecting a group of separate buildings into a compact plan. Examples are to be seen in the tower houses and in the larger buildings in towns. It was a planning device used in Italy first in the Roman period and then at the time of the renaissance after which it passed to other countries. When the East Lothian farmers employed this type of layout they were also taking into account practical considerations of efficiency and stock management. It is likely that arched openings to outbuildings had already been used in the coach houses of the large town buildings in Edinburgh, as well as at inns where such coach houses still survive. The forestairs up to the hay lofts and grain stores (**14**) could have derived from the forestairs in the old houses of the burghs in Fife (**16**) and in Newhaven or the larger outer stairs in the tower houses. These forestairs in burgh houses led to the first floors

13. *Below* Dunblane, Perthshire

14. *Opposite top left* Achamore, Gigha, Argyll

15. *Opposite top right* Begbie Farm, East Lothian

16. *Opposite bottom* Pittenweem, Fife

33   *The changes after 1750*

17. Kirbister Mill, Orkney

often being set over stone vaulted ground floors through which an internal staircase could not readily be made to pass. The earliest forestairs were of timber which could be swiftly pulled up for protection from invading soldiery when they came surging through the town battering the doors, bent on pillage and destruction.

The larger mills (**17**) and warehouses simply followed the same forms that had been in use in the burghs for centuries such as the three-storey mill of 1660 at Haddington or that at Kirkwall from 1614. The eighteenth-century builders freely borrowed the forms and details of earlier traditional building as they saw it at the time. Their contribution, and it was an important one, was to reconstitute the ingredients into building types delightfully simple yet convincingly composed because the builders had the secret of near perfect proportioning, as is discussed in Chapter 6, as well as the craftsmen's variety in technique that has not since been surpassed. Their joint response went far beyond the simple need to provide better shelter which had been the main concern of their forerunners in the countryside. They were expressing the artistic ideals of their time.

Buildings and their main characteristics

3 The pattern of building

Apart from some in the crofting areas, most groups of buildings did not originate by one person putting down a home and then others following at their own choice of place and time. The pattern of building was predetermined by boundaries adopted after thoughtful appraisal of needs and locations. Thus we have the regular grouping of buildings along streets and squares in many of the villages and towns of the eighteenth and nineteenth centuries (**12**). In the open countryside, short terraces of farm workers' cottages, farm houses and their steadings, were built in sites that were fundamentally practical and that suited local climate. As the grouping of buildings bears strongly on character, this chapter deals with some of the circumstances which shaped the pattern we see on the ground today.

The leaders of society in the early eighteenth-century countryside were confronted with a picture of planned burghs possessing market rights and traditions, very few villages and systems of farming of early origin, often communally run. Their first objective was to revolutionise agriculture, and to accomplish that they had not only to alter the outdated field systems and remove the older farm buildings, but also to select the sites for the

18. *Below* Dunblane. Perthshire

19. *Opposite top* Dirleton, East Lothian

20. *Opposite bottom* Biggar, Lanarkshire

Map I. Post-1700 planned villages

Key to Map I: planned Extensions to larger towns or villages later absorbed into large towns are excluded.

Map No.	Place Name	County	Date of Promotion or Start of Feuing
1	Aberchirder	Banff	1764
2	Archiestown	Moray	1761
3	Ardrishaig	Argyll	early 18th century
4	Athelstaneford	E. Lothian	
5	Auchenblae	Kincardine	1795
6	Avoch	Ross & Cromarty	pre-1750
7	Baledgarno	Perth	
8	Balfron	Stirling	1789
9	Bankfoot	Perth	1815
10	Beauly	Inverness	c.1760
11	Bettyhill	Sutherland	pre-1815
12	Blair Atholl	Perth	
13	Bowmore	Islay, Argyll	1768
14	Bridge of Earn	Perth	1769
15	Brodick	Arran (Bute)	18th century
16	Brora	Sutherland	1811
17	Burghead	Moray	1808
18	Brydekirk	Dumfries	c.1803
19	Callander	Perth	1730
20	Carlops	Peebles	1784
21	Catrine	Ayr	
22	Castletown	Caithness	1824
23	Charlestown of Aberlour	Banff	c.1812
24	Charlestown	Fife	c.1765
25	Collieston	Aberdeen	c.1800
26	Comrie	Perth	late 18th century
27	Cuminestown	Aberdeen	1761
28	Cummingstown	Moray	1808
29	Crovie	Banff	
30	Dallas	Moray	1811
31	Dairsie	Fife	1790
32	Dalswinton	Dumfries	c.1780
33	Deanston		
	Deer (5 villages in a group)	Aberdeen	
34	Fetterangus		1752
35	Longside		1801
36	Mintlaw		1813
37	New Deer		1805
38	Stewartfield		1774
	Deskford (3 villages)	Banff	
39	Deskford		
40	Lintmill		after 1760
41	Tochieneal		
42	Douglastown	Angus	
43	Doune (Deanston)	Perth	c.1790
44	Dufftown	Banff	1817
45	Dunnichen	Angus	
46	Easdale	Argyll	early 19th century
47	Edzell	Angus	1839
48	Evanton	Ross & Cromarty	1810
49	Fettercairn	Kincardine	c.1760
50	Findochty	Banff	1716
51	Fintry	Stirling	1794
52	Fochabers	Moray	1776
53	Fort Augustus	Inverness	1754
54	Friockheim	Angus	1830
55	Gordonstown	Banff	1720 and 1750
56	Garmouth (Kingston)	Moray	1784
57	Gatehouse of Fleet	Kirkcudbright	c.1790
58	Gavinton	Berwick	late 18th century
59	Gifford	E. Lothian	mid 18th century
60	Glamis	Angus	2nd half 18th century
61	Glencaple	Dumfries	1746
62	Grantown-on-Spey	Moray	1766
63	Gretna (Springfield)	Dumfries	1791
64	Guildtown	Perth	
65	Halkirk	Caithness	c.1790
66	Helmsdale	Sutherland	1814
67	Hopeman	Moray	1806
68	Houston	Renfrew	
69	Inveraray	Argyll	1743
70	Inverallochy	Aberdeen	
71	Kenmore	Perth	1760
72	Kerrycroy	Bute	
73	Killearn	Stirling	c.1800
74	Kilmartin	Argyll	
75	Kingussie	Inverness	c.1780
76	Kinloch Rannoch	Perth	1763
77	Kirkcowan	Wigtown	c.1800
78	Kirkpatrick Durham	Kirkcudbright	1785
79	Kyleakin	Inverness	1811
80	Latheron	Caithness	18th century
81	Laurencekirk	Kincardine	c.1770
82	Lauriston	Kirkcudbright	late 18th century
83	Letham	Angus	1788
84	Lewiston	Inverness	
85	Lochgilphead	Argyll	early 19th century
86	Longmanshill	Banff	late 18th century
87	Lumsden	Aberdeen	1825
88	Luncarty	Perth	
89	Lybster	Caithness	1802
90	Maryton	Angus	1824
91	Marywell	Angus	1819
92	Meikleour	Perth	
93	Millport	Bute	late 18th century
94	Moffat	Dumfries	late 18th century
95	Monymusk	Aberdeen	
96	New Byth	Aberdeen	1763
97	Newcastleton	Roxburgh	1793
98	New Lanark	Lanark	mid 18th century
99	New Leeds	Aberdeen	1798
100	Newton Stewart	Wigtown	1677 and 18th century
101	New Pitsligo	Aberdeen	1787
102	Ormiston	E. Lothian	c.1740
103	Padanaram	Angus	1824
104	Pennan (New Aberdour)	Aberdeen	1798
105	Pitcairngreen	Perth	late 18th century
106	Plockton	Ross & Cromarty	late 18th century
107	Port Charlotte	Islay, Argyll	1828
108	Port Ellen	Islay, Argyll	1821
109	Port Logan	Wigtown	
110	Port William	Wigtown	1770
111	Racks	Dumfries	
112	Rothes	Moray	1765
113	St. Combs	Aberdeen	1771
114	St. Fergus	Aberdeen	1806
115	Salen	Argyll	late 18th century
116	Sandhaven	Aberdeen	1838 and 1873
117	Spinningdale	Sutherland	1790
118	Spittalfield	Perth	
119	Stanley	Perth	1785
120	Strathpeffer	Ross & Cromarty	
121	Strichen	Aberdeen	1763
122	Swinton	Berwick	
123	Tobermory	Argyll	1788
124	Tomintoul	Banff	1776
125	Tyninghame	E. Lothian	c.1770
126	Ullapool	Ross & Cromarty	1788
127	Urquhart	Moray	c.1783

This list excludes most 19th century railway villages and many 19th century industrial villages and commuter towns.

(d) St. Fergus

(b) Aberchirder

(c) Friockheim

0   100   200   300   400   500

metres

(a) Fochabers

farms and homes of the people they had dispossessed. This process was progressively applied to the country over a period of about 125 years from 1725. Some families would move from the country to the burghs and the cities. Many, during the Highland clearances, emigrated but substantial numbers were settled in new villages and towns.

The planned towns and villages

Redistributing people and houses on any scale calls for organisation and planning. A large number of villages and small towns was established, some later in the nineteenth century (**I**,p.38). Thousands of farms and cottages were relocated and new churches, schools, workshops etc. – requiring new roads, harbours, drainage and water supply – began to reach across the open countryside. The new villages and towns in the eighteenth and nineteenth centuries were generally promoted by landowners. In some coastal locations the purpose was to expand the fishing industry, as at Findochty which was set up in 1716 for fishermen from Fraserburgh. In other instances the promoters wished to attract industry and provide work such as at Grantown-on-Spey in 1765 which prospered by the introduction of textiles, brewing, baking and candle making. Sites were selected with road access, good drainage, water supply and often in proximity to poor land where the villagers could be persuaded

Map II. *Opposite* Layout of traditional and planned villages

21. *Below* Findochty, Banffshire

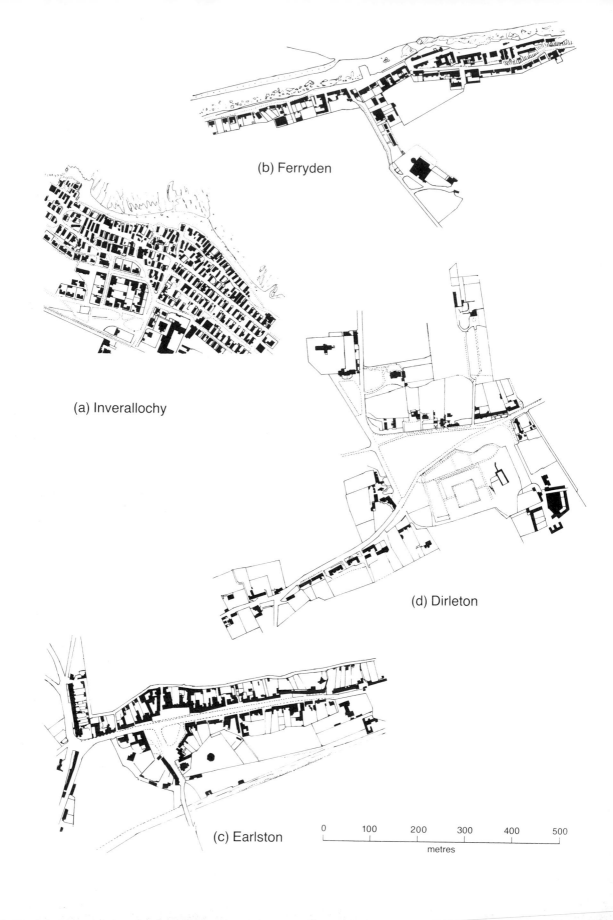

(b) Ferryden

(a) Inverallochy

(d) Dirleton

(c) Earlston

| 0 | 100 | 200 | 300 | 400 | 500 |

metres

22. *Right* Gatehouse of Fleet, Kirkcudbrightshire

23. *Below* Ullapool, Ross and Cromarty

Map III. *Opposite* Layout of traditional and planned villages

to effect improvements by drainage and cultivation. Master tradesmen, schoolmasters and, later surveyors and architects, produced plans and marked out the road lines and feus on the site. These promotions were widely advertised and the lots were bid for at roups (auctions). Inducements to prospective feuars took various forms such as a premium in cash or freedom to collect stone and clay from the land surrounding the villages. One enterprising Aberdeenshire owner in 1795 offered a prize of £5 and a silver medal to the first feuar in New Pitsligo to get a good grain crop off the village moor. Other 'big prizes on offer' were for textiles, bee-keeping and for the first two-storey house to be built with a slate roof. On such evidence a case may be made out for Scotland also having introduced modern sales promotion to town planning – an honour, however, which prudent Scots may wish to disclaim. The largest feus were about 13–14 metres wide (42–46 feet) and 45–50 metres deep (150–165 feet). The minimum ground size of the houses was sometimes stipulated, e.g. 9·7 metres by 4·9 metres (32 by 16 feet) about 39 square metres (420 square feet) on the ground floor and about 27 square metres (300 square feet) in the garret, an overall area close to present day local authority houses.

The plans of the late eighteenth and early nineteenth centuries were conceived as villages with recognisable shapes. The streets were boldly set out, focusing on squares, and providing sites for churches, workshops and inns. The first and one of the most ambitious was Keith in 1750 which is now too large to come within the scope of this study. Its long central street, central square, the two parallel side streets and the connecting cross lanes obviously evolved from the planning arrangements adopted by the mediaeval planners of the Scottish burghs. This plan-form was employed for many of the other towns, e.g. Fochabers 1776 and Aberchirder in 1764 (**II**,p.40). However, some were set out on triangular systems, such as Friockheim in 1827 (**II**,p.40) and Mintlaw in 1813 with a diamond-shaped square. Crescents were introduced at Longside in 1801 and at St. Fergus (**II**,p.40). The finest plans were characterised by well-known examples such as Inveraray, Gifford, Fochabers in 1774 and Gatehouse of Fleet in 1770, all associated with large estates and mansion houses close by which benefited by obtaining more ornamental precincts. The fishing villages took their plan-form from the coastline and were thus very picturesque (**23**). The later planning of groups of houses in the country after about 1850 seems to have declined into developers' feuing schemes which lost their sense of unity to the point of resembling building contractors' suburban speculations. These later developments occurred to meet the housing need of factory workers and miners and were conceived more as dormitories than villages, although there were notable early examples of much merit such as at New Lanark in 1789.

In the planned eighteenth-century village the siting of the buildings was controlled by the requirement that the layout conformed to the building line along or close to the public pavement. Nearly all buildings in this situation were erected with their roof ridges parallel to the road. Houses in fishing villages, however, were frequently placed with gable ends to the street and this resulted in some unique contrasts producing layouts combining spontaneity with discipline such as at Inverallochy (**III**,p.42). One result of this activity in town planning was the emergence of terrace houses in the countryside, planned along streets designed as single entities to which each builder of a house had to conform. This practice originated in the cities and developed into the sweeping

24. *Opposite* Milton, Ross and Cromarty

25. *Below* New Deer, Aberdeenshire

facades of terraces, crescents and squares representing Georgian architecture at its zenith. The small country towns and villages which were surveyed did not impose the same degree of control. Specification decided the length of frontage, the general form and the materials. Beyond that the builders or owners seemed to have acted with some freedom, and the overall effect of this policy can be seen today.

The informal terraces are easily recognisable in the later settlements and are more ordered than the grouping of houses in older villages (24). A certain amount of flatted houses were used to give a repetitive style of terracing. This did not not become a major feature of country building and was normally only found in larger towns but even there was not typical. The promoters of these new villages and towns demanded the use of stone and in some cases required two floors, either in two full storeys or in one storey and an attic storey (25). An important provision related to siting: the promoters, who were usually the landowners, wished to prevent any possibility of the feuars using open ground in front of their houses for household refuse or middens. All buildings, therefore, were required to be built up to or close to the edge of the feu adjacent to the pavement. This decision gave to the new Scottish villages a strongly urban aspect unsoftened by open gardens or abundant street planting. The control of building, however, was applied only to keep up appearances and did not attempt to impose a preconceived elevational plan calling for uniformity of style of buildings or of details.

Today a few of the large market squares have been built over with council houses or converted into traffic circuses. Fortunately the thoroughness of the old builders has preserved the buildings. Map I (p.38) indicating the location of planned villages shows that the most fertile area for the foundation of the new towns and villages was on the east coast between Caithness and Aberdeen where at least 41 new settlements became established, of which 25 were of eighteenth-century foundation. It was there that the $1\frac{1}{2}$-storey houses of the eighteenth and nineteenth centuries became the typical form of house. Those north of the Moray Firth consisted mostly of coastal villages. The remainder to the south were partly coastal towns and villages established to promote fishing and partly inland villages to facilitate the growth of the linen trade. Before, there had been almost no villages and in early times little security from strife. By the beginning of the nineteenth century, depopulation had been checked and work secured. New villages were instituted to a lesser degree elsewhere, in Kincardine, Angus, Perthshire and Inverness-shire. The Lothians and Berwickshire contributed fewer, but in these areas many older villages already existed. Sixteen new settlements came into being in the south-west, and 19 were set up in the west of central Scotland around Glasgow. The west coast and the Islands, with a sparser population and different farming methods, had only 15 new settlements.

There were at least 150 such planned communities introduced in Scotland during the time that most of the buildings examined in the survey were being built. If the later industrial and mining villages are included, the total would reach to over 200. Their influence on building cannot be exaggerated. They induced owners to build their houses to a standard which was well in advance of what had previously obtained. They made churches and schools possible

26. Monymusk,
Aberdeenshire

in areas where otherwise they could not have been justified. The earliest provided markets, which supported the new agriculture that was concurrently advancing and they later served new industries.

Farms in the landscape

The creative energy that founded village planning in eighteenth-century Scotland was inspired initially by the transformation of agriculture, the nucleus of this expansion being in the new farms. Starting in the Lothians, new farm buildings were rapidly introduced, first in the most fertile areas, and later in the remoter parts with less favourable soils and climate. They usually occupied holdings of over 100 hectares (at least 250 acres) and the steadings were based on plans far removed from the simple long rectangular farms that had generally preceded them. These buildings required larger areas of flat ground, good water supply and road access.

The siting of farms varied greatly and cannot easily be categorised into a few basic types. This is because the factors which determined the specific location of individual farms fluctuated to such an extent that it is difficult to generalise. Land ownership, field boundaries, farm boundaries, drainage, accessibility to roads, water supply, power supply, gradients, exposure, outlook and other factors determined the question for the original builder of where his farm should be positioned. However, some typical siting conditions can be observed by way of illustration:

(1)   crofts, the simplest of farm units, may be clustered together in townships or be located individually in isolated positions separated from others by moorland;

47   *The pattern of building*

(2)   in the glens, small farms may be sited on the river terraces above the cultivated slopes of the better land below, a policy also adopted in the locating of the early burghs;

(3)   the value of shelter to the farmer is demonstrated in many parts of Scotland where farms have been placed in the lee of the hills out of the direction of the prevailing wind;

(4)   in the mixed farms with sheep and hill grazing, the steadings lie conveniently between the arable land below and the grazing above, often standing well back from the roads and sometimes located in a cross valley running towards the main river; and

(5)   in central Scotland many farm buildings when rebuilt occupied the same site as the older buildings.

Perhaps when eighteenth and nineteenth-century farms were new and modern, their appearance may have seemed stark and unresponsive to their surroundings, but nature in the countryside has a way of assimilating any intrusions. Except in the far north, trees grow taller in the shelter of buildings, hedges and shrubs will also thrive, stone and other natural materials become softened with lichen and by the erosion of the elements in the open landscape. In short, farms grow their own background and setting.

In the north and west where trees in the open country have small hope of survival in the frequent gales, the farms for the same reason are low and sit

27. *Above right* Torrovaich, Caithness

28. *Right* Delgaty Castle Farm, Aberdeenshire

29. Dairsie, Fife

tightly hugging the land, their shoulders to the wind strongly braced against the blast. In the experience of such conditions this kind of siting makes sense and looks right. In the broad fertile plains of Aberdeenshire and the Lothians, farm buildings spread their parts under long, low roofs with the grandest gateways surrounded by classic pediments (**28**), ogival roofs and even domes. Interspersed and backed by trees, these expansive buildings in a wide horizoned landscape, look very fine and buildings and country match each other perfectly. Most of these farms, whether as isolated buildings or in groups, are capable of creating a powerful but not unwelcome contrast to the openness of the Scottish countryside. Built as they have been with suitable materials, in appropriate colouring and fitting their conditions of climate and topography, they have generally adopted a response to suit their surroundings. The harmony of this situation could be maintained provided new building or additions continue to follow the example of what has been shown to be seemly and in good taste. No matter how well the siting has been chosen and cultivated, new or altered building using wrong materials or planned with over-bulky dimensions, bad shape or poor design will defeat what could otherwise continue to be an example of fine siting.

Although farms, isolated cottages and scattered groups of houses represent only about a quarter of Scotland's rural buildings, they deserve attention out of proportion to their numbers because they straddle across the landscape in great profusion wherever pasture and cultivation is found.

The setting and form of buildings

Individual setting

In order to understand the setting of individual buildings it is best to look where the wall meets the ground. In the isolated country house or roadside group, common tradition has called for about 500mm (20in) of ground immediately adjacent to the wall, consisting of a narrow strip of earth containing the owner's own choice of plants and flowers. At the outer edge of the planted strip there may be a verge, usually nowadays of bottle-edged precast concrete. Stones on edge are also used and, in the older areas, long pieces of kerb-stone. Across part of the planted strip a stone platt is placed in front of the entrance door raised about 25mm (one inch) above the surrounding ground (**32**). Next there is normally a narrow access path used by the public and, beyond that again, a gravelled area before the road surface is reached. The outer area may sometimes serve for standing vehicles. No upstand kerbs occur between the house and carriageways, and only on rare occasions are grass verges between the pavement and the road planted by public authorities.

In the villages similar arrangements are found. The bottle-edged concrete or stone kerb at the planted strips is retained but the gravelled area is mostly absent (**30**). In the larger villages the planted area has often been either eroded and absorbed by the pavement (**31**), or it has been upgraded into a small private area enclosed by a wall (**103**).

In the town houses it became customary to build neat stone walls in front of shallow front gardens (**36**). These walls were surmounted in the late nineteenth-century examples with cast-iron railings of Gothic design, now almost entirely gone forever. During the crusade for iron in 1940, only railings of artistic merit could be left intact, and the experts appointed to evaluate aesthetic quality could not see at that time any merit in these distinctive designs. This sad fact is a very good warning against relying on the taste of one genera-

30. *Below left* Aberdour, Fife

31. *Below right* East Saltoun, East Lothian

tion to act as a standard when judging the products of an earlier generation. Only a few gates and balcony rails remain (d.26) to verify the worth of what was thrown away for a purpose which in the end proved of little help to the needs of industry at that time (d.25,e). The surroundings to the small town houses have been more 'municipalised' by the introduction of standard pavements and the elimination of planting strips. Thus the immediate setting is at once tidier and harder, more disciplined and less informal (33).

Houses and other buildings in the open countryside are generally related to their surroundings by being placed on level ground or lying along the contours on sloping ground with the front door usually on the lower side of the block. In the hilly areas in the north small crofts may be seen lying at different angles over the countryside but all placed running with the contours. The oldest houses arrange the wallheads to run at a gradient in sympathy with the slope of the ground below (3). It is not unusual to find the walls of the house to be met at ground level with a narrow path and beyond that the rough grass where animals may stray, lambs settle down or children play (1).

The later country cottages were built in terraces of three or four in areas where large-scale farming was practised and greater labour forces were required (34). Sometimes the later houses have been provided with recognisable front garden areas, the house being placed not within the steading as was originally done, but at a short distance and generally with an orientation related to the main access road. The houses set in the village streets of the older settlements are often without front gardens, the plots occasionally being placed across the road behind the back gardens of the houses in the next street or, in front of a main road beyond, such as at Embo. It was not only the cottages of the farm servants which came to be divorced from the steadings. In some parts of the country the farmer's house was eventually also set apart within its own walled garden like a suburban villa surrounded with planting and lawns (35). When the country comes close to walls of houses, farms and other buildings

32. Ascog, Bute

51   *The setting and form of buildings*

33. *Top right* Port William, Wigtownshire

34. *Above right* Burnside, Nairn

35. *Right* Callands Farm, Peebles

36. *Above* Dunblane, Perthshire

37. *Right* Tobormochy, Luing Island

38. *Above* Eaglesham, Renfrewshire

39. Hopeman, Moray

40. *Opposite* Eaglesham, Renfrewshire

54   *Buildings of the Scottish Countryside*

without the intervention of formal paths, lawns, roadside kerbs or front gardens, the buildings have the rural setting best suited to their situation (**6**). The minimum introduction of these features in the small villages also offers the best way of keeping country villages rural in character (**37**).

Storey height and built-form

The relative sparseness of population in Scotland's countryside ensured that shortage of land was not a problem. Land was obtainable with few exceptions for building, as well as for all the needs of agriculture, forestry and sporting activities, shortage being a comparatively recent phenomenon. In the towns, lack of availability of building land tended to create high buildings and crowded conditions. High building in the country generally is neither necessary nor wanted, although tall farm silos were for a time prominent in some locations. Yet, before the mid-eighteenth century, high building was witnessed throughout the countryside. Tower houses, reaching in an extreme case to over thirty metres (one hundred feet), were once a practical necessity for protection but later probably survived just as a style. After 1750, building followed the less pretentious forms and remained low and modest in scale.

The one and a half storey type is comprised of two forms of building. The single-storey form, with the eaves immediately above the lintels of the ground floor windows and the first floor rooms above in the attic space, is the more usual type (**38**). The other, probably the older form, has part of the upper floor contained in the outer walls which extend above the lintels of the ground floor window level to a point as much as a metre (3ft 4in) before reaching the eaves (**39**). This latter sub-division may be seen in all counties either in eighteenth-century buildings or as a later version in nineteenth-century Gothic design. These types are described more fully later.

Buildings with more than two storeys are most often found in the north-east and the central belt (**40**) and, in parishes where they were recorded, represented under 14 per cent of the buildings. This applies both to $2\frac{1}{2}$ and 3-storey samples. The greater proportion of complex roofs found in buildings incorporating different numbers of storeys is mostly concentrated in the north-east. The survey of remaining pre-1914 buildings showed that single-storey houses, schools and farm outbuildings are the dominant form in large sections of the countryside. Only in a few areas is this not so. For example, the north-east is more accurately identified as an area where $1\frac{1}{2}$-storey buildings take precedence. The Islands and the west coast also contain high proportions of $1\frac{1}{2}$-storey buildings among the samples recorded. Sutherland and Ross-shire samples include large proportions of $1\frac{1}{2}$-storey buildings as do areas in the Borders and the south-west. The large prosperous farms normally have 2-storey houses, cartsheds and stables. The small towns or large villages contain 2-storey buildings in all counties. The single-storey houses are evenly distributed but in the north-east $1\frac{1}{2}$ storeys are in the majority as indicated above.

The study of storey heights has been an essential key to understand building patterns in that it can distinguish character by the mix of heights which govern any area, not only in the widest sense of region or county, but also in districts within these wider areas. The computer analysis permitted a close examination to be made of distribution and the results have been taken into account, along with other features, in determining the character zones described in Chapter 8.

41. Biggar, Lanarkshire

Scale and elevational treatment

The number of storeys places a building in its position relative to other buildings and, this in turn, is affected by the height of internal ceilings (**41**). Where ceiling heights are low, a building is described as being small in scale, whereas high ceilings imply large scale. Naturally, in such circumstances the other attributes of scale respond so that when the eaves lie close to the ground the windows are less tall. The smaller scale buildings are usually narrow in plan and the roof ridges as a result do not rise to the heights of the classical villas or Victorian terraces with their tall windows and doors, high ashlar courses and the elevated roofs mounting high above the deeper plans typical of those styles. The study revealed large differences in scale, the older farms and houses in the north-west and in the Hebrides, belonging to the smallest scale. The

57   *The setting and form of buildings*

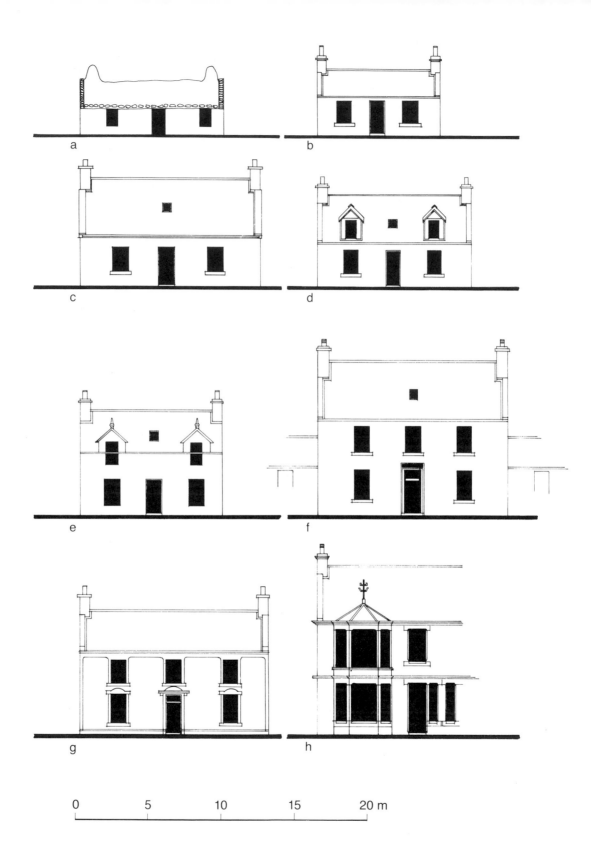

houses of the nineteenth century have higher ceiling levels and are often of medium scale. Later in the century, the rural scale approached that of the large towns. The twentieth century returned to a less ambitious scale, the progression being demonstrated in diagram 5. Some areas of the countryside have retained a fairly uniform scale but most parts have a mixed scale character. The greater informality of villages and countryside building, compared with the main urban centres, seems to indicate that the sudden changes of scale were introduced without much discrimination. The height of buildings is also affected by the height of the ground floor level above the ground outside. It was common for country buildings erected in the eighteenth or early nineteenth centuries to have a step of 100mm (4in) or less from ground level on to the floor at the front door (**59**). The later houses have two steps with a combined height to lift the floor at least 150mm (6in) above the ground. The late nineteenth-century houses sometimes had three steps (**69**). But probably none would have complied with current building regulations in this respect. Today the minimum required difference between ground and floor level is 425mm (17in). To combat ingress of water at the bottom of the front door in the early houses and farm buildings, the building was set out by the old builders so that the highest point

(d.4,a) An early eighteenth-century house in the north of Scotland has a low door, no step up to the door and shallow wood lintels over the door and windows. Thus the building belongs to the smallest scale. The elevation is reduced to the ultimate simplicity and the thatch has none of the sharp precision of the buildings that were to follow. The windows and doors are placed asymmetrically.

(d.4,b) This house is shorter, deeper in plan and has a higher wallhead with deeper lintels. The slate roof and stone chimneys and dressed skews introduced the more formalised approach to elevational treatment with symmetrical elevation. It belongs to *c.* 1800. A small step at the front door has been incorporated.

(d.4,c) This house from *c.* 1800 has a still higher wallhead to accommodate an attic floor, and is still deeper in plan.

(d.4,d) While lower in height, has dormer windows incorporated just above the eaves line. This type of elevation was adopted in 1½-storey houses consistently during most of the nineteenth century.

(d.4,e) Follows the form of the older 1½-storey building with the eaves positioned about midway between the sills and lintels of the attic windows. Small in scale but with a higher wallhead, it is in essence symmetrical but more intricate in design than the older houses.

(d.4,f) An example of the 2-storey formal classic frontage. Much more commodious, wider, deeper and with higher ceilings. This type of house developed from the middle of the eighteenth century, becoming more stylish over a period extending well into the nineteenth century. It could be plain or grander with classic front door and regular rybats. Compared with the first house, the contrast in every way is striking.

(d.4,g) Shows how the symmetrical 2-storey house could be adapted to the early Victorian styles of Georgian derivative design. Two steps up to the ground floor became usual in the nineteenth century.

(d.4,h) The tall Victorian semi-detached villa from *c.* 1870 shows how scale became still larger with higher ceilings (at least 3·3m – 11ft). The more vertical arrangement of the windows further emphasised this heightening of design which became very popular, although more so in the larger towns. Ornamentation was also more lively and lavish.

d4. Comparative scale of buildings

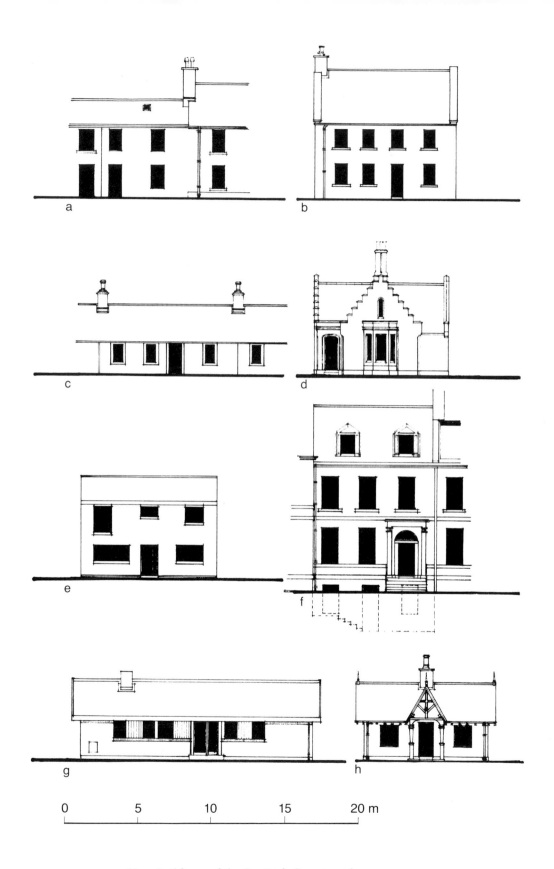

0   5   10   15   20 m

of ground in front of the building was immediately outside the door. The ground on either side of the door sloped away, so draining surface water away from the door. If the doorways in older houses are positioned below the road outside, this has been caused by the raising of the road level at some time after the house was built (**90**). Improvements of roads for traffic have often resulted in damage to the amenity of houses for the occupants.

How the heights and the scale of buildings have developed from the eighteenth century is shown in diagrams 4 and 5.

Houses

Houses in the countryside before the middle of the eighteenth century consisted basically of three types:

(1)   The tower houses, spread over all Scotland, but primarily located in the most densely populated areas, as well as near the border with England. These houses were normally built very strongly, with stone vaulted ground floors, first floor entrances and thick walls. They rise three to four storeys and are squarish in plan.

(2)   The houses of the farmers and clergy, built very simply with turf and stone, usually on one floor and in the form of a long rectangle.

(3)   The houses of the farm workers, very primitive, often built of wattle and clay or with turfs, provided with earth or clay floors and roughly rectangular in plan.

As was explained in Chapter 2, the advent of the mid-eighteenth century brought about a rapid change to a new type of building. The types which were adopted remained, in basic form, as the models for nearly all the houses built during the eighteenth and nineteenth centuries. The changes in building were not, of course, part of a simultaneous process affecting the whole country. These events began in one or two centres and gradually other parts of the country followed, in some places as late as several decades behind the front runners in the movement. Several examples of 'house form' are illustrated in diagrams 6 and 7.

The first basic type and the one most frequently built consisted of a single-

d5. Comparative scale of buildings

(d.5,c) The single-storey terraced houses show how the low-ceilinged houses survived well into the nineteenth century in some instances.

(d.5,f) Indicates how the town scale even in the less pretentious streets reached above the largest country houses. The flight of steps to the front door and the full-height windows to the first floor drawing room are typical characteristics usually absent from country houses. The principal floors had ceiling heights of at least 3.3m (11ft).

(d.5,e and g) The two twentieth-century houses demonstrate the flat pitches of modern roofs, the horizontal windows and informality, reduced in the 2-storey house to a kind of off-beat rhythm. The scale, however, in both houses has returned to the lower ceiling heights of the early nineteenth century.

(d.5,d and h) Examples showing the comparative scales of gatehouses in relation to other buildings.

(d.5,a and b) Are traditional examples of street building in the small rural burghs.

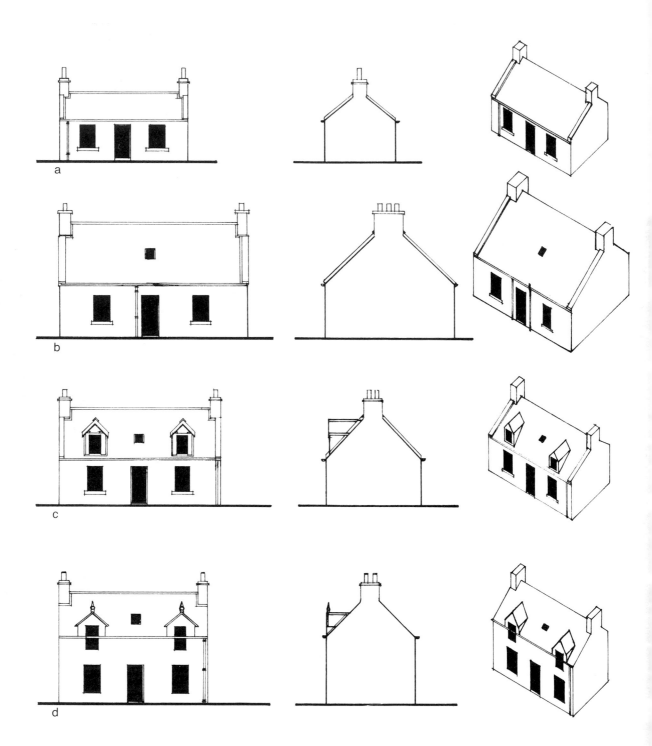

storey cottage (d.6,a). It is rectangular in plan which varies in length: 12 to 15m (40 to 50ft) was common in the north; an average 10m (33ft) was found in the south but lengths from just over 5m (16ft 6in) to as much as 21m (68ft) have been recorded. The widths vary also, from 5·1m (17ft) to 6·6m (21ft 6in) in old houses. In later houses these widths increased. The heights from the ground to the eaves in the earliest single-storey houses were as little as 2m (6ft 6in), but in later houses increased by degrees up to heights of 3m (10ft) from the ground.

The second type (d.6,b), with two floors, one of which was in the roof space, are generally described as 1½-storey and had alternative forms. The building had either the eaves at the same level as for a single-storey house (d.6,c) or its eaves level was at a higher position above the ground about midway between

d6. Form of houses

42. Pittenweem, Fife

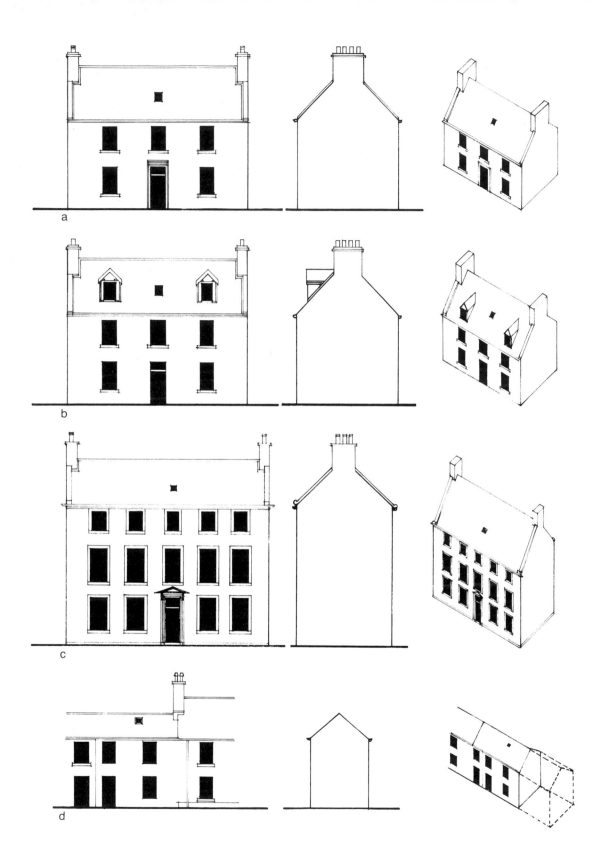

a

b

c

d

the first floor level and ceiling (d.6,d). The lengths of this form of building usually approached 12m (40ft). Lengths up to nearly 14m (46ft) were also found in some areas, especially in the north-east.

The depth of these types of houses tended to be slightly greater than in the single-storey houses. In d.6,d the heights to the eaves, from ground level, varied considerably from 2·5m (over 8ft) up to nearly 3·5m (11ft 6in).

The full 2-storey cottage (d.7,a) was adopted as a desirable type of house from about 1750. The earliest examples were often not very long, about 8m (26ft), but a 10m (33ft) length was a good average, especially in the nineteenth century, and up to 13m (42ft 6in) regularly appeared. Some of the later examples had lengths in excess of 13m (42ft 6in). The depths were similar to those shown in d.6,c. The heights from ground level to eaves varied from as little as 4·5m (14ft 6in) in the eighteenth-century houses to about 5m (16ft 6in) average in the north and 5·25m (over 17ft) in the south, with heights recorded of over 6m (19ft 6in).

Houses with more than two storeys (d.7,b) are a minor feature of most areas. $2\frac{1}{2}$ storeys were common in small towns (**42**) and also occurred in the largest country houses. They were usually narrow as when located in streets in towns, say 7.5m (24ft 6in). They were sometimes found in the country with lengths up to about 10 to 13m (33 to 42ft 6in) and heights from 5·5 to 6·25m (18 to over 20ft).

3-storey houses (d.7,c) were generally confined to the small towns, especially in central Scotland, and were usually narrow. All the above basic types may be symmetrically or asymmetrically arranged on elevation.

The most typical asymmetrical building (d.7,d) consists of $1\frac{1}{2}$- or 2-storey houses often found in pairs, or placed between gables of a row of buildings in a street, in a small town or village. The freestanding version of this type was rarer. The door was to one side and placed alongside the ground floor window. The two upper floor windows were usually positioned above the door and ground floor window. The house was normally rectangular, with its length greater than its height. The other version of this type was similar in the disposition of windows but its height often exceeded its length. Examples were also recorded with wide frontages, up to 9m (29ft 6in). A feature recurring in this type when built as a terrace was an extra door at the end placed hard against the gable, giving access by way of an inside staircase to a flat on the upper floor.

The essence of these houses lay in the following characteristics:

(1)   The clarity of their geometric shapes and forms.

(2)   They possess the orderly dignity and balance of Scottish character.

(3)   The buildings look strong and sturdy.

(4)   Although the overall shapes of the frontages are horizontal rather than vertical, this is counter-balanced by the verticality in the shape of the windows.

(5)   The average angle of the roof pitch is generally close to 45°, and excessively steep or flattish roofs are not typical of Scotland.

d7. Form of houses

It is within the framework of these salient characteristics that Scottish country building has been developed.

Farm buildings

Houses on farms do not depart in the essential elements of form from other houses. The composition of the whole farm with its byres, barns, stores, mills, etc. divides into certain basic types. Farm building evolved from small simple units (**43**) to large geometrical forms with inner courts closed on three or four sides and may be classified as shown in diagram 8.

Gables are normally found but hipped roofs are not unusual and are almost entirely confined to Peeblesshire farms. Some examples in the crofting areas have thatched hipped roofs or have been re-roofed in corrugated sheeting or bituminous felt. Farm steadings in the richer agricultural parts of the country were elaborated with horse-gang mills, multi-arched carthouses and noble entrance gates roofed over with a dovecot. In terms of building and architecture these clearly belong to the most important category of country buildings, excluding of course the mansion houses and castles. In some of these rich areas, and especially where coalfields lie convenient, the farmers of the mid-nineteenth century installed steam engines to drive the threshing machinery, bringing to these arcadian settings of the eighteenth century a whiff of the dark satanic mills of the following century. The age of the agricultural engine has had its brief sway but many of the tall brick chimneys, useless, still survive and are of interest to architectural historians and, unlike the factory chimneys in the industrial towns, are approved of by some architects for their design and contribution to architectural composition.

(d.8,A) The long rectangular plan is representative of the older small farm. It consists of a house with a barn attached at one end. The other end of the house may have a further farm building attached as is common in crofting areas. The barns sometimes have square or round-ended corn drying kilns, as in the Northern Isles and Caithness where summers are short.

(d.8,B) This type is similar to (d.8,A) but has an added shed placed approximately at right angles to the house. It is a common form and is often seen in crofting areas.

(d.8,C) The formal arrangement begins to emerge in this type. The buildings are grouped around a rectangular courtyard with one end left open, frequently employed in medium and large steadings.

(d.8,D) A type favoured in the more formal plans with two open courts for small or medium steadings as found in the north-west and north-east.

(d.8,E) A large version of (d.8,C) but with the house placed some way in front of the open court, common in Aberdeenshire, Banffshire and N. Kincardineshire.

(d.8,F) Like an extension of the principle of (d.8,A) but larger and more organised. The house is retained at the centre of the two wings; mainly found in small compact dairy steadings in the counties of Ayr (**45**), Renfrew, Lanark, Dunbarton and Argyll and the Western Isles.

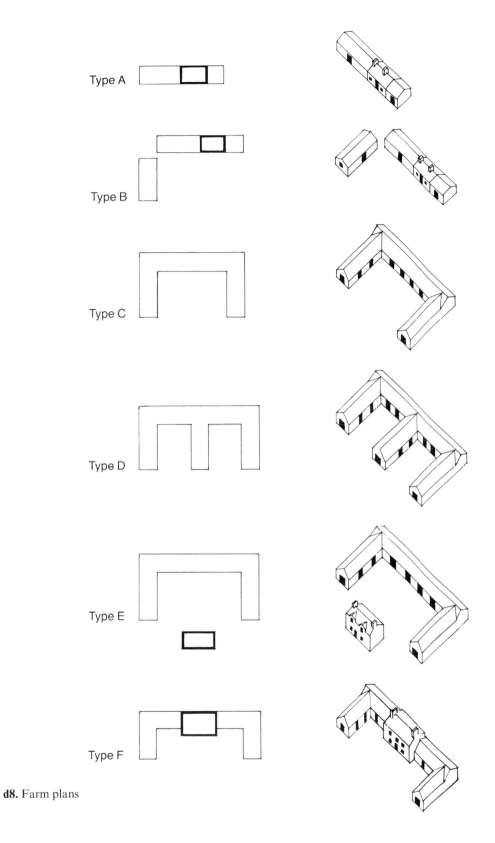

Type A

Type B

Type C

Type D

Type E

Type F

d8. Farm plans

67   *The setting and form of buildings*

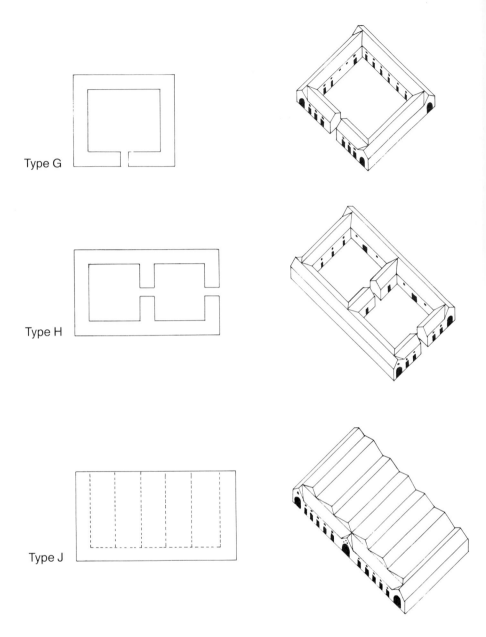

(d.8,G) An example of the large enclosed cattle court, usually located in big farms, where cattle in large numbers could be kept and fed during the winter. Found in Moray, Angus, S. Kincardine, Fife, the Lothians, Berwickshire, Roxburgh and the south-west.

(d.8,H) This provides an elaboration of (d.8,G) with greater storage space and room for cattle; found in the Lothians, Berwickshire, Roxburgh and the south-west.

(d.8,J) This type takes the form of a large roofed-in area of building, accommodating all the functions required of a very large holding. The house is large and detached. These farms may be slated or tiled, in some cases tiles being reserved for the steadings and slate for the farmhouse. Found in Angus, S. Kincardine, Fife, the Lothians and Berwick.

43. *Top right* Glachavoil, Argyll

44. *Above right* Berriedale, Caithness

45. *Right* Nethershield, Ayrshire

69   *The setting and form of buildings*

Other types of buildings

Countryside buildings vary to such an extent in form that systematic classification of form types has not been attempted. There is a tendency in the building of schools, mills, smithies etc. to adopt various forms according to site and function. Smaller structures like ice-houses, smoke houses and mort houses are nearly always simple in form and rectangular. It would be wrong to form a conception of buildings only on the basis of a knowledge of their salient features. In surveying the whole sweep of building, examples often arrest one's attention because they are atypical. They may relate to the overall form of the buildings that make regional character but they may not necessarily be stylistically consistent with that character. Although the national survey concentrated on the main ingredients that made up the staple diet of the architecture of the countryside, buildings that have some special quality or attribute are occasionally noted because the savouries and trimmings that lend zest and sweetness are worth mentioning.

Shops

A number of the early shop fronts have survived intact. In cast iron or timber, they now provide some of the most elegant frontages in many towns. They represent the charm of country life in the small towns of Scotland over one and a half centuries ago, and fronts can be found with classic columns in slender, fine detail, extravagant sprays of foliage, shields and other devices of the times. Fortunately, the more enlightened attitude towards traditional

46. The Holme, Kirkcudbrightshire

47. *Above left* Freswick, Caithness

48. *Above right* Ballindalloch, Banffshire

design in recent years will likely ensure their survival. These shops are worthy of a special study and should be recorded in detail. Advice on proper painting and maintenance would assist in their appreciation.

Gatehouses and Lodges

Gatehouses, placed on the roadside at the carriage entrances to mansion houses, have given owners and their architects an opportunity to display their inventiveness in architectural design and ornamentation (**46**). These buildings follow the countryside tradition in their choice of materials but seldom in their observation of the Scottish custom of striking a very dignified and respectable attitude to appearances. Most of the gatehouses are openly dressed-up, with classical or Gothic features and this romantic approach takes many forms. They also offered a rare opportunity for owners and their architects to 'throw their caps over the windmill' and contrive to disguise objects of utility as ornaments of imagination. In order to achieve their ends architects were sometimes given to forcing the plans into shapes derived not for their function but for their fancy. This has meant that the buildings are not always very conveniently planned and consequently are not readily adaptable. Nor from an architectural point of view may one easily add to such a building because it was usually conceived as an entity. In the future some greater thought will be needed if all these pleasing buildings are to be kept for the better artistic well-being of the countryside.

Dovecots

The great farming expansion also created fine dovecots. The oldest of the dovecots were erected one or two centuries before the period with which this book is mostly concerned. Many old dovecots of that earlier era are still preserved. Their solid bell-like shapes called 'beehives' and built in rubble, will always

71   *The setting and form of buildings*

appeal to anyone with an eye for architectural form (**47**). The other older type is that which is stepped at the top and is referred to as a 'lectern' with the stepped roof sloping in one direction only.

During the period covered by the survey, attractive dovecots were erected in square (**48**), as well as octagonal and circular plans variously executed in classical, 'Scottish', plain or ornamental styles (**49**). It is in the dovecots built within the farms that the most distinctive architectural effects are obtained. Placed above the arched entrances to the large courtyard farms (**29**) they provided architects and owners with a method of producing the wonderful compositions of farm steading, mill house, cottages and tower which form one of the most arresting prospects in the countryside of the richer agricultural areas.

General lessons

It would be remiss not to allude to the contributions made to the countryside by churches, churchyards and their distinctive monuments, castles, mansions, harbours, lighthouses, distilleries, large hotels, local monuments, memorial halls and minor structures. They are outwith the scope of the survey but they

49. Inverquhomery, Aberdeenshire

50. Mouswald Grange, Dumfriesshire

51. Strathpeffer, Ross and Cromarty

represent part of the overall picture of rural building and their interaction, visually and technically, with the lesser buildings is acknowledged.

There are many moderately-sized houses and farms that were built with surprisingly well-designed porticos – some in classical Palladian style or arches in the Florentine manner. For example, Strathpeffer has a rich collection of individual late-Victorian houses of excellent architectural quality (**51**). Findochty provides the unexpected answer to those who believe that the choice of colouring for buildings should be left to the experts. Inverallochy proves that delight in layout can come out of almost entirely ignoring the master plan (**III**,p.42). The crofters have raised corrugated iron to a point of respectability but only after it has rusted. Farmers in the south-west have produced their own style of black and white buildings as well as the Galloway cows (**50**). The large mills that were recorded from Orkney to the Lothians demonstrate how simple buildings may be large and without ornament or conscious design and yet look impressive, being built strongly with local stone and good slate (**17**).

The most rewarding outcome of the survey for the author has been the rediscovery that there is a countryside architecture which is distinctively Scottish. In the small towns from Stromness to Gatehouse of Fleet, in the small ordered villages, in the open countryside and on the farms, there are many changes in scale and style. But there is one constant: the architectural impression still conveys a proper awareness of Scottish character throughout.

52. Gatehouse of Fleet, Kirkcudbrightshire

5   **Elements of buildings**

Walls: materials and their use

The external walls of a building have been an essential medium of architectural expression since earliest times. Apart from the well understood devices of arranging windows, doors, arches, ornaments, projections and colonnades, walls provide a basic ingredient by the nature of the material that is employed and the manner of finishing its surface. Even in the small countryside buildings, these elemental processes have been put to work. Elevational arrangements concern the question of proportion and will be covered in Chapter 6. Here the use of the materials is considered.

Stone A feature of recent countryside building has been the rapid introduction of brick construction and harled finish. This change began after 1914 and, although the measure of its extent was not a matter of investigation by the survey, other statistical sources indicate that even today less than 75 per cent of all the buildings that exist are stone built. That the survey confirmed stone as the dominant walling material will not surprise Scots. For centuries visitors to Scotland have remarked on this fact and people from the brick areas in England are even today still struck by this contrast to their own countryside more than by anything else. Without the benefit of statistics the finding is that stone is Scottish and the chief contributor to character in the architecture.

There are good reasons for singling out stone in this way. First, the material that was employed belonged to the land where it was to be used for building. It therefore naturally possesses local colour. Secondly, by its composition – closeness or coarseness of grain and degree of stratification – it naturally displays many different textures. Furthermore, it is capable of differing applications of surface treatment from very rough to polished. Thirdly, it may be gathered or wrought and built in units in a wide range of sizes. Finally, the ways in which it may be fashioned by masons are nearly limitless. To sum up, nature and civilisation have not combined to produce any building material more conducive to the creation of character and style than stone. The fulfilment of the primary objective of the survey, which was the investigation of building character in the countryside, called for a very close examination of how stone has been used. For convenience, its many varieties have been grouped below into sandstones, whinstone, granite and flagstone which is a form of sandstone.

Sandstone
Sandstone, including freestone, is the chief adornment of Scotland. It would seem almost to have an affinity with the people, for wherever rural population is congregated, sandstone is to be found with only about two notable excep-

tions. The explanation derives from geology because the more fertile agricultural areas where people are settled generally coincide with the underlying rock formations which provide good building stone. Therefore when agricultural methods were transformed and the countryside flourished after the mid-eighteenth century and new building was in demand, countrymen turned to stone, their next greatest resource after land. It was then that this great wealth was uncovered. Over a large extent of the country old stone quarries were being worked and new ones uncovered. In some parts the sandstone was so abundant that it lay almost open for the taking in a great many varieties. In texture and grain it ranged from coarse to very fine, from open to very close and dense.

Equally the diversity of colour can be observed: deep red, red white, reddish, rusty-iron colour, buff, yellow, orange, dark brown, purple or heather colour, cream, pale and dark grey approaching black, light blue, greyish red, yellowish, red variegated with grey spots, white with tinges of brown or yellow, bluish grey, straw coloured and deep yellow. These are some of the descriptions by those who were living at the time when the walls were new and the colour fresh. The survey, after nearly one and a half to two centuries, still recorded these colours but in more muted tones. There may be in some minds doubts about these descriptions of colour. People coming from the southern countries are accustomed to the bright positive colouring in buildings which sun and clear skies invite. Their eyes are not attuned to the softer colours which suit the less dazzling Scottish light. Perhaps even Scots themselves have become dazzled in front of the unreal exaggerations of their colour TV screens to the extent that they may fail to recognise this quality in their buildings. But the gentle colours of natural stone are still there.

The countryside in Scotland was generally fortunate in that much of it lay well outside the orbit of nineteenth-century industry. While the country buildings remained relatively clean, the buildings in Glasgow and the larger towns in the west did not escape. The soft rich tones of Lanarkshire building stone for a short time must have brightened the lives of Glasgow's tenement dwellers. It may well have inspired the Glasgow school of brilliant colourists towards the end of last century. But this bright city environment was rapidly enveloped in the black carboniferous shroud of the 'palaeotechnic' age. The polluted air not only led to poor health and the drudgery of work to keep home and contents clean, but it must also have blighted the spirit and left an inheritance of social problems among people who by their nature have need of more than the material ends in life. In the descriptions of the character zones, the contribution which colour makes to the local character will be demonstrated. In the country as a whole, the sandstone counties follow down along the east coast from Caithness, Sutherland, Ross-shire, Nairn and Moray to Banff. They commence again in Kincardine, continue through Angus, East Perthshire, Fife, the Forth Valley and the Lothians down to Berwick and Roxburgh and cross Lanarkshire to Renfrew and Ayr. There are isolated areas in Dumfries.

Ashlar
The techniques of working and building sandstone are influenced by quality. The coarse-grained stone was used principally for rubble. The fine-grained stones were reserved for rybats, lintels, sills, chimney copes and skews. Its use

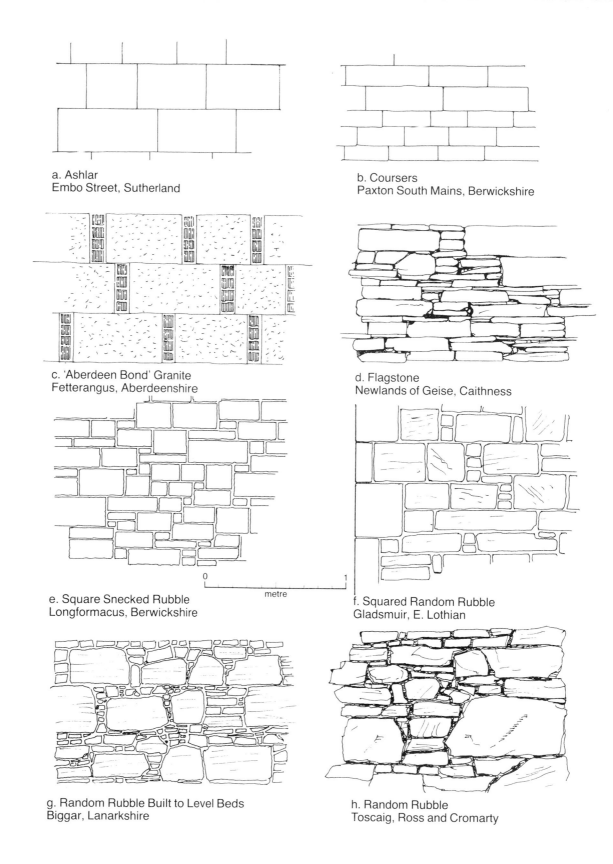

a. Ashlar
Embo Street, Sutherland

b. Coursers
Paxton South Mains, Berwickshire

c. 'Aberdeen Bond' Granite
Fetterangus, Aberdeenshire

d. Flagstone
Newlands of Geise, Caithness

0   1
metre

e. Square Snecked Rubble
Longformacus, Berwickshire

f. Squared Random Rubble
Gladsmuir, E. Lothian

g. Random Rubble Built to Level Beds
Biggar, Lanarkshire

h. Random Rubble
Toscaig, Ross and Cromarty

for ashlar or snecked work can be observed in many small buildings in most parts of the country (**53**). Although the stone was often fine enough for the most demanding of hewn work, polished ashlar was not commonly encountered in the countryside examples surveyed (d.9,a). Its appearance will be noted in the smaller towns and in many of the fine farms built or rebuilt during the nineteenth century. The quarries producing stone which was suscep-

d9. *Opposite* Masonry walling techniques

53. *Above right* Sanquhar, Dumfriesshire

tible to a very high polish usually sent their products to the cities or to contractors erecting mansion houses in the country. One of the computer maps illustrated that ashlar work, not necessarily polished, is found in the north-east and in the central belt where populations and the small towns and villages are mostly located. Ashlar is also frequently employed in Victorian public buildings such as small village schools, if only in ornamental portions of the building. It was apparently seldom regarded as appropriate for mills or warehouses.

Coursers and square snecked rubble

As the nineteenth century progressed, masons extended their techniques. Where stone of a higher grade was available they began to produce a finish that was less natural than rubble but not so finished as ashlar (d.9,b). The stones were square-dressed on the beds and joints. The face was provided with whatever texture was required within the limitations of the grain. The stones were built usually in equal courses rather stiffly and finished at the openings with ashlar rybats or starts and tails (21). Square snecked rubble (d.9,e) is a more complex and more handsome method of building in this style. The stones consist of three basic shapes – headers, stretchers and snecks. The headers provided the square deep stones built into the depth of the wall for strength. The stretchers were built against the face or backing of the interior of the wall and are about half the height of the headers. The snecks were the small stones inserted by the mason to break the horizontal bond of the beds, thus limiting the length of the beds to about 1 to 2 metres (3 to 6 feet) to give strength to the structure. The two styles eventually spread over nearly the whole of the countryside and in the suburbs of the towns. Its strong representation in the areas of reasonably good freestone has established it as one of the indicators of local character in some regions as will be seen later.

Rubble

Generally where masons used sandstone or freestone as rubble they were recognising the deficiency of the quality of the stone available. Such stone was described as coarse and gritty. The so-called 'bastard free-stone' was known to be rather porous and apt to crumble, while others were believed to retain dampness. In some quarries the upper stratum of weathered rock was found to be friable and 'crumbles in the northern weather'. Such low grades were known and presumably avoided. The better grades, in the hands of competent masons, provided large stones and small stones which were fitted together patiently to produce the characteristic walls of buildings all over the country.

Rubble was put together in various ways using different sizes and shapes of stones. The main variations come from the degree to which the masons modified and shaped the stones before building them into the wall. At one extreme the stones are employed as selected by the mason without any intervention by him in breaking or splitting the stone (d.9,g,h). Very large stones may be positioned at foundation level and at corners for stability. The stones thereafter were laid by making up the levels before each stone was placed over the one below through inserting small snecks or pins consisting of the small bits of stone, to give a base on which the stones to be positioned could sit firmly.

Similar small stones were employed to fill any gaps in the vertical joints between a stone and its neighbours on either side (**54**). Some instances are, of course, found where no mortar has been used and the beds and joints are dry as in dykes and some farm buildings. In walls built with stone which was more readily open to splitting the courses were laid approximately level, and over-thick mortar beds were thus avoided. But the joints remain at their natural angles and gaps were again fitted with small stones of various dimensions to suit the occasion (d.9,f).

Within these basic approaches masons may have further modified their technique by various methods of pointing – from fine thin joints lying at the edges of the stones to thick over spread pointing to give a much smoother appearance. The survey showed, however, that much good rubble work has been spoiled in recent times by repointing, using bad techniques and wrong colours. The procedure to adopt in repointing is obvious: repeat what has been done before if the pointing appears original. If not, examine and find an original unspoilt example in the vicinity and copy.

A practical problem confronted builders of houses and other buildings when rubble was employed. Because of the comparative severity of the Scottish weather during part of the year, the junctions require to be well made and protected. Windows and door openings in the walls needed to be formed to achieve a tight fit with the joinery. This required a true straight finish of the stonework and obviously that could not be obtained in most types of rubble building. It induced masons to use a superior stone for forming these openings (**20**). They cut and dressed the stone in various ways to form rybats, margins or starts (d.10). The stones thus produced were built in along with the rubble walling. The method ensured a vertical plumb opening to which the sash and case windows could later be fitted giving a close joint and vertical positioning so necessary for this type of window to operate properly. It will be noted that this procedure differs from the English brickwork technique which provided for the building-in of the wooden casements along with the walling. The sills and lintels in Scottish rubble walls were also usually of dressed stone. Older buildings were recorded with wooden lintels and no dressed sills (**111**).

It has sometimes been observed when old rubble buildings were demolished that the walls appeared to have been erected in two parallel leaves forming a vestige of a cavity between the outer and inner leaves. There have been instances where this interior space has been found to contain a filling of small

54. Oban, Harris

stones, lime mortar, and even clay and earth, turf or peat. The front and inner faces of the walls had to present a reasonably even surface. The interior of the wall where the walls were thick had to take up the differences in the surface brought about by the varying depths of the stones employed. In good rubble work the walls were solid and the mason skilfully bonded his stones across the thickness of the walls as well as along the surfaces. However, in the Western Isles two-leaved stone walls were regarded as the soundest protection from damp penetration. Lime mortar was universally adopted for building rubble except in the very old buildings where clay was used. No examples of clay mortar were noted during the survey, but very close examination could bring to light any that may still survive.

Whinstone

Where sandstone, freestone or granite could not be found locally, Scots country builders used whinstone. It is available in many of the counties although not used in all of them for building. Some counties have relatively few examples of whin walls in buildings. Whin was used neither in Orkney nor Shetland, nor was it much used in Kinross, Ross and Cromarty, Angus, Kincardine, Aberdeenshire, the north-east and Caithness. It dominated Selkirk where it was the one building stone available in any quantity (**55**). It was in use in most of Peeblesshire and its distribution made it a primary walling material in the Borders and north Dumfriesshire. It is to be seen in the Lothians, Fife, Stirlingshire, the south-west and the west and in the Western Isles.

The material varies in consistency and character over the country. In some areas it is found to be hard and intractable – 'hard, amorphous, blackish and no cleavage' as one contemporary Peeblesshire writer described it.

Elsewhere it could be of a fine colour, capable of being neatly dressed but hard to work. Its physical characteristics call for skill in shaping and preparing the stone and in building it. It was usually employed for rubble (d.9,g) although instances of coursed work can be found. Because the surface of the material

55. *Above right* Boleside, Selkirkshire

56. *Opposite* Wigtown

57. Insch, Aberdeenshire

does not absorb and hold moisture in wet weather as sandstone does, whin had to be built in such a way as to discourage water that had penetrated through the mortar from running inwards towards the interior face. This was done by tilting the beds outward. Masons who mastered this technique of building in whinstone belonged to the elite of their craft. As in sandstone or freestone rubble, whin walls were usually built with dressed stone or, in the south-west, brick at the openings for doors and windows (**58**).

In colour it has been referred to as blue whin and grey whin, but the geological intrusions of bands of various minerals often lend to the surface of the stone a prismatic quality of semi-latent colouring.

Granite

This material was recorded in the walls of buildings in four main centres: the counties of Aberdeen, Kincardine, Banff and Kirkcudbright. It is present in other areas where it has less widespread influence on the local character. Some granite was worked in the past in Selkirkshire, Midlothian, Wigtownshire, Stirlingshire (mostly for use in road making), Argyll, Sutherland in the farthest north, Perthshire, Angus, Banffshire and Shetland. It was so abundant in Aberdeenshire that it lay in places scattered on the surface for immediate working and use. One contemporary declared that it had 'brought gold to Aberdeen'. The material has great potentiality for enriching architecture. Normally it polishes to a gloss finish. Its speckled colouring gives the finished surfaces, whether rough or polished, a lively appearance.

The granite builders in the countryside never used polished granite for walls. That belonged to the city and the interiors of buildings. The country technique, however, gave the walls of the buildings a novel appearance (**57**). The stones were squared into blocks often only slightly longer than a square. They tended to be moderately large in scale. Usually each stone along the bed was separated from its neighbours on either side by a series of small squarish stones built one above the other so that the combined height of three to five small stones equalled the height of the larger stone (d.9,c). The technique seems to have developed towards the end of the eighteenth century and is encountered wherever granite was used.

The colours available in granite were blue purple, white, black tinge, red grey, dark blue, light grey and sand coloured. Openings were formed in granite but they were also often framed by another material, notably brick in the south-west.

Flagstone

Flagstone is found in the north-east of Caithness and in Orkney where it is geologically part of a basin which extends from the mainland of Scotland to beyond the Orkney Islands. The material possesses an extraordinary property in that its stratified composition allows it to be easily split into thin sheets like slate and yet in its thicker forms it is not dissimilar to rough sandstone (**119**). It represents almost the ideal building material. So diverse are its uses that it may be split fine for slates, used as large thin slabs for roof covering, split thicker for wall building, cut to form lintels and employed for paving and floors. Internally, it served for larder shelves and forming water storage cisterns. Even in the fields the divisions are formed by neat precise fences consisting of rows of slabs set into the ground and standing erect shoulder to shoulder along the margins of the fields. When built into walls the faces of the stone are rough and horizontally striated (d.9,d). This is the sort of texture much admired by modern architects although here it was being created nearly two centuries ago. In the low, flat almost treeless landscape it is difficult to imagine any walling material that could be more apposite. These areas offer countryside building at its very best in terms of character. The buildings are modest and rarely assume any architectural pretensions. What they do achieve is an affinity with the landscape of the country, the essential objective of all country building but nowadays too seldom even attempted.

The flagstone is frequently described as grey but it has much richer colour properties. Local writers described it as a very beautiful blue which was the best quality obtainable. When built or long exposed to weather, warm rusty colours also became evident. In Orkney the slatey sandstone was given only limited dressing. Even when built dry it was known to have little tendency to shift even in the raging winds that periodically blast that part of the country. The stones are relatively long and shallow, being laid in even courses of varying heights with considerable differences in the heights of the courses. The pointing is positioned back from the face of the stones in most examples. Lintels and sills are formed roughly in the same material. This technique is used not only in houses and agricultural buildings but also in the larger commercial buildings such as the many impressive mills in Orkney.

Flagstone buildings were found in Sutherland and in Argyll. It was also quarried in Angus and Arbroath, the flags being used locally for paving as well as being exported to England and the Continent for street paving, kitchen floors etc. Angus, however, being also rich in the more orthodox sandstones, did not exploit flagstone to the same extent as in the north.

Other building stones

Other types of stone were used only sparingly and have no influence on the national character of building. Graywacke, a bluish gritty sandstone, is found

in the Borders and the south-west of Scotland as well as in other isolated instances in other parts. Limestone occurs in East Lothian and Midlothian. For the most part limestone, which was scarce in many areas of Scotland, was worked for agricultural purposes and for mortar and plaster. Some areas had to import lime from England or Ireland. Cockleshells were also used for plaster.

Brick and other material

It was not the lack of refractory clays that precluded brick from becoming a part of the Scottish countryside. There have been few areas in the country that have not had brickworks. Scotland is a stone country because that is what she chose to be. The survey confirmed that buildings of brick prior to 1914 were but infrequently encountered. Only four parishes in the south-west of the country recorded over 30 per cent of the samples with brick walls.

Parishes with up to 30 per cent brick construction were recorded in the Lothians and the area of Scotland extending from Angus, in a south-west direction to Dunbarton. As a building material relating to character, it therefore has only local significance. There are, however, cases where brick has been used in an effective fashion. As previously indicated brick rybats, in place of stone where granite or rubble is the primary wall material, have become familiar features in some areas. Brick has also been used along with stone in other parts of buildings, especially chimneyheads (**58**).

The reaction of Scottish people to brick walls in building seems to have been unfavourable. This may be because of an inherent belief deeply implanted in the mind that brick belongs to industrial buildings, associated with cheapness and poverty. Some find brick buildings depressing, even when seen in areas to the south, where it belongs to a fine tradition. With this sentiment, Scots may never have been happy about using facing brick, no matter what colour

58. Cairnryan, Wigtownshire

or texture it provides. Architects with an enthusiasm for brick walls may have to submit to this attitude and recognise that, in the service of conservation, their proposals for brick buildings should be directed where they properly belong, that is to areas where brick is established as part of a local tradition.

Early brick buildings were recorded in the Borders, e.g. Ednam village, planned and built at the end of the eighteenth century and a large house in Berwickshire built in the first decade of the nineteenth century. Evidence of even earlier use of brick walling suggests that, as a minor technique, it goes back a considerable time also in Scotland.

In some instances alterations and additions have introduced newer materials for walling. Concrete blocks and sheeting like corrugated iron and asbestos cement are shown to be well established in some areas. Other types of material beyond those mentioned above such as timber, hung slates etc. are found in small proportions in agricultural areas, except Orkney and Shetland. Generally they do not represent as much as 30 per cent in areas where they were recorded. No examples of the ancient form of walls using turf and stone were encountered during the survey, although a few relics are known to exist. Solid clay and clay and wattle walls still survive in the east and the south-west, but their minor position in the overall national reckoning does not call for more than this passing reference here, although historically, they were of much greater importance.

Farms and other buildings

The materials used in building walls generally are also found in farm buildings, although the less traditional materials appear more frequently in farms than in the other buildings. There has been more timber and asbestos sheeting used in gables and in the sides of barns and sheds. Some look temporary and will be replaced eventually. There is yet time to reconsider the strategy for dealing with the rapid change in mechanisation and farming methods which leads in turn to building alterations, demolitions and new building. The most pressing difficulty confronting the farmers and others is how to find uses for older buildings to justify their retention and upkeep.

In the matter of walls, many farms still retain fine nineteenth-century cart sheds with openings or 'eyes' too low in height to admit entry of the powerful machinery now available and necessary for working the farms (**14**). Horse-mills are only retained if the farmers wish to keep them for sentimental or decorative purposes (**29**). In some cases entire farm steadings have become redundant and lie virtually unused, verging towards dereliction with walls deteriorating due to neglect. Fortunately, some splendid examples can be found where farmers of their own volition have rebuilt barns and sheds using the old materials and adding with the same materials anew in such a way that experts could not detect the change. Traditional materials may still be had if the will is there to seek them.

Schools and public buildings were commonly executed in stone (**60**). They were well built and usually well maintained, coursed work being normal in such buildings. Warehouses, small industrial buildings and old houses converted to commercial use have mostly followed the techniques and use of materials found in domestic dwellings. It was noted, however, that some industrial buildings such as grain stores and mills are falling into disrepair through lack of use.

Field and boundary walls

Field boundary walls, called 'dykes' in Scotland, provide an insight into the skills of masons and the adaptation of their techniques to suit the limitations of the material to hand. Notable are the fine walls, round copes and end posts of the Angus red stone walls. Rubble walls with stone-on-edge copes are widespread and some have a rough oversailing course below the header top course for the protection of the faces of the walls. Some walls are finished with low and high vertical stones in the 'cock and hen' style. Other walls hardly deserve that appellation, consisting only of heaped field stones providing rough barriers. In Caithness, the stone slabs constitute the distinctive field fence in that county. In the Borders and other whinstone areas, farmers had drystone field walls built, and in the granite areas of Deeside drystone dyking achieved a perfection which has not been surpassed elsewhere in the country.

These walls lend their character to their surroundings to the extent that they could in many cases tell an observant traveller in which part of the country he had arrived without reference to anything else. Field walls in the dairy farms in the south-west are finished with thin rubble deliberately chosen to look slim and precarious. It is said that they were to keep in cattle for no beast, however adventurous, would risk trying to climb over them.

Applied wall finishes

Applications of various coatings to stone or brick walls have become common practice in this century. Wet dash harling has been regarded as a traditional material. Coating with lime was also used, especially for interiors of cowsheds and stables. Where stone was soft and liable to exposure from severe weather it was finished in a thick coating of lime as was recorded in the north-east in the early nineteenth century. The survey did not show harling to be a major walling finish in the country. It appears most frequently in the east of Ross-shire, in Nairn, Banff and north Aberdeenshire. The north-west coastal strip and the outer Hebrides also have concentrations. In the remainder of the country fairly uniform distributions occur in the central belt and down the Ayrshire coastline. Elsewhere, isolated pockets emerge where heavier concentrations of population are found. The older lime harling looks softer and less mechanical than the harder more uniform dry dash finishes which have become popular in recent years.

Lime wash and rendering as a form of wall treatment was definitely bred in the west of the country. Like a shield against the south-west winds and driving rain it stretches from the south of Dumfries along the Solway and up the west coast to Caithness (59). Its origin may lie in the poorer capacities of local stone to resist water penetration in face of the weather conditions typical of the west coast. The desire for brighter colour which the west coast people seem to have may also have inspired this style of finish. In recent years it seems to have intensified and begun to spread east like a contagious infection.

Beyond these limits, the practice is counter-productive to maintaining character because it induces owners to paint over fine stone and whin walls removing the inherited character and substituting a finish which is out of keeping. Painting over blackened harling, using shades in harmony with the local established colour, is acceptable. The survey did not disclose a great many cases

59. *Opposite top*
Gatehouse of Fleet,
Kirkcudbrightshire

60. *Opposite bottom*
Dirleton, East Lothian

of external wall painting in areas where it is not traditional. There was sufficient evidence, however, to suggest that the practice may be growing in places where it does not belong. It is a matter needing attention in face of the indiscriminate advertising by manufacturers inviting owners to colour their buildings. The map which presented the result of this part of the survey showed colouring penetrating even along the west of Shetland.

The choice of colour is a matter of vital importance in the maintenance of character in both existing and new buildings. In the wider landscape the significant building colours derive from the basic materials used on roofs and walls. The colour of chimney pots, doors, windows and barge boards has greater consequence at closer range. The survey took account of colour because of the key part it plays in the landscape and the results demonstrated the positive contribution natural stone colours can make to character and local variation. It has clearly identified the capacity of stone, slate and tile to give unity to buildings and to the landscape. It has left no doubts that an over-zealous application of white paint on walls is another example of one generation's taste wrongly overruling another's. Colour on wood is ephemeral, but once applied to stone or harling it commits the process for all time or leaves the walls sadly disfigured, fading and streaked. The drift of white over the countryside from west to east was started in the 1960s by the 'black and white' fashion much loved then by architects and architectural photographers before the widespread development of colour photography. Thus in areas where painted walls were traditional, new colours were introduced which were foreign to the locality. Even more damaging, white was applied to stone walls for the first time merely to conform to a transient fashion.

Surface treatments of stone

Stone lends itself to a great many forms of surface treatment and the three main nationally employed examples are:

1. Left rough (d.10,a)
(a) The exposed face of the stone is left as it is received from the quarry, i.e. rock faced, only being subjected to rough shaping with the hammer (d.10,m); or
(b) the face of the stone is left as it was formed naturally on or near to the surface from where it was gathered, this finish usually being more rounded and smoother than the rock faced stones (d.10,i).

2. Tooled (d.10,c,g).
(a) The face is dressed with a tool to make it roughly smooth but not polished (d.10,l); or
(b) the stone face is tooled by punching or droving to give a mechanical texture, the latter leaving broadly spaced deeply cut grooves or being very finely tooled to provide close horizontal grooves giving the appearance of a fine comb (d.10,d,f).

3. Polished
The stone may be chiselled and polished to provide smooth ashlar. Finish to this pitch is seldom found in the open country areas but is familiar in the smaller towns (**12**). Ashlar finishes are especially used in contrast to rubble face work on the main walls (d.10,p).

d10. Stone finishing

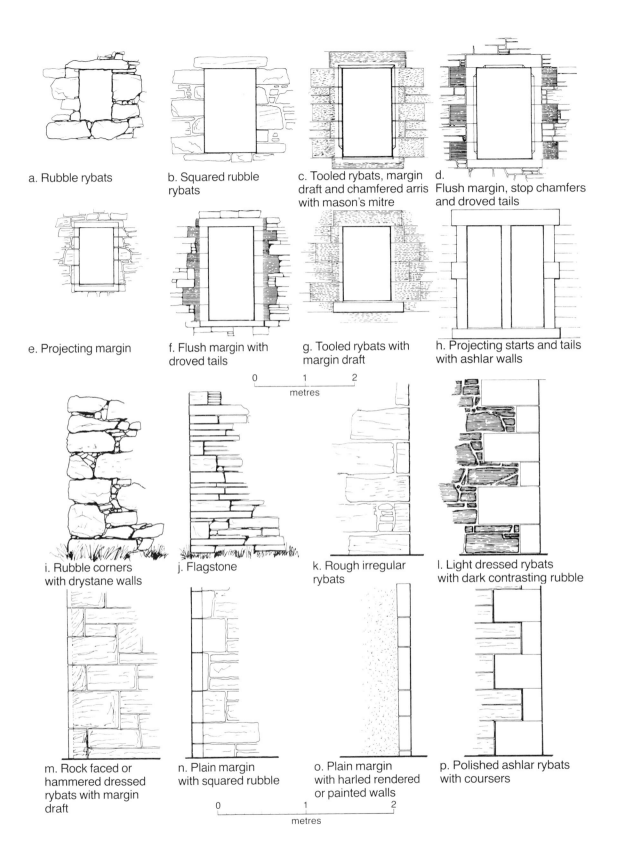

a. Rubble rybats

b. Squared rubble rybats

c. Tooled rybats, margin draft and chamfered arris with mason's mitre

d. Flush margin, stop chamfers and droved tails

e. Projecting margin

f. Flush margin with droved tails

g. Tooled rybats with margin draft

h. Projecting starts and tails with ashlar walls

i. Rubble corners with drystane walls

j. Flagstone

k. Rough irregular rybats

l. Light dressed rybats with dark contrasting rubble

m. Rock faced or hammered dressed rybats with margin draft

n. Plain margin with squared rubble

o. Plain margin with harled rendered or painted walls

p. Polished ashlar rybats with coursers

0 1 2
metres

Corners, margins and embellishments

The erection of stone walls in buildings involves the techniques of finishing at the corners and at windows and doors. Corners are sometimes treated by forming chamfers at 45° across the corner of dressed rybats or margins. These chamfers are usually finished at the bottom rybat by forming a stop-chamfer splayed out and converging to meet the true right-angled corner (d.10,c). Stop-chamfers may also be formed at the top rybats and at the lintels (d.10,d). Alternatively the chamfer may be made to run round the top rybat and along the lintel by forming a 'mason's mitre' at the intersection (d.10,c). Sometimes stop-chamfers are moulded. Chamfering was very popular in Gothic-style buildings but also appeared in much earlier buildings (**41**). It performs the useful function of protecting the corners from damage by removing the sharp arrises which are otherwise susceptible to chipping.

Although margins belong to windows and doors as an element of building, their close connection with the art of the mason calls for a passing reference to them. When they are formed in stone in Scotland they are usually narrow in the smaller-scale buildings – about 115mm (4½in) (d.10,e). They do not project very far beyond the face of the wall – very often not more than about 10mm (⅜in), or are even set flush. The smooth face of the margins thus formed is differentiated from the tail of the rybat, which is finished with contrasting tooling to give a broken texture, conforming to the rougher surface of the adjoining rubble walling (d.10,e,n).

In later building, starts and tail stones were employed and there the projection of the margin became larger; nearly double that used in the older technique (d.10,h) (**76**). It should be noted that on traditional stone walls the stone sills were not provided with a large projection. Some are set flush with the wall face (d.10,c,d). In other cases the corners are formed in the rybats by making relatively smooth ingoes and finishing the front of the rybat by a margin draught – a narrow band of fine horizontal droving about 35mm (1⅜in) wide. The rest of the face of the rybat is left rough or tooled with 'pecked' or other contrasting finish (d.10,g).

The countryside, even in the small houses, was not deprived of the mason's accomplished performances for other embellishments. Classical doorways with stone entablatures and pilasters or pillars are frequently found, and cornices have sometimes been employed. There are also all the trappings of Gothic to be seen on occasions, carved finials, panels, coats of arms and date stones (d.11).

Main principles and future prospects

The walls of the country buildings demonstrate how builders could employ different methods of stone treatment to offer variety in finish. Briefly their approaches have ranged from the very simple to highly-worked finishes:

(1)   The stone was built into the walls subject to no more than reducing it to manageable sizes. This applied to rough granite, schist, whin and coarse sandstone.

(2)   The squaring of the stones to allow them to be built on level beds in courses. This technique was applied to the finer granite and various types of sandstone. The method of building included coursers and snecked rubble.

d11. Stone carving and ornamentation

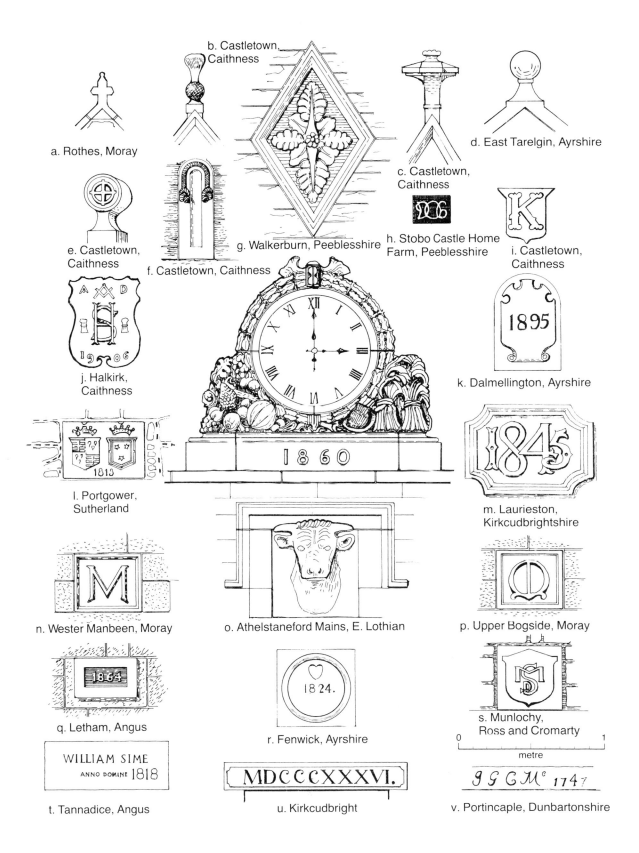

a. Rothes, Moray

b. Castletown, Caithness

c. Castletown, Caithness

d. East Tarelgin, Ayrshire

e. Castletown, Caithness

f. Castletown, Caithness

g. Walkerburn, Peeblesshire

h. Stobo Castle Home Farm, Peeblesshire

i. Castletown, Caithness

j. Halkirk, Caithness

k. Dalmellington, Ayrshire

l. Portgower, Sutherland

m. Laurieston, Kirkcudbrightshire

n. Wester Manbeen, Moray

o. Athelstaneford Mains, E. Lothian

p. Upper Bogside, Moray

q. Letham, Angus

r. Fenwick, Ayrshire

s. Munlochy, Ross and Cromarty

t. Tannadice, Angus

WILLIAM SIME
ANNO DOMINE 1818

u. Kirkcudbright

MDCCCXXXVI.

v. Portincaple, Dunbartonshire

0   metre   1

93   *The elements of buildings*

(3)   The highly worked or tooled stone concerns sandstone built as ashlar, coursers, snecked rubble and polished ashlar. Polished granite was not used in the country.

(4)   Treating the surface of the built walls with harling, colour washing or painting, traditional in the south-west and west but also found in local areas elsewhere, e.g. in Inveresk where orpiment, the golden colour wash, has been maintained for centuries.

If the future walls of rural buildings are to retain the character which was developed so patiently and faithfully for nearly one and a half centuries, ways will have to be found of conforming to the fine qualities which these walls possess. New walls will have to be of a texture to conform to the walls in the vicinity. They will also have to comply with the prevailing colour. Furthermore, this colour will have to have some of the properties special to the colour of the stone – its variation, its capacity to change with the light and atmosphere, its comfortable capacity of ageing gracefully. New materials will have to be built in units of similar dimensions to those in the area of the new building. The sizes of the units will usually appear better if not too uniform. In some areas uniformity will be damaging to the local character. The material should look solid and sturdy.

If the walls are in an area where harling is traditional, they should still look solid and the harling is better if lime harling. If it is in an area traditionally associated with painted walls, the colours should conform to the original range of colours. The paint should be of a matt finish. Where margins or rybats are the recognised idiom of the area, they should only be used if they are designed with the regard to finish and scale which pertain to the older buildings. Further detailed enquiry into the methods of achieving such ends could point the way for future building development in the countryside: towards building twentieth century walls with eighteenth and nineteenth-century perception.

Roofs: materials and their use

Roofs come next in importance to walls in country buildings. Like walls, roofing consists of a synthesis of materials, technique and craftsmanship and has a controlling influence on character. When in the seventeenth or early eighteenth century Scots came to consider the roofs of their new houses, they chose slate if they could afford it. Slate was held in high regard. This opinion, maintained for centuries, had its due effect. Scotland, as well as being a stone country, is also a slate country. The results of the survey confirmed this.

Slates and stone slabs
Analysis of the survey data showed the location of slate roofs in the countyside and gave a vivid indication of how much Scots depend on slate to keep their buildings dry. In a high proportion of areas slate represented 95 to 100 per cent of the recorded samples. In many of the remainder the figure is from 80 to 95 per cent and, still further, a large area has 40 to 80 per cent of buildings roofed in slate. Slate at first came mostly from local quarries, although the reputation of slate from the west of Scotland resulted in some importation

to some areas as far as the Borders. Scotland produced several kinds of slates. First, what is commonly recognised as slate, the argillaceous or clay rock that splits into the relatively thin sheets, was quarried in many parts of the country. Second, certain sandstones were capable of splitting into thicknesses of under 12mm ($\frac{1}{2}$in) and were used widely for roofing in some areas. Lastly, the flagstone of the north of Scotland could be split into large pieces of up to 3m (10ft) long and yet no thicker than about 12mm ($\frac{1}{2}$in), producing a roofing material unique in Britain, when used as full-length slabs on the roofs rather than as slates (**27**).

As in stone for walling, these materials offered a variety of colours and textures. The colours of the true slates ranged over grey, blue, very dark blue, purple, azure blue, greenish, light blue and greyish blue. Aberfoyle produced both green and purple which were usually mixed in the one roof. In texture the finer slates are very smooth and dark in colour. The coarser slates are less dense and normally lighter in colour.

The stone slabs were produced from various quarries. Some are grey, and some blue. The Angus stone slates have a coating of talc which gives them the attractive elusive tint of blue within the warmer stone colour. Muddy-brown stone slates may also be observed in some parts and the stone slates have a more broken uneven surface than true slates. Their much thicker sections also give an overall rugged appearance to the roofs (d.12,b).

The stone slabbed roofs are almost 'modern' in their appearance, but as they were laid in various widths and lengths, the mechanical repetitiveness of modern manufactured materials is absent. Instead the slabs with their varied colours and uneven surface finish are a fitting accompaniment to the flagstone walls with which they are associated (d.12,f).

In the countryside, slates were fixed and arranged as in normal practice with the double gauge laps and pinned with slate nails. Single lap open slating was reserved for stables and byres to combat condensation and timber rot by providing ventilation. Some counties in the country were without local slate of any kind, e.g. Ross-shire, Kinross, Clackmannan, Renfrew, Ayr, Roxburgh, Berwick and the Lothians. The Borders and the south turned to England for supplies, especially after the advent of the railways. Selkirkshire used Welsh slates. Dumfries and other counties took slates from Lanarkshire, Westmorland and Lancashire as well as Wales. Berwickshire imported slates by boat. The west of Scotland was the chief supplier to those areas in the north where

61. Sordale, Caithness

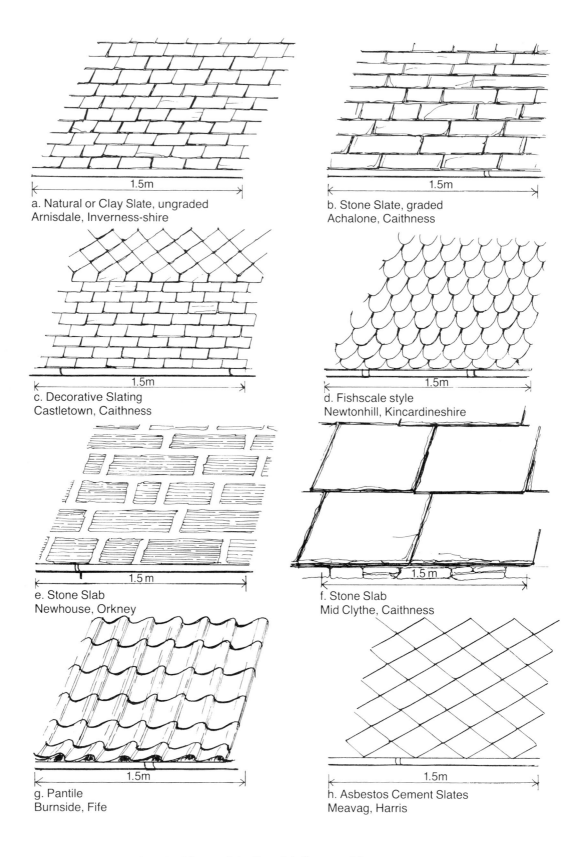

a. Natural or Clay Slate, ungraded
Arnisdale, Inverness-shire

b. Stone Slate, graded
Achalone, Caithness

c. Decorative Slating
Castletown, Caithness

d. Fishscale style
Newtonhill, Kincardineshire

e. Stone Slab
Newhouse, Orkney

f. Stone Slab
Mid Clythe, Caithness

g. Pantile
Burnside, Fife

h. Asbestos Cement Slates
Meavag, Harris

slates were absent, or of poor quality or insufficient quantity.

In terms of the distribution of stone slabs and slates the study revealed that Caithness and Orkney, lying over the same geological basin, share the same characteristics in roof material as they have been shown to have in walling materials. Angus is the other area with a good representation of stone slates. A belt of stone slates also stretched across the centre of Peeblesshire. In Dumfriesshire thin slabs of mica sandstone were used as eaves slates, being brushed over with tar before the fixing of the upper courses of clay i.e. true, slates.

Slates are very versatile as a roofing material, permitting carpenters to adopt various shapes of roofs and complicated intersections. The slates could be dressed to form mitres in hips and valleys, to be fixed round curves in turrets (**49**) (d.24,g) and the rounded cheeks of dormers. This facility gave the builders the opportunity to incorporate intricacies in their designs that were impossible to achieve in pantiles or stone slabs. From this circumstance the dormer window developed in all its forms and became, as will be shown later, a major contributor to character in some areas. It was not usual for the earlier roofs to be provided with a bell-cast at the eaves. The carpenter's wood sarking followed the one slope down to the edges of the outside of the wall and the slater placed his first row of slates immediately above to lip over the cast-iron gutter. After that the slates were added row by row on the same slope up to the eaves. The sides of the slated roof at the eaves were bedded up with mortar tifting

d12. *Opposite* Roof slating and tiling techniques

62. *Above* Eaglesham, Renfrewshire

by the slater so that the end slates against the upstand of the skew sloped away from it to divert water in windy weather from being blown against the stone and hence into the building. The junction between the skew and the slates was finished with a triangular fillet or flashing made of lime and sand which did not tend to shrink or crack. A wide stone wall below, however, was a necessary concomitant for success of this technique because some dampness may evade the defence so put up but would become absorbed and dry out in the warm stone chimney gable. A thin brick wall could not give such protection without the addition of a metal flashing at the join between the slate and the skew.

Grading of slates

By far the greater part of the roofs in the sample were shown to be laid with ungraded slates (d.12,a). This meant that the slaters employed one size of slate throughout on a roof and maintained the same lap from the eaves to the ridge (**66**). Large areas in the counties of Roxburgh and Berwick used standardised English or Welsh slates as did Ayr and Renfrew. The result is that in these areas a major proportion of their roofs are laid with slates that are not graded so that each row of slates from eaves to ridge is of equal depth. The large slates, whether graded or ungraded, predominate along the southern border of the country, especially in Kirkcudbrightshire (**63**).

Almost all stone-slated roofs in contrast had graded slates. Stone slates show almost always a very marked degree of difference in size between the very large slates at the eaves to very small ones at the ridge. This technique has practical justification in that the part of the roof with the greatest number of joins between slates is at the top of the roof which is not called upon to withstand a great deal of water. The larger slates with fewer joins lie along the lower slopes where the surface water collects from the upper parts of the roof and poses the greatest threat of penetration. Also by this arrangement the slater is able to make use of all the sizes of slates as they become available from the quarry and thus economise in material. Furthermore, the larger slates are the ones most likely to pull away from their nails by reason of their considerable weight. If these large slates were nearer the top, they would slide down, gathering momentum and overshoot the gutter to fall below to the danger of the occupants. An advantage of grading, not necessarily incidental, lies in the very distinctive and stylish appearance that buildings, especially low buildings of the countryside, derive from this method of roofing (d.12,b).

The small or medium graded slates are located along the west coast in the south of the country, in the northern part of the central belt, on the east coast especially in the far north, and in the area of Angus and Kincardine.

Decorative slating

The craft of the roof slater developed as the nineteenth century progressed. The romantic movement liked to see decoration, and the slaters obliged by producing various decorative effects. Slates were set diagonally on occasions to produce a diamond pattern; sometimes these diamond patterns were arranged in bands to alternate with bands of horizontally-laid slates (d.12,c); or the bands were further differentiated by adopting different coloured slates,

e.g. purple and green. In some parts, especially in the Buchan area, the slates were dressed with semi-circular shaped ends to produce 'fish-scale' patterning (d.12,d). In other parts the slates were shaped to give an octagonal pattern.

Pantiles
Most counties without local slates made good the deficiencies by importing slates from others better endowed or from England, whichever was the most convenient source. Berwick and the Lothians, also without local slates, did import from both England and the north-west. Slates were, however, confined to the more important buildings such as the farmhouses, the larger houses and the houses in villages. In the smaller cottages in the country and in the farm byres, barns and mills, pantiles were used from the end of the eighteenth century (d.12,g). Some of the Lothian pantiles were reputed to have been imported

63. Kirkcudbright

64. Pittenweem, Fife

from the European continent. Pantiles were also used in Stirlingshire and along the northern coastline of the Forth in Clackmannan and Fife (**64**). Apart from these areas, only isolated parts of the countryside especially along the east coast used clay tiles for roofing. The pantiles in the counties bordering the Forth estuary are differentiated by colour and shape. The East Lothian tiles possess the warm terracotta colour, the Berwickshire tiles are pinker as are the Midlothian tiles, while the Clackmannan tiles are browner. The shapes differ also in the heights of the rolls. Tiles happen to respond well to the red soil of East Lothian and the soft colouring of the east coast landscape just as the blue slates of the west fit the Highland landscape of distant blue hills and the pale blue smoke from the peat fires. The pantiles do not readily admit complex roof patterns but this did not deter local roof tilers from shaping their tiles rather clumsily, but not in a less workmanlike manner, round the octagonal roofs of horse-mills (**29**) and the polygonal roofs of other agricultural buildings such as meal mills.

The tiles laid on tile battens were usually fitted without any jointing but there are many examples where the side laps have been filled with mortar or 'torched' to prevent driven snow from penetrating into the attics of houses. Pantiles are provided with small projections or 'nibs' at the back near the tip of the tile which, with nailing, hooks over the horizontal tiling battens to prevent the heavy tiles from sliding down the roof slope. Sometimes owners have spread tarpaulins over the roof joists to protect their ceilings. Nevertheless, a pantile roof when well laid, and thereafter maintained, may provide years of service as their persistence in these parts of Scotland proves. Modern equivalents made of natural clay are reasonably close in style and character to the Lothians patterns but resemble more closely the English shapes upon which they are based. The unique green pantiles of East Lothian appear to have ceased to exist. The old custom of providing several rows of slate along the eaves of the pantile roof to form a skirt is still commonly seen.

Thatch

There was a time when practically every building in rural Scotland, apart from the tower houses and the churches, was roofed in some form of thatch. Although from about 1750 thatch began to be superseded by the more permanent roof coverings better equipped to resist the extreme weather of the winter months, it remained longer where good material such as reeds or heather was available. In the northern more remote counties the change from thatch was much delayed, especially in the Islands. Now few thatched roofs survive, the last outposts being the Islands with sporadic examples in the Highlands (**111**), Borders, Midlothian and Fife, as well as in some other outlying areas.

The regional methods of Scottish thatching did not vary much. The roofs consisted of couples or crucks overlaid with saplings or young trees or branches operating as purlins. Thereupon lighter timbers were arranged close together to form a base for turfs which were cut in large rectangular slabs and laid lapping like slates. The top covering consisted of straw, reeds, heather or ferns (**3**) which was usually tied down with rope or plaited straw (**10**). This whole thick blanket of material was often held in place by ropes occasionally weighted with stones passing over the top and hanging down the side of the walls, or was covered by plaited straw ropes or nets. The material had to be maintained annually and, at longer intervals, removed and replaced. When the whole apparatus worked and withstood the furious rages of Atlantic gales the interiors of the houses were no doubt warm and protected. When the combined attack of rain and winds dislodged the thatch then disaster faced the occupants. Some forms were reputed to last for several score years and improvements were introduced by combining it with other materials. The complicated varieties of local techniques are fully explored in Fenton and Walker's *The Rural Architecture of Scotland*, reference to which is strongly recommended.

The roofs are picturesque and attractive to view, yet they seem to be in decline. The technique of erection is slowly being lost and if this, the oldest type of roof in rural Scotland, is to survive positive action will be required to retain the necessary skills and derive ways of overcoming the problems of upkeep which the modern ways of heating houses impose on thatch roofing. Thatch which does not receive the drying warmth of coal or peat fires becomes too wet and starts to disintegrate. This is followed by leaking, rotting of roof timbers and overstraining of the carpentry due to the excessive weight of the damp thatch and turf. The future of thatch may also be in doubt from another quarter. Some local authorities do not accept thatch as a roofing material permissible under the building regulations. Householders may also be confronted with problems in obtaining affordable insurance cover for a thatched roof.

Regarding the distribution of thatching, analysis revealed that between 50 and 100 per cent of roofs in some parts of Lewis and Uist are covered with thatch and some other parts have between 10 and 50 per cent. Such high percentages are reached much less frequently in Skye and on the mainland of Scotland.

Metal sheeting and other materials

It is not unusual to find that where the thatching has been damaged or become in need of major maintenance, the owners have protected it with an overlay of corrugated iron. Metal sheeting for roofs has a long history in the north of Scotland. Corrugated iron became an accepted method of roofing by about the middle of the nineteenth century, and it has been used independently or combined with thatch as mentioned above (117). Its rich rusty red on ageing is not an inappropriate colour for those northern parts of Scotland where it seems to have settled. The disadvantage arises in its temporary nature and the noise which it produces under heavy rainfall, which is too frequently met in the north and west of Scotland for the comfort of some of the affected householders. Some conservationists, not necessarily also the householders, would wish to see this form of sheeting retained as a foreign but 'naturalised' element of building in certain parts. A means of insulating the interior of such roofs from sound impact may have to be devised if this established tradition is not to be lost, especially since reducing such immoderate levels of precipitation appears to be beyond the ken of modern science.

Other thatch roofs have been stripped and re-covered with asbestos cement sheets, bituminous felt, felt slates, etc (d.12,h). Bituminous felt is not a material new to Scotland. Scots have invented so many of the devices of modern society that it might dismay but not surprise them to learn that it was probably a Scot who also invented felt roofing. It was openly advertised as a roofing material in Inverness in 1809 but was used in the previous century in the west of Scotland. In 1811 a building in Dunbartonshire was roofed in thick brown paper dipped in tar, laid and then painted over with pitch. The sheeting materials recorded during the survey may all be assumed to be of more recent times. Many such roofs are confined to farm outbuildings but some houses in the north have also reverted to various forms of sheeting for replacement of former roof coverings. Some of the materials used do not accord with the established character, being badly in conflict with the local colouring and presenting a discordant intervention of suburban tiling or mass-produced sheeting associated with engineering and large-scale industrial estates. Investigation and advice as to how more sympathetic solutions can be found is clearly called for.

Metal or other forms of sheeting have become intensively employed in the Islands, where in some places up to between 90 and 100 per cent of the roofs are covered in such materials as corrugated iron or asbestos cement. Where crofters have removed the thatch the sheeting lies over the roof timbers to reach the eaves, not towards the front of the thick stone walls as with the thicker thatch but near the inner face of the walls, causing problems of dampness. The sheeting also appears fairly frequently along the north coast and down the west coast of Kintyre. As well as the Islands, the Highlands and most of the countryside north of the Forth, contain examples of this material. It is becoming almost universally employed in roofing new and re-roofing old farm buildings. If it is accepted that these roofs rarely accord with their surroundings but are apparently capable of serving their functional purpose economically, then it must be recognised that this is one of the major problems of protecting the character of the Scottish countryside and calls for very thorough investigation.

Ridges, eaves and pitches

Ridging
The finishing of the ridge of pitched roofs is chiefly a practical matter. The earliest examples are of cut stone which gives a smart appearance to a dark slate roof like piping in a Highland soldier's tunic (d.13,o). Clay tile ridges of a light stone colour, usually V-shaped, have also been noted in fairly early buildings (d.13,p). The most consistently used are the lead and zinc ridges, which are familiar to everyone, with the sheets uniformly spaced out and joined by forming a roll and lapping the ends over and fixing down with straps (d.13,q). The pantile roofs have small round ridge pieces made of the same material as the pantiles and filled with cement, bedded and carefully pointed. In the latter part of the nineteenth century, elaborate tile ridges were introduced for slate roofs. They were finished on top with a continuous fret or 'cockscomb'. This style greatly suited the Gothic flavour of the buildings which were becoming popular (d.13,s–y).

Eaves
It is difficult to say when gutters were first introduced to the countryside. The gutters are nearly always half-round cast-iron, fixed with straps nailed to the wood sarking. The great majority of eaves consists of the gutter so fixed that its inside lip lies close to the face of the wall of the building. Some would like to imagine that the builders provided a convenient plinth course projecting beyond the face of the wall to give a vestigial cornice in deference to the classical style. In a few cases where there are margins to the doors and windows, a similar margin is run along at eaves level as a feature, but it has no noticeable overhang (**85**). The eaves were emphasised by the Gothic stylists who introduced overhanging eaves with fascia boards and exposed rafter ends (**55**), while the classical architects provided cornices for the eaves (**40**) and sometimes ogee gutters for architectural reasons. It has to be accepted, however, that the national style of Scottish country building has plain eaves with no more of a projection than about 130mm (5in), consisting of a half-round cast-iron gutter.

Roof pitches

The survey showed that flat roofs are not a feature of the Scottish countryside, although a flat roof of 10° to 12° pitch was experimented with in Scotland as early as the beginning of the last century. However, it seems not to have been more than an isolated trial. Pitched roofs are a Scottish tradition as they have been in other countries of northern Europe. The survey investigated the pitch of the roofs contained in the samples to determine if there were any marked differences. The normal pitches lie between 39° and 44°. Not a county in Scotland exists where there are not relatively high percentages of roofs coming within this range, and it is in the counties of north Aberdeen, Banff, Kincardine and Angus that these pitches predominate. The rest of Scotland farther to the south has the principal examples of roofs ranging in pitch from 33° to 38°. The very low-pitched roofs of below 32° are well represented in Lewis and in central Scotland. The range between 45° and 50° are found in Berwick and are much in evidence in the north-east and north-west with some in the Hebrides. Lastly, roofs of above 50° form less than 40 per cent of the roofs where they occur. A few widely-distributed cases appear where this steeper roof is found in the higher bracket of percentages of up to 55 per cent.

One determinant in the angle of roof pitch is the covering material adopted. Some materials in a severely wet climate demand steeper pitches because of their porosity. Others need a moderate pitch because the weight, if fixed like slates, would cause the material to become insecure if the pitch is too steep. Thatch was sometimes laid at low pitches and the survey confirmed that the higher frequency of lower pitches is in the thatch areas in the Hebrides and Shetland.

General form

There were few examples of hipped roofs shown up in the survey. Only in the older Highland cottages of thatch and in some of the buildings of the larger farms, as in Peeblesshire, are hips observed in significant numbers (**77**). Gabled buildings steadily grew in numbers from the middle of the eighteenth century and this progression was not seriously challenged until the advent of the modern bungalow.

The thatched roofs very often have a flat saddle at the top instead of a sharp ridge. This makes the thatcher's job easier in effecting a practical transition between the opposite sides of the roof, for giving continuity to the thatch and streamlining the outline of the roof against the wind. The appearance is accordingly not angular and, as the stone rubble walls below also tend not to have angular corners, the whole aspect of a thatched house or byre in the Islands or the north seems closer to nature and landscape than buildings erected today. The double equal pitch is by far the most common form, providing a simple symmetrical gable at either end. On this primary shape are erected the gables and dormers which are the subject of a later section (p.126).

The predominant features for roofs over the greater part of Scotland can be summarised as follows:

(1)   They are pitched and gabled.

(2)   The pitches are on average between 40° and 45°, but significant numbers occur both above and below these averages.

(3)   Slate is the predominant material, being mostly dark in shade and grey-blue or blue-purple.

(4)   Red and brown pantiles are a sufficiently important exception to the use of slate that their retention should be secured.

(5)   There are various alternative sheeting materials which contribute to local character.

Chimneyheads and other roof elements

Chimneyheads

In large towns and cities the roofs and chimneys are not always prominent and from some positions not visible. In villages and the open countryside the chimneys are nearly always seen and often conspicuous. In any research into the character of country buildings, chimneys merit individual attention. The survey has shown that builders and architects treated the construction of the chimneys in many ways, partly yielding to the rigours of climate and partly indulging in exercising imagination and originality.

Chimneyheads are understandably associated with gables in Scotland because most detached buildings have gabled roofs and most chimneys pass

65. Dirleton, East Lothian

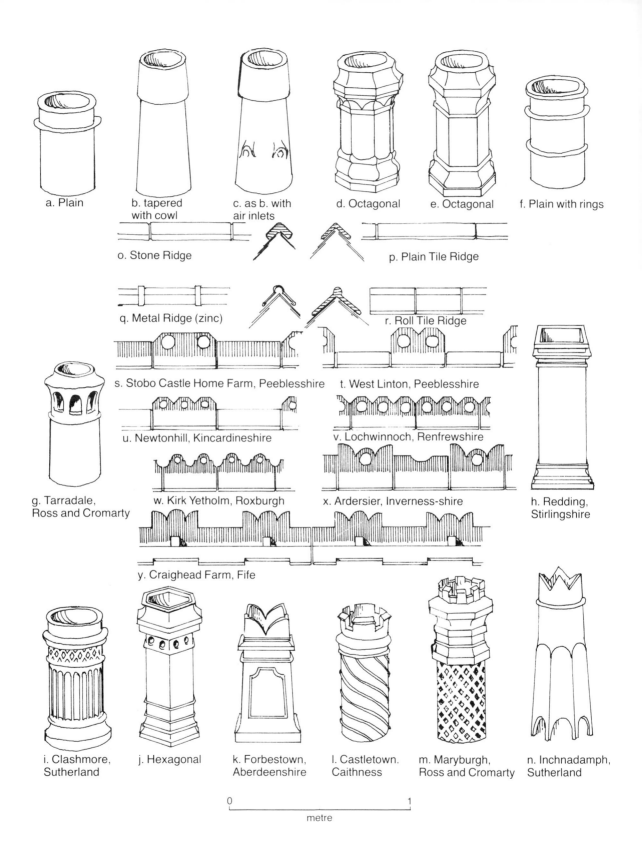

a. Plain

b. tapered with cowl

c. as b. with air inlets

d. Octagonal

e. Octagonal

f. Plain with rings

o. Stone Ridge

p. Plain Tile Ridge

q. Metal Ridge (zinc)

r. Roll Tile Ridge

s. Stobo Castle Home Farm, Peeblesshire

t. West Linton, Peeblesshire

u. Newtonhill, Kincardineshire

v. Lochwinnoch, Renfrewshire

g. Tarradale, Ross and Cromarty

w. Kirk Yetholm, Roxburgh

x. Ardersier, Inverness-shire

h. Redding, Stirlingshire

y. Craighead Farm, Fife

i. Clashmore, Sutherland

j. Hexagonal

k. Forbestown, Aberdeenshire

l. Castletown. Caithness

m. Maryburgh, Ross and Cromarty

n. Inchnadamph, Sutherland

0   1
metre

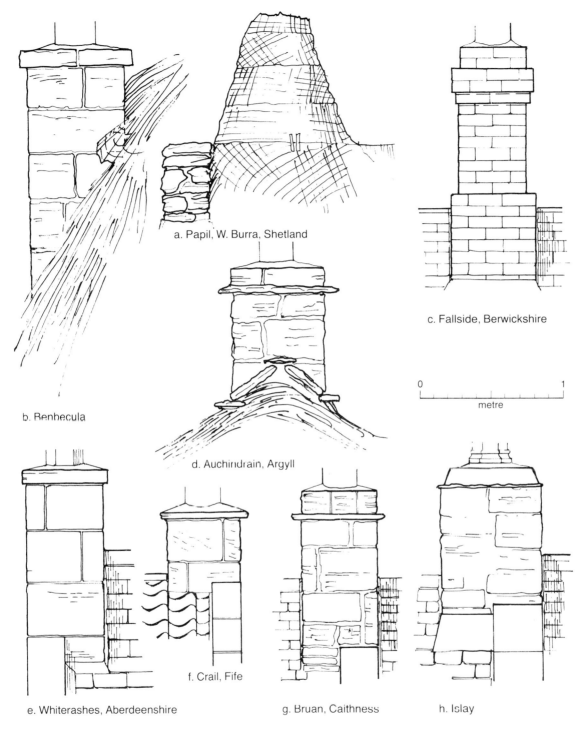

a. Papil, W. Burra, Shetland

b. Benbecula

c. Fallside, Berwickshire

d. Auchindrain, Argyll

0   1

metre

e. Whiterashes, Aberdeenshire

f. Crail, Fife

g. Bruan, Caithness

h. Islay

d13. *Opposite* Roof ridges
and chimney cans

d14. *Above* Chimneyheads

up the end wall of buildings. For this reason it is rare for chimneys to emerge at points on the ridge at a distance along from the gables. However, as some rural buildings are terraced, chimneys also emerge at intervals along the roof, centred on the ridge. In Scottish terraces, the custom has been for only the first house built at the end of a row to have two gables. Thereafter each house added possesses only one gable and borrows the other from its neighbour. Chimneys are sometimes accommodated by using extra flues but more often a new set of flues, if required at the end of the house, is built against its neighbour. The survey seldom showed double chimneys which had been planned from the beginning to accommodate two sets of flues placed side by side. The chimneyheads are nearly always only one flue thick, i.e. about 525mm wide (21in) and most are surmounted with a cope.

All chimneyheads have chimney pots, in Scotland known as 'cans', excepting those where the cans have been removed, or the chimneys are constructed of wood or thatch. Not all are rectangular in plan. In some areas the designers have elaborated the construction by building rows of square individual stone chimneys rising from a sub-stack (65) and set at 45° so that the angle, instead of the face, of each individual chimney faces the front of the building (d.15,d). On some occasions the stonework is harled or painted to conform with the treatments on the main walls of the building. Cases do appear, however, when the stone in the stacks is left natural, where the walls have been coated with harling or paint. During the eighteenth and, for a part of the nineteenth century, the masons frequently built-in a projecting string course or drip at the foot of chimneyheads at the front and back of the stack to protect the junction of the masonry and the roof covering, be it thatch, tile or slate (d.15,f and h). In some areas where thatch was used, drips were also built-in along the inside face of the chimney for the same reason. They were positioned higher up and horizontal just sufficient to clear the rounded top of the thatch (d.14,d). In slate roofs drips were sometimes built-in at the same angles of the roof to keep close to the surface of the slating.

Materials
Buildings in most parts of the country where stone has been used have stone chimneyheads. The construction is of stone as large as is practicable. The heights of the courses in ashlar-built chimneys may vary between 250mm and 300mm (10in and 12in). Some parts of the country have flagstone chimneyheads using narrower courses. In most stone chimneyheads, lime mortar would have been used for jointing, the flues being lined or 'parged' internally also using lime mortar. Wooden or thatch chimneys were rarely noted during the field survey (d.14,a).

Brick chimneyheads were recorded in various districts (d.14,c) *and* (d.15,b). In many cases they may have been replacements of stone chimneyheads which had deteriorated. Although the chimneyheads are all sturdy and well put together, they are subjected to the full force of rain and wind in their exposed position and chimney fires have caused fracturing of the masonry in many instances. If the original stone was also soft, these combined hazards could limit the life of a chimneyhead. In this connection it is relevant to note that many brickwork chimneys built after 1914 were constructed with the outer

d15. Chimneyheads

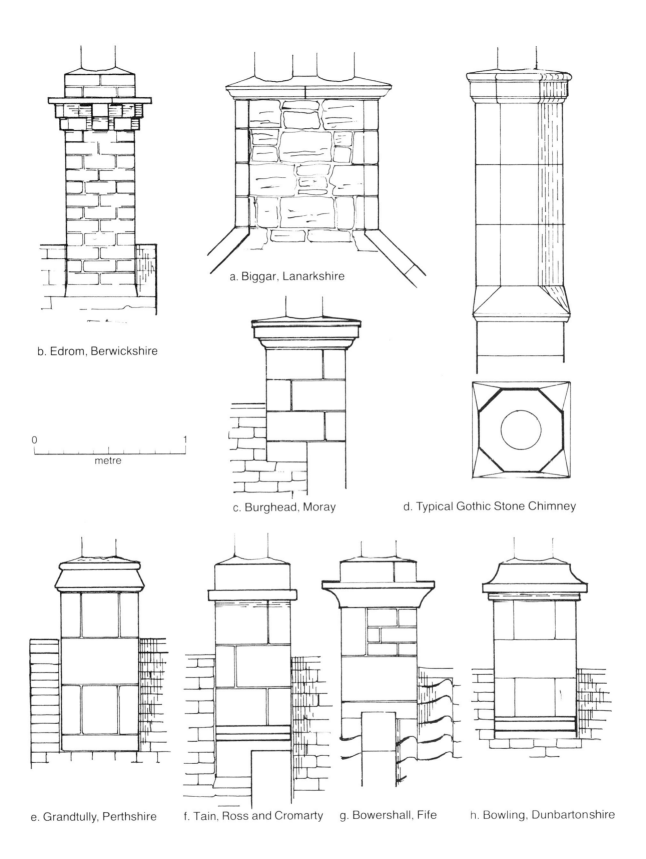

a. Biggar, Lanarkshire

b. Edrom, Berwickshire

0   1

metre

c. Burghead, Moray

d. Typical Gothic Stone Chimney

e. Grandtully, Perthshire   f. Tain, Ross and Cromarty   g. Bowershall, Fife   h. Bowling, Dunbartonshire

walls only 110mm thick ($4\frac{1}{2}$in). Thus the chimneyheads were restricted to an overall width of 450mm (18in), compared with the traditional width of 525mm (21in). Further rebuilding of these slender stalks has perforce been undertaken at great expense. The traditional brick chimneyheads, whether in replacement or in an original design, have an average width of about 575mm (23in).

Copes

Chimneyheads in the north of the country and on the Islands seem in many instances to have been constructed from the beginning without copes. The best stone was usually reserved for the copes when they are fitted. The masons worked the stone in a variety of ways, and basically there are five types of copes:

(1)   A plain cope consisting of a slab varying in thickness and projecting beyond the face of the stack (d.14,b,e).

(2)   A cope built flush with the main stack (d.15,f) consisting of a blocking course sitting on the top of the chimneyhead, well dressed and often 130mm (5in) deep but varying. Immediately below this course a narrower necking course was laid projecting beyond the face of the stack all round (d.15,g,h). In flagstone areas the necking course may be as narrow as 35mm ($1\frac{1}{2}$in) but in most other areas it is found in depths of about 70mm ($2\frac{3}{4}$in).

(3)   The cope may consist of stone about 150mm (6in) deep, with a splay on the face, slightly projecting beyond the main stack.

(4)   This splayed cope may be further elaborated with mouldings above and/or below the splay (d.15,e).

(5)   Moulded copes occur in some of the buildings built later in the nineteenth century (d.15,c,e,g,h).

The brick chimneyheads were nearly always completed with brick copes (d.14,c). In the north the copes followed type (2) for stone design, the top blocking course being formed by a course of bricks built on edge. The necking is of the same depth but it projects about 51mm (2in). In the south the formation of the cope was more elaborate and the blocking course was usually built with two courses of brickwork. Above the top of the copes, lime mortar was added in the form of weathered haunching round the chimney cans.

Dimensions

The frequency of severe gales in parts of the country led to masons taking the understandable precaution of reducing the height of the chimneyheads. In such areas the masonry extends above the ridge only to about the thickness of one or two courses of stone and the thickness of the cope. Cases have been noted where the total height above the ridge is limited to as little as 150mm (6in). Taller stacks are found in the less exposed areas and in towns. The height above the ridge usually extends to about two courses of stonework and the depth of the cope, i.e. 600mm (24in). Taller stacks constitute a very low proportion of the samples surveyed. Climatic conditions also influenced the width of the stacks. It has been estimated that stacks with single rows of flues may increase to at least 600mm (24in) across in exposed open country.

Skews

The building of skews or dwarf parapets along the edge of pitched roofs at the gables is a technique of long standing. It seems to have originated in those countries in Europe where buildings were built of stone or brick. The timber houses in the mountainous regions and in the north of Europe developed the method of running the roof material over the gable walls, sometimes producing large overhanging verges. The stone skew is normal in Scotland and open verges appear to have been introduced only in the middle of the nineteenth century. They were favoured by railway companies for country stations, by the estates for gate lodges and by architects in many Gothic designs (**76**). The survey showed that several distinctive types of skew finishes evolved.

66. Eaglesham, Renfrewshire

Crowsteps

This older form of finishing the top of the gable has its own Scottish style distinct from the continental style. The masons of the seventeenth and eighteenth centuries obeyed certain simple rules which architects in the Gothic period of the last quarter of the nineteenth century did not always follow. Even such a master as Sir Robert Lorimer in the twentieth century departed from the older 'correct' methods. Only a few examples were recorded during the survey, the most typical being in Fife, Cromarty and Dunblane (**13**) and belonging to the eighteenth century and earlier (d.16,a). Each crowstep consists of a plain ashlar block of varying length. The step is about 250mm high (10in), the breadth of the step varies between about 150mm to 200mm (6in to 8in). The width or 'tread' of the step depends on the pitch of the roofs which usually varied between 52° 30′ and 55°. The average width was about 150mm to 180mm (6in to 7in).

There was not sufficient evidence to determine whether the early masons weathered the top of each step in any particular direction. The top step finished against the chimneyhead to give the same width as the other crowsteps. If there was no chimneyhead, the cap stone was the width of the crowstep or very slightly greater. The crowstep started at the foot of the gable as an ornamental putt which had the same width or tread as the remainder of the steps but with a refinement which distinguishes the original from most of the later nineteenth century examples. The putt projected out from the front wall of the gable about 50mm (2in) less than the full width of the crowstep. Thus the face of the first crowstep above the putt stone was set back from the face of the building by about 50mm (2in). Herein lay the graceful transition from the vertical frontages to the slope of the pitch of the gable end.

Old crowsteps in Orkney were seen to diminish in size up a gable but were cruder in design and workmanship than Lowland examples (**122**). The Gothic examples took on fanciful shapes, were sometimes large and with piended tops, and belong more to the continent of Europe than Scotland. Most Gothic designs also made the face of the first crowstep beyond the skew putt flush with the front of the building, whether through design preference or carelessness has not been discovered (d.16,b).

Plain skews

Most skews recorded in the survey consisted of plain skews. These are found in broadly two forms. The narrow skews are about 200mm (8in) wide, are laid on bed on the slope, giving about three to five lengths between eaves and chimneyhead (d.16,c). They are placed about 120mm (5in) above the level of the tiles or slates and the junction is formed by a lime-sand triangular flashing. The width of the gable below is very much thicker when built of stone so that any water penetration that might occur is absorbed in the masonry and may dry out if not severe, particularly as the gables are usually fireplace walls and dry. Good quality fine grain stone was used for skew copes. In some areas the skews are very much wider, about 300mm (12in) (d.16,d). When there is a stone drip course at the base of the chimneyhead, the skew usually fits immediately under it.

d16. Skews and crowsteps

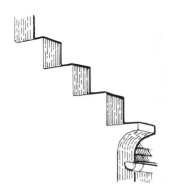

a. Crail, Fife

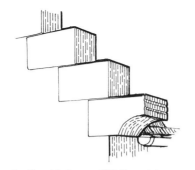

b. Buckieburn, Stirlingshire

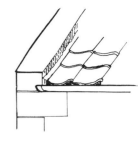

c. Bowershall, Fife

d. Cairnpark, Dumfries

e. Biggar, Lanarkshire

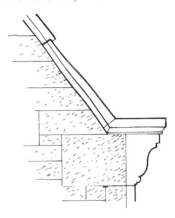

f. Letham, Angus

g. Greenlaw, Berwickshire

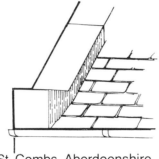

h. St. Combs, Aberdeenshire

i. Athelstaneford, E. Lothian

j. Insch, Aberdeenshire

k. Arnisdale, Inverness-shire

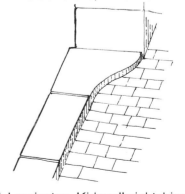

l. Laurieston, Kirkcudbrightshire

113 *The elements of buildings*

Ornamental skews

As the nineteenth century progressed, the plain skews did not serve so well for some of the later styles of architecture, with the result that designers turned to more elaborate forms and skews were made a vehicle for decoration. Kneelers with squared projections were introduced. The tops of skews were piended (d.16,e). Some skews were stepped with overlaps like slates (d.16,f). However, skews of these types were found to be very limited in number (102).

Skew Putts

Several different methods have been recorded of finishing the end of the skew where it meets the wallhead. The most common is for the skew to continue down on the slope and stop when the underside of the skew meets a point just beyond the outside face of the front wall, so that the top oversails the face of the building at an angle (d.16,g). Occasionally where thinner skew stones were used, this stone also overhung along and over the side of the gable (d.16,d). In some parts, principally in Aberdeen, the skew finishes at the bottom against a plain horizontal skew putt which acts as an anchor to the sloping skew stones above (d.16,h,j). In the older eighteenth century buildings (20), the skews were often finished with a scroll skew putt with ogee moulded or ringed shafts (d.16,i). In the later types the skew putt finished with a projecting moulding (d.16,f).

Open verges

When the skew is omitted, the slates are sometimes sloped just beyond the ends of the gables and the 'tifting end' pointed and slightly raised to prevent an overspill of surface water down the face of the gable. In the west and south-west the slates were stopped short of the verge against a raised lead-covered fillet to prevent their dislodgement and protect the gables from rainwater driving over the edge (d.16,k).

Projecting verges

More common in the mid-nineteenth-century buildings are the projecting verges. These occur in three forms:

67. Bridgend, Argyll

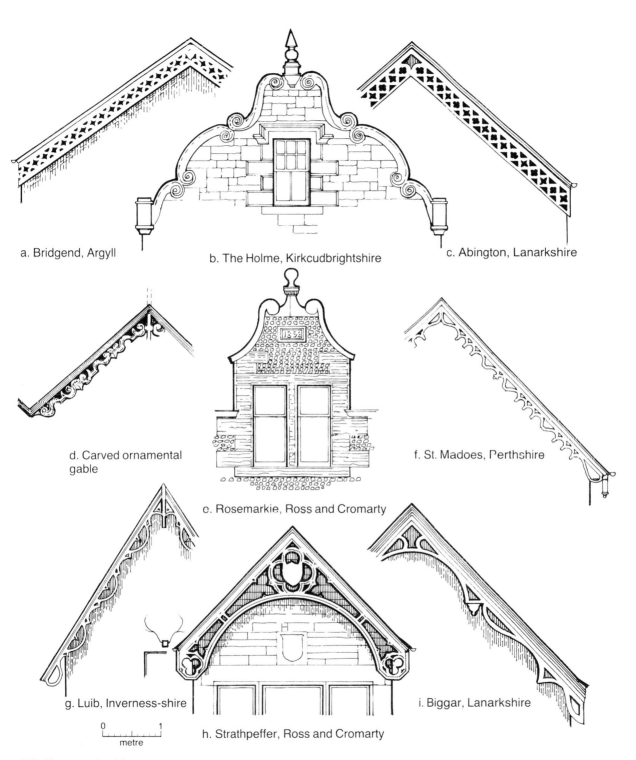

a. Bridgend, Argyll

b. The Holme, Kirkcudbrightshire

c. Abington, Lanarkshire

d. Carved ornamental gable

e. Rosemarkie, Ross and Cromarty

f. St. Madoes, Perthshire

g. Luib, Inverness-shire

h. Strathpeffer, Ross and Cromarty

i. Biggar, Lanarkshire

0   1
metre

d17. Verges and gables

115   *The elements of buildings*

(1)   the projection is supported underneath by the projecting ends of the purlins, which are usually half-rounded on the lower corners;

(2)   the ends are finished with a plain barge board; and

(3)   the ends are finished with an ornamental barge board either fretted and scalloped at the edge or cut into elaborate open fret with flowing linear designs reminiscent of the contemporaneous Victorian lace curtaining.

Examples of the third type are astonishingly rich and belong to the late Victorian age of decorative Scottish architecture, which also produced original ironwork and carved stonework (d.17,a,c,d,f and g–i).

Raised skews

In some cases skews were observed to rise far above the level of the slated or tiled roof. This feature could be of Victorian origin (**19**) or be accounted for by the possible existence at a previous time of thatching on the roof which would, of course, need a greater height of upstand.

Chimney cans

Patterns of chimney cans vary considerably over the country. They are very rarely plain except for modern replacements. The fireclay employed has traditionally maintained a golden or buff colour. Black and terracotta were seldom met with during the survey. There are too many shapes and designs to list them all, but some basic types are noted as follows:

(1)   Round in plan with a rim on top (d.13,a).

(2)   Round in plan with moulding on top and along the bottom.

(3)   Round and tapered from the foot towards the top and surmounted by a fireclay top or cowl, also tapered in the same direction but wider at the foot to fit over the top of the can below (d.13,b).

(4)   Octagonal in plan and moulded at top and bottom (d.13,d,e).

(5)   Octagonal in plan and moulded, but fitted with vent holes at the side near the top of the can.

(6)   Hexagonal, octagonal or round in plan as (2) or (4) but with small vents set near the (d.13,c) bottom and projecting at an angle in front of the face to counteract down draught. Vents in the top are shown in (d.13,g,j).

(7)   Ornamental designs of numerous kinds with spiral ribbing, basket weave, castellated tops, classical motifs, etc. (d.13,h–n).

Modern replacements frequently consist of very short, plain, round fireclay cans. Traditional cans seem to have averaged about 600mm (24in) in height and were used under most conditions. Shorter traditional cans were also recorded and in the south, where more moderate weather is experienced, taller cans have been used for stylistic reasons as well as the practical objective of inducing more draught. In farms the treatment of chimneys followed the same traditions as in domestic buildings; and even in some industrial buildings, where a fireplace existed, the same types of chimney can were used.

Ironwork

There is much of interest in ironwork to be found in the countryside (d.25, and d.26). Apart from shop fronts, ornamental ironwork demonstrating great skill in design and craftsmanship was recorded. Most of it belongs to the second half of the nineteenth century and, as has already been indicated, a great deal of it was taken for melting down in the 1940s. The best can be seen now only in the balcony rails of the Victorian villas and in small pieces of ornamentation. Some of it is of an order of excellence to call for care in maintenance (d.25,e). Some good designs were observed also on metal finials used on stone dormer gables and at the apex of bay dormers (d.25,a–d,f). Mostly they have been wrought and in a few cases have been cast. Unfortunately, because of their relative inaccessibility, maintenance is difficult and not infrequently examples have been found to be damaged with parts missing.

Doors and porches

Doors

Scottish doors, traditionally, are broad and short. In the seventeenth century, they were seldom narrower than about 940mm (3ft), many were over one metre (3ft 4in) and some were even 1·2m (3ft 11in). The heights, on the other hand, were often no more than 1·8m (5ft 11in) although in large or important buildings heights of 2·25m (7ft 3in) were used. Three forms of doors were common:

(1)   The framed-and-lined door with broad lining boards, plain and seldom studded, which could be one or two leaved.

(2)   The four-panelled door of traditional design.

(3)   The six-panelled door with equal almost square panels.

The survey did not give decisive information on how the doors in the new houses evolved after the mid-eighteenth century because doors are so vulnerable to wear that many of the original doors have been replaced once if not more often. The types of doors that were noted are as follows:

Framed-and-lined

(d.18,a). Old framed-and-lined doors were noted on farms and agricultural buildings in the north of Scotland. The lining boards were of broad or medium widths, clapped over a rough frame which was wholly contained on the back. This type of door was often made in two leaves (d.18,b). Simple hasps or sliding bolts were fitted, often to a short back plate or a back board extending the width of the door and on front for greater strength. This construction was also used for two-leaf stable doors.

(d.18,c,d). The framed-and-lined door with narrow width V-jointed, groove and tongue joints, belongs to a later date and is still produced. The stiles and top rail were made the full thickness of the door. The mid-rail and the bottom rail were placed behind the lining. Cross diagonal braces were also introduced. The stiles, rails and braces may be stop-chamfered. Most of the country versions of this type of door have projecting verges fitted at the foot of the door

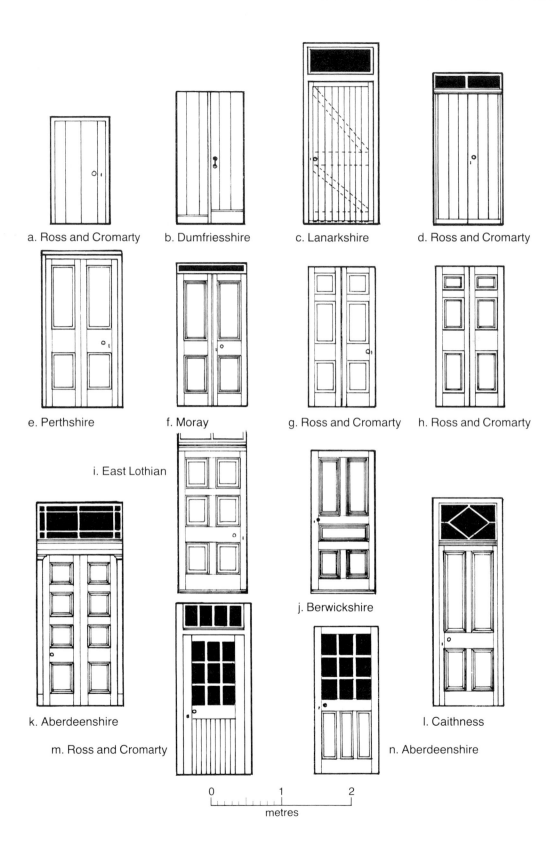

a. Ross and Cromarty b. Dumfriesshire c. Lanarkshire d. Ross and Cromarty

e. Perthshire f. Moray g. Ross and Cromarty h. Ross and Cromarty

i. East Lothian

j. Berwickshire

k. Aberdeenshire

m. Ross and Cromarty

l. Caithness

n. Aberdeenshire

0   1   2
metres

Buildings of the Scottish Countryside

to prevent water which is running down the face of the door from being blown into the house at the threshold. The construction of this type of door is very intricate in its jointing techniques.

Panelled

(d.18,e,f). The four-panelled door is found in most counties and is usually made with broad stiles, rails and muntins. Normally the mid- or lock rail is placed at a convenient level below the centre of the door. The panels are plain and the mouldings, which run on the stiles, rails and muntins, consist of a simple ogee or even a plain splay. Later this type of door was fitted with more richly worked moulding round the panels.

(d.18,g–l). After the middle of the nineteenth century a richer form of door was adopted in many houses with various arrangements of panels, e.g. five-panel, six-panel etc. Bolection mouldings were used and, in the classical designs, fielded panels and beaded panels were introduced. From this period some magnificent examples of Scottish joinery may be seen, still surviving well after more than a century. Some of these doors in the later large houses, are wide and heavily made with very thick stiles. The wide form of door of the earlier periods already referred to, tended to continue in the doors described. The average width is about 950mm (3ft 1in). Some are as narrow as 850mm (2ft 9in) but there are a great many, probably up to one-third of all front doors, in excess of one metre (3ft 4in) wide.

Fanlights

The heights of the door openings were nearly always controlled by the height of the lintels on the ground floor windows. This resulted in the curtailment of the door heights to permit a fanlight to be inserted above (**74**). Many of these lights are very shallow, even as little as 100mm (4in) in height. They are

d18. Door styles

68. Stonefold Farm, Berwickshire

119   *The elements of buildings*

often divided by three astragals and are very rarely fitted with decoratively patterned panes. The doors are about normal height – 1·95m (6ft 6in). Unlike the architects in cities and towns, the rural builders did not emphasise the fanlight.

Surrounds and other features

The doors normally have the same types of surround as the windows. Rybats go with rybats and margins go with margins. In the more classical designs the surrounds to the doors received greater emphasis, especially at the lintel where simple entablatures were added in some examples. In such cases the margins tend to be wider than the window margins. Not all front doors could be recorded because many are now inside after the addition of a new porch.

The renewal of front doors in the Scottish countryside has bred some alien and hybrid specimens, e.g. there is the proliferation of flush doors which are very well designed to direct all the surface water into the house with the utmost dispatch. Omission of panels, mouldings or grooves which would have directed the stream of surface water away from the jambs and stops, ensures that on a windy wet day, water will be given every opportunity of finding its way into the space between the door stiles and the door standards.

(d.18,m,n). Some framed and lined doors with 4 to 6-paned lights in the upper third were for some years very popular in the mid-twentieth century. The 'superior' type doors of all descriptions may be seen fitted by owners in the belief that, as their houses are more than a hundred years old, mass produced 'period' doors are bound to be suitable. There are plenty of 'Tudor pub' and some 'Tudor ecclesiastical' doors. Some enthusiastic owners have resorted to improvements of the flush door, based on the Odeon Cinema era. Very superior owners put on framed-and-lined doors with black metal band hinges, even risking a few mock studs. 'Suffolk' latches may be seen by those who do not avert their gaze.

Porches

Considering the large number of porches which have been added to buildings in the north of the country, it is surprising that the original designers did not provide for them at the outset. Possibly people after enduring the spartan existence in earlier turf and clay habitations found a porchless house very adequate. Yet there were some who knew better. One Factor in 1835, writing regarding the building of the new manse at Glenshee, commented on the good sense of a porch or a freestone flag inside the front door for . . . 'it is impossible to prevent the west wind from driving the rain over the lobby and rotting the floor'. In *General View of the Agriculture of the Hebrides* in 1811 it was stated that necessity compels gentlemen there 'to build porches before their main doors which, notwithstanding the constant trouble and awkwardness accompanying them, are never comfortable: but still they are better than doors altogether unsheltered to the pelting of the pitiless west.' In face of such evidence the building of porches cannot be criticised in principle. But the form of the porches is not always in keeping with the main building either in shape, scale or proportion. The survey showed that the forms of porches vary and they may be described in the following broad categories (d.19, d.20).

d19. Porches

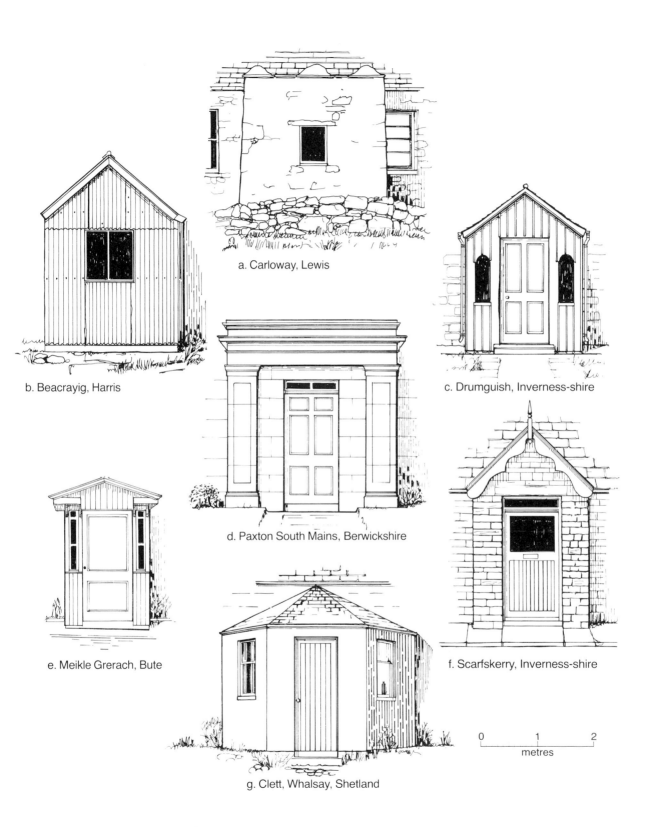

a. Carloway, Lewis

b. Beacrayig, Harris

c. Drumguish, Inverness-shire

d. Paxton South Mains, Berwickshire

e. Meikle Grerach, Bute

f. Scarfskerry, Inverness-shire

g. Clett, Whalsay, Shetland

0   1   2
metres

121 *The elements of buildings*

Enclosed

The enclosed porch (d.19,a–g) consists of a solidly-built addition to the building against the front door. If it is contemporary with the building, the walls of the porch will be the same as the walls of the main building. If the porch is a later addition it is likely to be built in a different style of stone construction or built in other materials and roughcasted in most cases. The roofs are usually sloping, finished in slate, corrugated sheeting or felt. The normal roof arrangement is that which presents the gable to the front of the porch.

The alternative consists of a lean-to roof or a flat roof. Sometimes the porch has a two-way pitched roof running parallel to the main building and thus forming a boundary wall gutter. Nearly all such porches are single storey except for some of the Gothic porches. The door is not necessarily placed at the front of the porch but is put on the leeward wall, and thus the front may contain a small window. This type of porch may also have a pyramidal roof. Although enclosed porches are most frequently encountered in the Western Isles, Shetland, Caithness and Sutherland, they are also to be found in the open country and the hill lands in other areas such as the Borders. Enclosed porches are not so common in the villages, especially the planned villages, because the space free at the front of the house is either too small or completely lacking.

Portico porches (d.19,d) are those stone-built porticos erected as part of a building in the classical style. These have classical elements and generally belong to the last half of the nineteenth century. They are usually built in polished ashlar.

Light framed porches (d.19,c,e) are the lighter-built porches consisting of timber, with timber lining and pitched roofs finished in slates (**69**). These are proper porches in that they are fitted with an outer door. They have been built in some cases with the house and, if there are pedimented dormers in the building, the gable of the porch follows the style of the dormer pediments. This type of porch is neater and more decorative in style than the heavier solid types shown at (d.19,a,f). The entrance side and front are normally filled with painted timber lining.

69. Highfield Farm, West Dunbartonshire (West of Loch Lomond)

Details of enclosed porches
(d.19,a–g). These porches are very plain and without any ornamentation. The outer doors may be lower in height than the original door. In Shetland and the north of Scotland they are sometimes relatively large and are horizontal or nearly square in elevation. The smaller version with slated roofs do not necessarily have any gutters. There are usually one or two windows as well as a door. In the farming areas such porches are found built in common brick and colour-washed like the main walls of the building. The ridge of the roof of the porch, where it runs at right angles to the front of the main building, has to be arranged so that the top of the ridge meets the wall below the sill of any upper floor window which has normally been positioned above the original front door. In 1½-storey buildings where the eaves occur about a metre above the top of the original door, the ridge at right angles to the main front wall is mostly arranged to abut the wall immediately below the gutter by flattening the pitch of the roof of the porch.

(d.19,d). This type comprises some classical porches with scholarly details, having a slightly Scottish flavour. The roofs are usually flat and are concealed behind a blocking course. The blocking course surmounts a cornice and frieze, supported by flat classical pilaster surrounds, and inset slip lintel and jambs all in ashlar. Some of the richer versions have detached columns. These porches appear more arresting when they are found on an otherwise plain colour-washed building.

(d.19,b). This type of porch, when made of corrugated sheeting, is presumably practical and is tolerably acceptable in the areas where sheet metal roofs have become part of a regional style.

(d.19,c,e,f). When well designed these porches can be made to fit the overall composition where the architectural style of the original house has been taken into account. In particular, when added to a 1½-storey building and furnished with a roof of the same pitch and decorative details as those of the dormers, the porch can introduce a pleasing feature of interest.

Open
Open porches (d.20,b,d,f) are more common in the southern areas and in the Highlands. The basic form consists of a projecting canopy over the front door with pitched roof and gable end, supported against the wall at the back and on pillars at the front. The pillars or posts may be turned and carved, squared and chamfered, in single posts or twin posts, or in the Highlands they may be fir tree trunks with the stumps of branches left protruding to give a rustic effect. The pediments may be plain and lined, built herringbone fashion, filled in with struts and with straight or curved brackets. Some in the Highlands may even be hung with antlers. Dwarf side walls in certain areas were added where the supporting posts terminate at the top of these walls, keeping the ends off the ground and reducing the danger of timber rot.

This type of porch only protects the visitor from rain falling vertically and it assists in keeping the platt before the front door from becoming very wet. They provide the most decorative of porches and the best designs belong to this type.

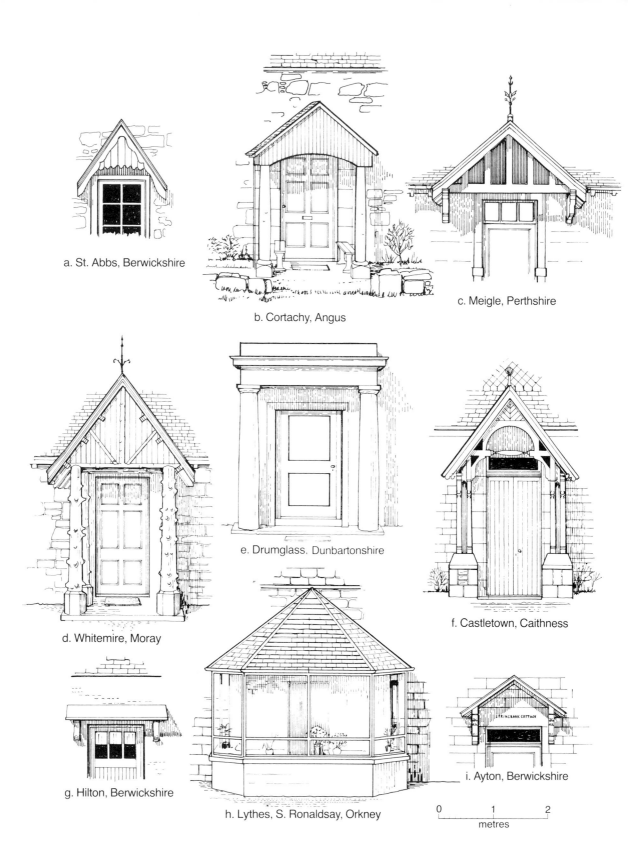

a. St. Abbs, Berwickshire

b. Cortachy, Angus

c. Meigle, Perthshire

d. Whitemire, Moray

e. Drumglass. Dunbartonshire

f. Castletown, Caithness

g. Hilton, Berwickshire

h. Lythes, S. Ronaldsay, Orkney

i. Ayton, Berwickshire

0   1   2
metres

Colonnaded

(d.20,e). Colonnaded types include the classical versions with stone pillars and a frieze.

Bracketed

(d.20,a,c). Bracket hoods or canopies are not so customary in the country. Some examples were noted, especially in the Gothic style of building. They are nearly all finished in slates and built of wood.

Cantilevered

(d.20,g,i). Small narrow hoods or pediments over doors may be regarded as the rudimentary form of canopy and are listed here because they do appear in street buildings where larger projections would not be feasible.

Sun porches

(d.20,h). There were many recordings of the modern type of porch, including glass conservatories and glass and timber enclosures with flat roofs. Few of these kinds rank high in architectural merit, but perhaps they satisfy the requirements of the occupants because, on a good day, they often present a sunny inviting interior.

Details of open porches

(d.20,b,d,f). The open porch has given considerable scope to designers and added dignity and charm to many otherwise plain but well-proportioned buildings. Given the small degree of protection from weather that open porches offer, it seems that they have been engendered by decorative rather than functional aims. They are seen at their best when the supporting posts are reasonably slender and sufficiently far apart to leave the door unobscured. Like the pediments of dormer windows, the gables of these porches are arranged with decorative features such as fret and scalloped barge boards, finials, chamfered and elaborately turned strutting with curved members and brackets and herringbone patterned weather-boarding. Sometimes the ceilings are lined with timber and sometimes left open. The supporting pillars may be cylindrical or square and provided with neatly carved capitals and bases. The gables are also on occasion left open and the various triangular openings between the struts infilled with scalloped trimming to form inner openings with flowing leaf designs. Some of the designs, especially in gate lodges become so exuberant that they dominate the remainder of the buildings.

Nearly all are splendid examples of Victorian originality and design and bring to the countryside some of the magic and romanticism of the spirit which inspired the poets and artists of that age.

(d.20,e). This porch does not pretend to be a work of imaginative art. Its contribution is restrained and academic, similar to (d.19,d). The principal difference lies in the forward columns which are cylindrical and decorated with doric capitals with or without bases and unfluted. They usually belong to houses of formal and balanced classical design.

(d.20,a,c). Bracketed canopies were also favoured in the late Victorian era.

d20. Porches

They are associated with open verges and purlin ends supported by elaborate brackets with carved timber drops and curved members stop-chamfered and surmounted by spire-like finials.

Windows and dormers

Windows

Up to 1914, over a period of nearly two centuries, country joiners hand made well over one million windows, rarely ever departing from the sash-and-case design. It suited the widths of the openings due to the limited span of stone lintels. It gave the right protection against draughts and rain penetration. If wider widths were required the joiners coupled two or more windows together still adhering to the sash-and-case form. Variety, however, was introduced by dividing the sash into panes using astragals where the mouldings were scribed and the joins made with tenons. Machines are still able to turn out excellent sash-and-case windows but modern building legislation has now tended to impede their adoption.

Windows, like doors, have nearly always been regarded by Scottish builders as fittings, i.e. they were not part of the basic wall structure which was under the exclusive control of masons and so were not called upon to support the walls or roofs above as is done in some brick building in England.

Sash-and-case

The small country buildings before the eighteenth century had few, if any windows. Apertures for light and ventilation existed but were probably more often closed with wood shutters than glazing. From the start of the rebuilding in the mid-eighteenth century, glazing was nearly always provided. The availability of glass thereafter allowed larger windows to be fitted. In form they followed the design of the tower house sash-and-case windows but with lighter members and larger panes. All over the country the sash-and-case window appeared.

The thickness and style of the sashes and astragals followed the Scottish Georgian pattern of the mid-eighteenth century. The broad astragals of the mid-seventeenth century and later were not adopted in the countryside building until about 1875. The shape of the sash-and-case windows was, in most examples, near to the vertical rectangle, a side and base of which when joined by the diagonal formed a 60°–30° triangle or a triangle very close to that in shape. 57°–33° is not uncommon and any triangle between these two may be found in the windows of any county in Scotland. Some windows are taller, with 64°–26° diagonal. Very elongated Georgian-type windows with steeper base angles of 65°–67½° were only infrequently noted. The later Gothic windows are often very elongated, but as they are usually coupled by a narrow mullion, tended to 'read' to an overall nearly square shape (**94**). Shortened windows occur occasionally in the upper floor windows of 2-storey houses. These have base angles ranging from 50°–40° to 54°–36°. Square or nearly square windows are

very unusual except in the Gothic type of building where the square is made up of multiple windows.

The size of windows is on average 850mm by 1·45mm (2ft 9¾in by 5ft 9½in) but varies greatly according to the shape and scale. For example, in windows with angles varying by 2°, windows of the example above with a constant height could vary between 825mm and 900mm (2ft 9in and 3ft) in width. Dormer windows tend to be narrower than the main windows by about 100mm (4in) to 200mm (8in) and the heights are often reduced correspondingly. The older form of dividing window sashes into smaller panes was used, but not to the extent of their counterparts in the towns. The country windows were smaller in order that the practical consideration of obtaining large enough panes of glass would not be so onerous. The divides which were used are as follows:

70. Marybank, Ross and Cromarty

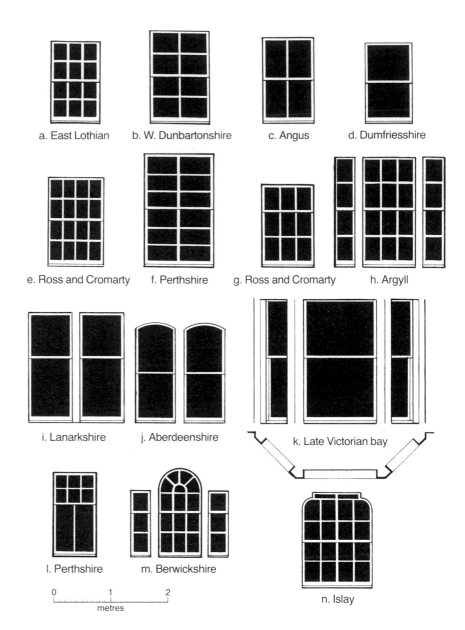

a. East Lothian b. W. Dunbartonshire c. Angus d. Dumfriesshire

e. Ross and Cromarty f. Perthshire g. Ross and Cromarty h. Argyll

i. Lanarkshire j. Aberdeenshire k. Late Victorian bay

l. Perthshire m. Berwickshire n. Islay

0 1 2
metres

d21. Window styles

(d.21,a,h). The 12-pane Georgian window was recorded in various parts of the country. Its presence is particularly evident in the Lothians, Fife and in some northern areas. The unequally divided 6-pane window is related in style. (d.21,g).

(d.21,f). 12-pane horizontal panes are found in some areas. There is evidence that a small proportion of this type has been fitted as a substitute for earlier Georgian 12-pane windows. It has not been possible to ascertain whether others are original, belonging to the Regency and post-Regency style, as occurred in parts of England on the south coast and in Spa towns etc.

(d.21,c). Shows one of the most common types. The upper and lower equal sashes are vertically divided to give a 4-paned window where the panes are almost similar in shape to the overall shape of the window. This is referred to as '4 similar panes'.

(d.21,b). This is similar to (d.21,c) except that the upper and lower sashes have been further sub-divided to produce 8 panes.

(d.21,d). The normal sash and case window is often left without astragals, giving 2 full panes. Less common than the 4 similar panes (d.21,c), it is nevertheless found in most parts of the country but may in some cases have been a later substitute for an earlier 12-pane window.

(d.21,i). Has the meeting rails positioned to give unequal top and bottom panes, the upper being smaller than the bottom. These became popular in the 1870s and were almost universally exploited by the Gothic designers. They were often placed in pairs, separated by a thin stone mullion. A variation (d.21,j) has curved heads to the upper sashes.

(d.21,e). 16-pane windows, once commonly known as 'weavers windows' were not recorded very often.

(d.21,l). Towards the end of the period under study, windows were modified in various ways. The sashes were sometimes divided unequally and redivided by astragals again to give a smaller 6-light upper sash and a larger 2-pane lower sash. This style of window survived in popularity up to *c*. 1930.

(d.21,h). Composite windows in larger houses or in town houses were introduced, such as the 3-light window. This has a central 12-pane sash-and-case Georgian window, 2 stone mullions and 2 side lights of 4 panes each; 2 in the upper and 2 in the lower sashes. It was noted very infrequently during the survey. (Variation in Venetian style d.21,m.)

(d.21,k). The Victorian designers introduced the bay window with great zeal. It became an essential part of the larger Gothic semi-detached and terraced houses of about 1870 and later, and is mostly found in the larger villages and towns.

It is pleasant to meet on some buildings of classical design, circular or oval windows, sometimes glazed in one pane, sometimes divided with astragals to give interesting shapes. They add fineness to a design which is as welcome as it is surprising in normal surroundings.

All the above types of windows, in various combinations, were used in most of the counties of Scotland. The strengths of their popularity varied and this fact will be shown as one of the character-forming contributions to regional variation.

Modern alternatives

The survey produced evidence to show that the character of some country buildings has been adversely affected by the removal of original windows and the substitution of new styles. The alteration normally takes two forms. In one it merely takes place by putting a design by the English Joinery Manufacturers Association (EJMA) of casements in replacement of a sash-and-case window, or alternatively in some cases a pivoted wood window is employed. Both these types of window are heavily framed and look clumsy and awkward in comparison with the fineness and elegance of the sash-and-case windows.

In the second form of alteration, the older vertical window is enlarged by widening and a large 'picture window' is fitted, usually out of scale with the remainder of the building and not conforming in any way with the design and proportion of the whole elevation. This type of work spoils the design and destroys the architectural composition. Cases of this misplaced 'improvement' may be seen in the main street of many small towns where the fashion has

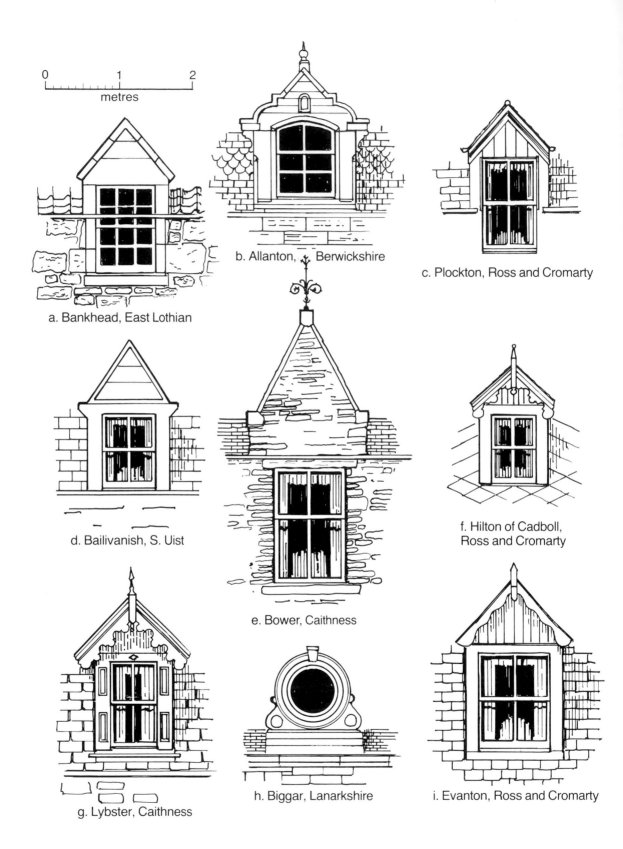

a. Bankhead, East Lothian

b. Allanton, Berwickshire

c. Plockton, Ross and Cromarty

d. Bailivanish, S. Uist

e. Bower, Caithness

f. Hilton of Cadboll,
Ross and Cromarty

g. Lybster, Caithness

h. Biggar, Lanarkshire

i. Evanton, Ross and Cromarty

been pursued to the extent that few houses have escaped. Other types of window which do not conform well with overall designs are those employing glass bricks and small leaded lights, but their appearance is fortunately rare.

Margins

In some areas, margins round the windows alter the scale and underline the significance of the windows in a design. Such margins are usually painted, sometimes directly on to the rendering. Margins do not now appear to be so popular and instances can be seen where former rendered margins have been painted over with the same colour as the walls, thus obliterating them. But the wide seatings of the sills still remain and are made to look ugly and jut out without purpose like protruding ears. Margins are hardly ever wider than 145mm (5¾in) and normally less according to the size of the window. The popular belief that all margins measure 150mm (6in) in width is a misconception and 125mm (5in) is fairly common.

Ingoes

Nearly all Scottish windows are set well back from the outer face of the wall. The depth of this 'ingo' is about 150mm (6in) but varies slightly with a tendency for greater depth to be employed in the north – 150mm to 175mm (6 to 7 in) – with shallower depths in the south. The technique, evolved for added protection from driving rain, has been supported by recent research which has demonstrated that the vulnerability to water penetration at window openings in walls increases in proportion to the amount by which the ingo is reduced, especially in dimensions below 100mm (4in).

Dormers

Dormer windows belong to the Scottish architectural tradition. They were treated with elaborate detail and ornament during the sixteenth and seventeenth centuries when they reached perfection of their kind. The builders at that time knew how to fit a dormer to a roof to look well and thus add a powerful flourish to a building. The dormers were usually arranged to breach the eaves line and lend an emphasis to the vertical element in the overall design of the architecture. It is useful to note certain simple methods that were adopted:

(1)   The fronts of the important dormers were placed flush with the face of the building. Sometimes their sill level was positioned slightly above the cornice level. More commonly the sill level started below the eaves so that the horizontal meeting rails half way up the windows were in line with the eaves.

(2)   The windows were often slightly smaller in size than the main windows of the rooms on the floors below, both in width and height. Without this reduction, dormer windows give the illusion of being larger than the lower windows. The widths of the window openings were often about 775mm (2ft 7in) or less. The heights were in the region of 1·350mm (4ft 5in). The stone surrounds to the dormers were comparatively narrow – 195mm to 225mm (8 to 9 in).

(3)   The pediments were set at about 50° to 52·5° but some could be of a flatter pitch. Their finish could range from relative simplicity to rich embellishment.

d22. Dormer windows   (4)   Some dormers in the older types had the cheeks built to splay slightly outward on plan from the front to back further up the roof, to direct rain water away from the point where the side of the dormer met the slope of the roof – the most vulnerable part of the construction to ingress.

(5)   The dormers were built with the best close-grained stone and had slated roofs.

Dormers of the old type were built in tower houses and town houses. Their design must have been well known throughout Scotland in the eighteenth century. However, they were very much symbolic of the older fashion and were associated with the gabled frontages in towns, the ogee gables and the turrets. Perhaps they seemed to the new establishment of the eighteenth century to have overtones of Scotland's former connection with other countries of the European continent, Jacobean rather than Hanoverian. In any case dormers did not accord with the new fashion of monumental city streets with sweeping cornices and string courses. These dormers were barred and not incorporated in the plans of the designer. Later independant owners did not feel the same autocratic urge about preserving the myth of living behind the facade of a large classical palace and added dormers later.

In the country, designers were not so fastidious in their attitude to dormer windows. From the start of the rebuilding in the eighteenth century the tradition of dormer windows remained unbroken. The style changed but the principle stayed. The survey showed that large areas of the mainland, north of the Highland fault, contain a majority of $1\frac{1}{2}$-storey buildings. Nearly all these buildings have dormer windows. The builders adopted many styles and the joiners took the opportunity to display a rich range of techniques. Just as in the seventeenth century, dormers in these areas became vehicles for displaying style, character and ornamentation. The builders positioned the dormers at various points on the roofs. The roofs in the north-east were very suited to dormers because, as the computer disclosed, most of the roof pitches fall within the steeper ranges of 39° to 50°. Dormer windows in low-pitched roofs are less practical. The dormers are sometimes placed partly below the eaves in the fashion of the preceding centuries but the majority were raised in position to eaves level or more often above, the front being up to one-third of the roof slope above the eaves (**70**).

The styles may be classified as follows:

Flush
(d.22,a and d.23,c). Eighteenth- and early nineteenth-century dormers. Face flush with front wall of building. Sill positioned below eaves level. Stone fronted and gable ended with a skew. Sash-and-case window, often with 12 panes.

(d.23,c, d.23,f, and d.24,a,c,e,f). Similar to (d.22,a) but erected in the middle to late nineteenth century. Sometimes open verges or projecting verges. Pitch at least 45°. Sometimes hipped or crowstepped.

(d.23,e and d.24,d). The oriel dormer is set at a lower level or slightly below the eaves and projects beyond the face of the main wall of the building. Sometimes corbelled or cantilevered on brackets. Usually in the form of a bay. Hipped roof.

Flush (Plain) (d.22,b,d). Set at the eaves and flush with the front wall. Sometimes in stone, but usually in timber. Gable with projecting verge. Sometimes scalloped with barge boards and finials in timber. Gable filled in with weather boarding, vertical or herringbone pattern. Sometimes the vertical apron is superimposed and hung from verges and carved at the foot. Gable pitch at 45°.

d23. Dormer windows

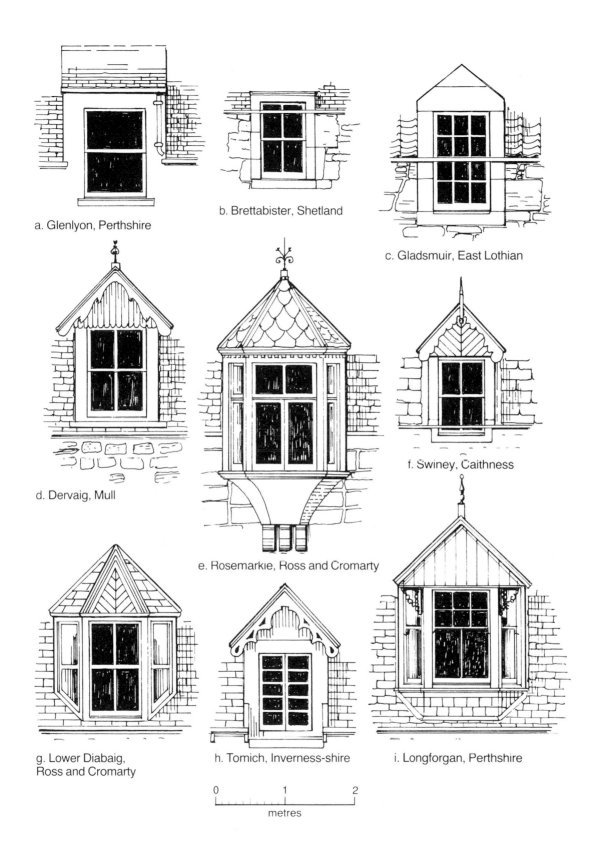

a. Glenlyon, Perthshire

b. Brettabister, Shetland

c. Gladsmuir, East Lothian

d. Dervaig, Mull

e. Rosemarkie, Ross and Cromarty

f. Swiney, Caithness

g. Lower Diabaig,
Ross and Cromarty

h. Tomich, Inverness-shire

i. Longforgan, Perthshire

0   1   2
metres

133   *The elements of buildings*

Details and embellishments

Nearly all of the early nineteenth-century dormers with gable ends have pitches of about 45°. They form the most interesting and best-designed group, especially in the north-east of Scotland and in the northern counties. As already stated, the windows are smaller than the main windows on the frontage below but usually of the same style, i.e. sash-and-case and with panes divided into four. The jambs, of timber, are narrow and set on a lead apron. The projecting verges and barge board above hug the top of the window and do not stand high above it. The eaves at the cheeks of the dormer project well over the face as there is normally no gutter provided and the surface water from the dormer roof must be cast well clear of the sides to guard against penetration. The pitched roof above is normally slated even when the dormer has been formed on a pantiled main roof. The late William Maclean, probably the last real craftsman slater in Scotland, pointed out that for pantiled roofs to be successful they must be kept simple. Gables with valleys, dormers etc. could not be properly formed in pantiles.

It was in the infill of the pediments that the joiners excelled themselves in design and craftsmanship. The pediments are surmounted by turned wooden finials onto which the barge boards and the verges abut (d.22,f,g,i, d.23,f; d.24,f). These are finely proportioned. Usually square on section in the middle

Flush (Bay) (d.23,i). As above but bay window usually with slated roof.

Set back

Set back (Plain) (d.22,f,i). As (d.23,i) but set up the roof at about up to one-third. Some of the finest designs occur in this group.

Set back (Bay) (d.24,g). Bay dormers set up the slope of the roof back from the face of the building above the eaves are usually hipped, sometimes with a metal finial. Occasionally the corners of the bay are rounded in plan and covered with vertical slating. Bay dormers are designed in two ways. The simpler type has the sills of the front and side windows all at one level so that the bay sits up at the front and the space under the sill is usually covered with hung slating.

(d.23,g). The more intricate and neater bay dormers have the front sill of the middle windows positioned down close to the roof on a lead apron. The two side lights are also placed with the sills close to the roof but as a consequence, these sills have to be made sloping up from the mullions and the bottom sashes are also sloped upwards.

Other types

Flat topped (d.23,b). Flat-topped dormers with various forms of elevational finish at eaves, e.g. (d.24,b) flat pediment, flat circled end etc.

Mock (d.22,e). Mock dormers with pediments placed over normal top floor windows for decorative effect. Late nineteenth-century.

Forward sloping roofs (d.23,a). Dormers with one-way pitched roofs running from back to front.

Special (d.22,h). Special dormer types have been recorded such as oval shaped, circular and half circle. Normally positioned over stairway and hall below. Victorian and small with classical motif and daintily positioned.

Gabled (d.24,h). Gables have been recorded over dormer windows especially in mid- to late-nineteenth-century designs, often with projecting verges and steep pitched roofs.

d24. Dormer windows

a. Dallas, Moray

b. Uphall, West Lothian

c. Peaston, East Lothian

d. Cruden Bay,
Aberdeenshire

e. Stewartfield,
Aberdeenshire

f. Dunbeath, Caithness

g. Longforgan, Perthshire

h. Fortingall, Perthshire

0   1   2
metres

135   *The elements of buildings*

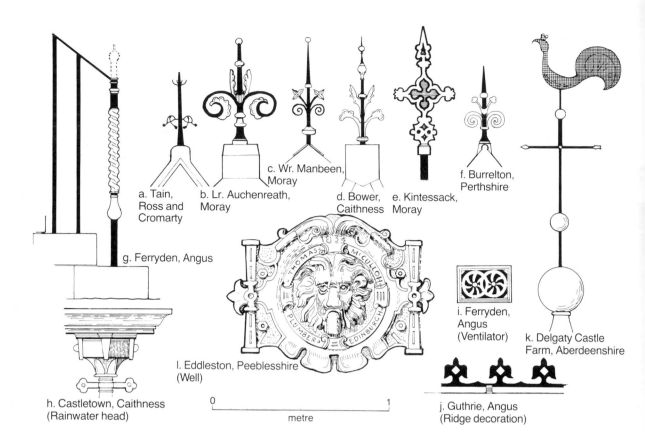

a. Tain, Ross and Cromarty

b. Lr. Auchenreath, Moray

c. Wr. Manbeen, Moray

d. Bower, Caithness

e. Kintessack, Moray

f. Burrelton, Perthshire

g. Ferryden, Angus

h. Castletown, Caithness (Rainwater head)

i. Ferryden, Angus (Ventilator)

k. Delgaty Castle Farm, Aberdeenshire

l. Eddleston, Peeblesshire (Well)

0 _____ 1

metre

j. Guthrie, Angus (Ridge decoration)

d25. Cast and wrought ironwork

length for practical reasons, the finials have turned, moulded, tapering finishes at both ends. The barge boards are often pierced and fretted or scalloped with small piercings.

The success of the early nineteenth-century dormer lies in its scope for creating style. The examples from the survey also demonstrate that the builders had a good sense of scale and reduced the size of the window and dormer to the extent that compared to the main windows they appear in a proper proportion: smaller than the main windows but not too noticeably.

The design of the flush dormer (d.22,a) is arranged so that the bottom of the skew cuts diagonally across the top outer corner of the lintel thus bringing the skew down close to the top of the window. The later type of dormer looks too high and clumsy when the lintels run across the full length of the face of the dormer and the sloping skew is placed above.

The cases of the windows in the dormers shown on (d.22,f,g,i) are set back from the face of the wooden jamb by about 35mm ($1\frac{3}{8}$in). In (d.22,a, d.23,c) the sash-and-case windows are built into the reveal about 150mm (6in) from the face of the jamb. Dormers are often completed with a stone finial (d.22,b; d.24,e). In the older examples this could take the form of a thistle or fleur-de-lis. Later examples have, delicately carved, a finial with a circular face and small, thin, curved neck below to give an appearance on face like a sphere sitting on a curved tapered stand (d.11,e). The side elevation shows the circular end

to be cylindrical in shape and extending the full width of the skew as does the curved shaped neck.

In the later Victorian types the designs return to thistles etc. (d.11,b).

The rich ornamentation of the seventeenth-century dormers was not repeated in the country buildings of the late eighteenth and nineteenth centuries.

Where hipped roofs are employed over dormers (d.23,e,g) the piends are in almost every case covered with metal ridge pieces over a roll. Gutters to these dormers were usually a later addition and are always found in the Gothic form. In the Gothic period it became common to incorporate in some dormers (d.24,a) projecting verges supported on open wooden struts with chamfers and stop chamfers and moulded vertical finial posts.

The late Victorian architects evolved bracketed hoods over dormers and put heavily moulded cornices under the great projecting verges. The hipped roofs were often close piended, using concealed lead soakers. The exposed open framing sometimes incorporated curved or arched members (**71**). In the last stages of the Victorian versions the architects produced designs with heavy stone pediments having large horizontal club skews often corbelled out from the face. These dormers became top heavy and comic like the overlarge creations of Victorian milliners. (d.24,c). The Victorians also liked to produce false dormers of the type shown in (d.22,e), placing above the window tall steep-pitched

71. Moffat, Dumfriesshire

137   *The elements of buildings*

pediments with metal finials. They lend to a design the romantic element associated at the time with the tower houses and castles.

The flat-roof dormers of (d.23,b; d.24,b) when small and neat appear to be original and not unattractive. Some have a classical theme which accords well with the rest of the treatment of the building. There were fewer of the modern box dormers recorded than might have been expected and this may be due in some areas to the vigilance of planning authorities. It may not, however, be the form of modern box dormers that offends the designs of the older buildings but more the failure of designers to observe the scale of dormers in relation to the building as a whole.

Dormers with roofs sloping in the same direction as the main roof but at a flatter pitch (d.23,a) are seldom found in the mainstream of dormer design in the countryside.

Roof lights

Closely related to dormer windows are the small lights or ventilators with a circular glazed openings set in the front with architectural advantage to both exterior and interior (d.22,h).

Ventilators

Eyebrow ventilators are frequently used in the roofs of byres, stables, etc. In the corrugated iron roofs and thatch the ventilators are sometimes placed in the stone rubble walls either as triangles formed in stone slabs or in fireclay pipes.

Loft Doors

Loft doors in farms are a typical feature with a dormer-type pedimented roof and a framed-and-lined door, usually set in stone jambs and lintel.

Chapter 8 which deals with the character zones, demonstrates that in some zones certain types of dormer are very strongly represented. They are a strong ingredient contributing significantly to variety in local style and character.

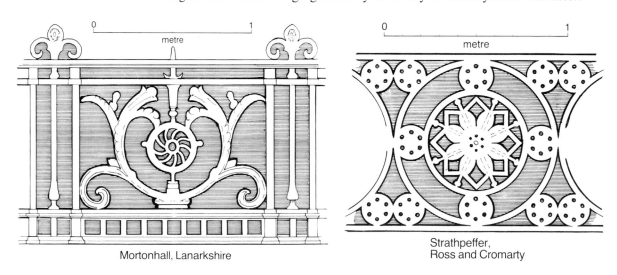

Mortonhall, Lanarkshire

Strathpeffer,
Ross and Cromarty

6 An analysis of design principles

It has been shown how Scottish builders had the advantage of well-chosen sites in the country and in the planned villages and towns. Excellent materials for walls and roofs were usually available and, if the local products were less amenable for fashioning to their purpose, the builders had the skills to adapt their techniques to overcome the disadvantages. Yet a building when put together in such auspicious conditions, displaying fine craftsmanship and beautiful textures and colours, may not necessarily look wholly satisfactory. As indicated earlier, success only comes when the composition is well proportioned and the various parts are related in shape and size so that they are felt to be well balanced. This prerequisite the builders understood well. Analysis of their composition has proved, perhaps unexpectedly, illuminating.

It has long been recognised that buildings which are well proportioned possess qualities which make them look right. This is because the various elements – windows, doors, cornices, pilasters, string courses etc. – are given attributes of shape, size and position so that they relate in geometrical or mensural terms to one another. This fundamental truth of architecture seems to have been known to the ancient Egyptians because their monuments have been found to conform to such systems of proportions. Greek and Roman building was controlled mathematically and Vitruvius recorded among the essential ingredients of a work of architecture the term 'Eurhythmy' – 'beauty and fitness in the adjustments of the member'. The various parts of a building required to be 'of a height suited to their breadth, of a breadth suited to their length and in a word when they all correspond symmetrically'. This led him to the use of the module as a unit of design to which all the parts of a building conformed. Later investigations in mediaeval and renaissance times into the application of proportioning, relating to selected numbers or modules, have been re-examined in modern times by architects such as Le Corbusier.

These theories were generally conceived as applicable only to large buildings such as churches, public buildings or mansion houses. It might, therefore, have been felt to be absurd to connect them with the ostensibly artless and homespun farms and cottages of Scotland. However, the analysis of survey photographs, contrary to such previous assumptions, has established that composition in small buildings also may be governed by geometry.

The analysis was directed towards the large selection of photographs which had been taken to give elevations almost true to scale. A random sample of over 1000 of these photographs was extracted and tested to find to what extent the relationship of the overall frontage of each building and its doors and windows conforms to any system of related proportions. The result was that 57 per cent responded to overall control of proportions comprehensively or nearly so. 'Comprehensively' here means that all major shapes came within an overall proportional principle. Those close to this perfect stage contained one or two shapes that did not strictly conform, often because the length of a building was curtailed at one end or an asymmetrically placed door had introduced non-conforming elements into the otherwise perfect arrangement. A further group of buildings in the sample amounting to 28 per cent were fair examples of controlled proportioning which, however, embraced only some of the parts or contained slight inaccuracies in shapes or positioning of the parts. These results meant that in only 15 per cent was proportioning inconsistent or wholly absent.

The test showed that the basic properties derived from the rectangular windows. The square, however, applied especially to the overall shapes of the elevations. Single-storey buildings often divide into multiples of squares from 2 to 5 in length (d.28,a–d). The shape of the elevations in 1½- and 2-storey buildings frequently consisted of 2 squares in length (d.28,e). Sometimes the front was slightly elongated so that the two square shapes lie on either side of the centrally placed door (d.28,f). Alternatively the building may be slightly narrowed so that the two square shapes overlapped exactly across the width of the door (d.28,h). Less frequently the overall shape is similar to the shape of the vertical windows but of course set horizontally (d.28,i), or the elevation is arranged so that, when vertically divided into three or four equal divisions, each has the same shape as the windows set vertically (d.28,g,j).

The square has also frequently been employed as a basis of proportion especially in Gothic elevations or in building where the windows are tall and the diagonal of the rectangle approaches $63\frac{1}{2}°$, i.e. the window shape consists of two squares in height. The window shape mostly used, however, is the rectangle where the angle of the diagonal is 60°, i.e. the ratio of the base to the height is 1:3. This rectangle has a special geometrical property in that, when it is equally divided horizontally into three, the rectangles so formed are similar to the main rectangle, i.e. they also have diagonals of 60°. Other window rectangles were regularly recorded such as those with 58° diagonals where the proportion of base to height is 5:8. When this is divided into two the resultant shape of 5:4 has the diagonal angle of $51\frac{1}{3}°$ which has occasionally been revealed as the angle of the controlling shapes in elevational proportioning of buildings in some parts of the country (d.30,h,i). The majority of rectangular windows have diagonals that range between about 57° and $63\frac{1}{2}°$. The methods adopted for testing the geometrical systems of proportions are shown on the illustrations (d.29 and d.30).

The subjects surveyed leave no doubt that, for the most part, care in proportions is manifest in all parts of the designs. In the buildings such as the thatched and rubble-built dwellings and byres of the early eighteenth century the simple forms employed are intimations of the finesse in proportioning that was to come later.

The frontages of these buildings tended to be arranged in squares which are usually accepted as having stable properties in design. The example shown in (d.30,a) consists of masonry walling punctuated by the door or small windows at such intervals that the length of each part of the wall thus distributed equals approximately the height of the wall from ground to eaves.

The most responsive elevations are of two storeys, symmetrical and with a central door and five windows, three on the upper floor and two on the ground

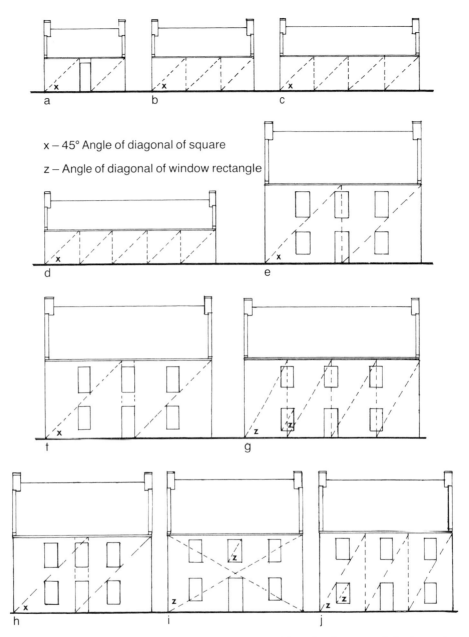

x – 45° Angle of diagonal of square

z – Angle of diagonal of window rectangle

floor. (d.29) has been selected here from out of hundreds to explain how the key to the system applies. It is the elevation of an early nineteenth century house in Perthshire but is in general arrangement typical of many others from various parts of the country. In this example the angles of the diagonal of the windows are 58°15′ and 31°45′ (d.29,a). The rectangle forming the elevation of the frontage is made up of two squares each lying on opposite sides of the door as illustrated on (d.29,b). In this type of arrangement, rectangles formed by one of these square shapes and the central vertical panel formed by the width of the door when vertically bisected, gives two vertical rectangles of

d28. Proportion: shapes of buildings

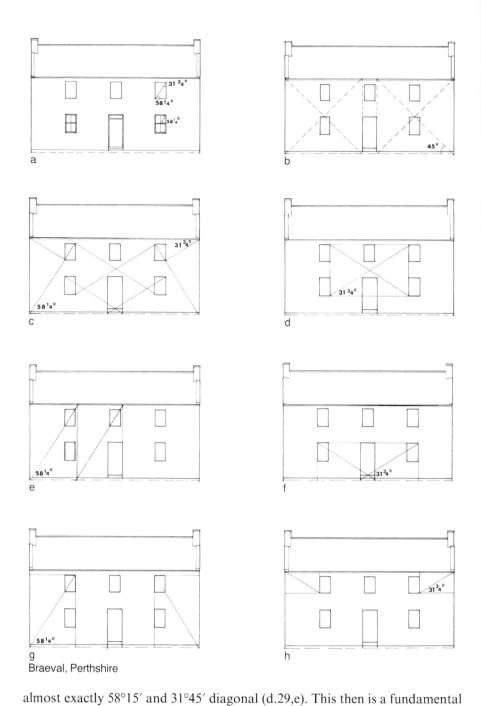

a

b

c

d

e

f

g

h

Braeval, Perthshire

almost exactly 58°15′ and 31°45′ diagonal (d.29,e). This then is a fundamental property in the overall shape that relates to the square and the window shapes. The position of the central window is determined by the position of the door at the centre of the composition. The positions of the end windows, locked into their proper place by no less than four rectangular controls, all geometrically similar to the window rectangle, become perfectly located with the overall composition. The four controls can be observed in the following illustrations:

d29. Proportion: analysis of elevation of house in Perthshire

(1)   (d.29,d) shows the large central rectangle formed by the inner jambs of the four outer windows. It has a 58°15′–31°45′ diagonal.

(2)   (d.29,f) shows the lower two outer windows related to the central door by two rectangles formed by the outer jambs of the two lower windows and the opposite jambs of the door. These also have diagonals of 58°15′–31°45′.

(3)   (d.29,g) shows each of the upper floor windows positioned by rectangles formed by the corner of the elevation, the top of the window and inner jamb of the window and the ground level. This rectangle is also similar to the windows with a 58°15′–31°45′ diagonal.

(4)   (d.29,h) adds a further control to the placing of the end upper floor windows lying in top corners and formed by the eaves, the jamb of the window and the projection of the sill line. These also have diagonals of 58°15′ and 31°45′. It will also be observed that the window divide of astragals and sashes provides four panes with rectangular shapes of nearly 58°15′–31°45′ (d.29,a).

The two-storey house referred to above is a type which occurs in every county in Scotland. Most seem nearly the same in general appearance, yet so few exactly repeat the geometrical arrangements that exact replication is rare. One might at first entertain the notion that geometrical proportioning such as described above would restrict the options open to a designer to exercise individuality. The diversity of perception among the builders has simply produced almost an endless variety of well-balanced and aesthetically satisfying elevations (d.30).

(d.30,b) illustrates an example based on the square. It is not unusual also to find the shape of the square, in addition to the 'window rectangle', determining the proportional positions of minor parts of an elevation as well as the major parts.

The geometrical basis of design did not fade with the introduction of Gothic style into the countryside. At one time 'pure' classicists used to invite everyone to dismiss the advent of Gothic as a style which threw out the rational classical canons of beauty and refinement for the new romanticism. The analyses show, however, that the sense of order was too ingrained in the Scottish character to permit the control of proportion to be relaxed. (d.30,b) illustrates that the Gothic design of this house is regulated by the square. Indeed the square set diagonally could be regarded as the fundamental framework on which the composition is built. It may only be accidental that this pattern of framework is reminiscent of the leaded lights in a Gothic church.

In the later designs, unravelling the pattern of the proportioning systems requires caution. It would not be correct, without evidence, to read into the minds of the designers exactly what their objectives were or how they went about achieving them. Unlike the worthy Vitruvius or the Renaissance masters, the creators of countryside buildings left no recorded theories or treatises. For that reason it would be rash obviously to hurry to the conclusion that they practised the procedure of geometrical proportioning or 'tuning'. Yet it would not be unreasonable to assume that their natural instinct for disciplined thinking coupled to the spirit prevailing in the eighteenth and nineteenth centuries for classical order and balance frequently led to design reflecting these influences. The logical cast of mind sometimes emerges in architectural design even in today's world where harmony and balanced proportion have not been a

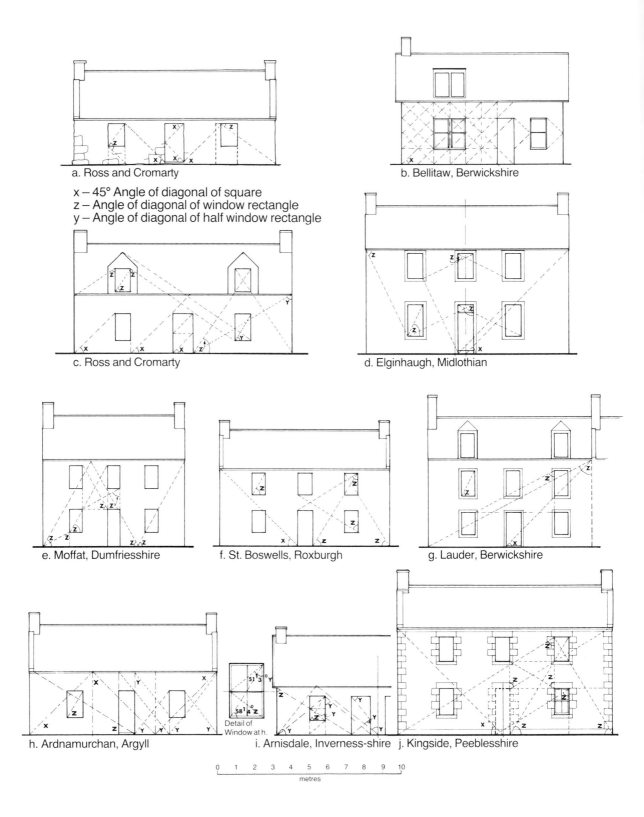

a. Ross and Cromarty

x – 45° Angle of diagonal of square
z – Angle of diagonal of window rectangle
y – Angle of diagonal of half window rectangle

b. Bellitaw, Berwickshire

c. Ross and Cromarty

d. Elginhaugh, Midlothian

e. Moffat, Dumfriesshire

f. St. Boswells, Roxburgh

g. Lauder, Berwickshire

h. Ardnamurchan, Argyll

Detail of Window at h.

i. Arnisdale, Inverness-shire

j. Kingside, Peeblesshire

0 1 2 3 4 5 6 7 8 9 10
metres

central theme. Appreciation for organised proportion in lines and shapes may still be discerned in the architectural designs of some students, suggesting that this deep-seated impulse is not extinct. Further, in recent times some notable architects have shown from their works that they have possessed a perfect sense of proportion in the same way as musicians may have a perfect sense of pitch.

It would not be beyond expectation therefore to find that the builders in the Scottish countryside, working in an age when order and balance were regarded as imperative, created well-proportioned designs without effort. For historic reasons most of the buildings covered by the survey were built in the late eighteenth and nineteenth centuries. They belong to the same family as the elegant town houses in the cities and the mansion houses in the country. They merit the appellation of Georgian, Georgian derivative and Gothic no less than their better recognised urban counterparts. The consistency of refined proportion in these small buildings which applies over the whole countryside seems to have remained largely undetected for too long.

The study has made it evident that the essence of country building in Scotland can be drawn from three sources.

(1)   The setting in the open country where buildings submit to the influence of landscape, topography and climate and merge with local colour or, as in the west, take up the challenge of more spectacular surroundings and respond with contrasting colour. The setting in the villages or towns produces a very acceptable blend of conformity to height and widths but elevations that are not standardised.

(2)   The use of local materials and the sound building techniques applied to them by the craftsmen.

(3)   The system of related proportions applied by the builders.

Thus building in the country was thorough, techniques were adaptable and developed by skilful and conscientious builders. The concise elevations were presented directly and logically, not necessarily without wit, but seldom displaying the lighter touches or fancy or waywardness. All of it down to earth and practical, as one would expect of country people.

On the facts now revealed most of us will have to revise our estimation of the status of country buildings. The existing examples still unspoiled cannot any longer be flawed by permitting ill-conceived alterations to destroy the integrity of their carefully arranged compositions. Scots will have to re-learn to appreciate and recognise the 'music' of well-proportioned design. If some are blind to good proportion as others are tone deaf or colour blind, they should be dissuaded from ruining the harmony of these productions for others by altering them and introducing discords and leaving behind architectural dissonance. They are not major masterpieces like the large city buildings and the mansion houses. In musical terms they belong to the preludes and miniature suites, the orderly accomplishment of the designs being very apt for the neat country rows, the well-shaped farms, the planned villages and the landscape in which they have been placed.

In new works, building proportions ought not to be relegated below building regulations. It would be a poor future for Scotland's countryside if the most fundamental attribute of her buildings in the past were to wither because legislation had reduced design to a mere exercise in modern technology and

d30. Proportion: various analyses

bureaucratic niceties. Architecture denotes more than well-disciplined arrangements of elevations, however, and in the Scottish heritage of country buildings it does not simply consist of fine proportioning.

The Regions

The development of regional styles

One may easily imagine how out of place a single-storey house from East Lothian would look, with its pink random rubble walls and terracotta coloured pantiles, if it were to be set down in a Kirkcudbright village among two-storey houses with white-painted walls, contrasting margins and roofs of large light grey slates. Insert one of the white Kirkcudbright houses into an Aberdeenshire village, between granite-built houses with steeper roofs of dark-blue slates and oriel dormer windows, and it in turn would appear decidedly odd. By the same token, place the Aberdeenshire house among the flagstone walls of Caithness, then move the Caithness house to fill the gap left by the first move in the East Lothian village, and both would seem incongruous in their new locations. All these buildings are patently Scottish in appearance but are subject to the sort of regional variation that is found in most countries. The differences derive from three factors: climate, geology and stylistic influences stimulated by social, economic and cultural impulses.

Climatic factors
Materials and construction in Scottish building have to resist the impact of a ferocious climate. Climates can be measured and compared, although Scots are inclined to discredit the description of theirs as temperate. From the point of view of building, it is the combination of rain and wind that requires great attention. Its intensity is highest in the Highlands and on the west coast and in the Islands. About one-third of the country to the west lies within the zone graded by the Building Research Establishment and the Meteorological Office as severe in terms of driving rain with exposure gradings of mostly 7 but in parts reaching as high as 15 and 20. The rest of the country lies within the moderate zone, between grades 3 to 7, with the national average being just over 4.

Couple these indices with maps showing rainfall and wind on which the indices for exposure are based, and, obviously any architect or builder setting out to design a building for permanent purposes in the country, has to select materials and techniques to stand up to harsh treatment. Records often refer to the adverse situations that can arise through lack of adequate measures against the forces of wind and rain. Siting, materials and design change across the country in the face of ever-increasing severity as one progresses westwards, the severity being most acute in the Islands.

As climate may affect form and siting of buildings and their construction and materials, so it may influence character. In zones of high winds, buildings are found to be low in height when out of the shelter of a town. Roof pitches where the most severe winds are encountered tend to be below average in steepness. In more sheltered areas pitches are inclined to be above average. Two-storey buildings are more common in the sheltered east coast and the south.

Harling as a protection to rubble stonework has been applied most extensively in the western areas of Argyll, Inverness-shire, Ross and in the Western and Northern Isles. Further evidence of its use in the west appears in the counties of Bute, Dunbarton and parts of Ayr and Renfrew. Its fairly common presence in the north-east may be partly due to stylistic influences. Lime washing in the south-west also started as a protection to rubble and as a barrier against water penetration but perhaps has now been superseded by painting for its decorative effect.

In the areas of severe wind and rain, the windows are below average in size and more widely spaced and deeply recessed. The narrowness of the windows may be accounted for by the shortage of long stone lintels but that does not explain the shorter heights. From Argyll northwards, the use of fanlights above doors becomes less frequent, to the extent that in the Islands there are very

72. Gatehouse of Fleet,
Kirkcudbrightshire

149   *The development of regional styles*

few compared with the rest of the country. Low lintel heights did preclude them, but their weakness in resistance to admission of the cold would not recommend them to local builders. In parts where the exposure is severe, houses in the open countryside will be found sited with their gables to the prevailing winds. Also, they often have shorter thicker chimneyheads, thicker walls, shorter cans, skews at the gables and no projections at the eaves apart from the gutter. Where open verges have been adopted in the west, the edges of the slates are protected by the lead-covered timber plate to prevent damage, as already noted (d.16,k). The most obvious consequence of adverse weather is found in the hillier areas of Perthshire and in the west northwards from Argyll. To protect the front doors builders adopted the solution of introducing porches which are more often encountered there than in the milder south.

These simply stated consequences of climate describe many of the buildings recorded in the Islands, the west coast, in about half of Sutherland and in some parts of Wigtownshire and Ayrshire and for some of the buildings in the higher altitudes of the open country in Selkirkshire. Climatic conditions also invite the corollary that in these areas where the more moderate weather prevails buildings may be taller, roof pitches average, chimneyheads taller and less robust and chimney cans taller. Windows may be larger, more closely spaced and less deeply recessed. Open and projecting verges and eaves may be expected.

Solitary buildings in those areas of most severe climate and cool summers will have surroundings with less foliage and trees and will appear more stark in effect. In the warmer, less exposed areas of the south and east there is usually a greater profusion of planting seen round farms and isolated buildings. Such conditions describe parts of the Border valleys, the counties of Dumfries, parts of Kirkcudbright, Berwick, the Lothians, Fife and the other counties up to the Highland fault and some of the central belt.

Geological factors

Geology has had a major formative effect on the character of country building because the builders used local materials won from the surface of the land or from quarries. The distribution of sandstone over the country was associated with the most fertile soils so that stone was available where it was most needed. Geological maps show the location of the most important rock structures suitable for building stone. Research for the study revealed an extensive presence of quarries but many others unrecorded were undoubtedly worked and later abandoned. All counties thus enjoyed a good distribution of building stones and only a few were seriously deficient. Slate was the other natural material which had a major influence on the external appearance of buildings. It was worked in Argyll at the famous quarries of Ballachulish and Easdale but many other local sources were uncovered in nearly half the counties of Scotland while other counties produced stone slate. Lastly, clay was worked to produce brick and tiles. The extent of these local works has not been fully appreciated in recent times. Their number was extensive and indicated that there were few counties in Scotland that did not contribute to brickmaking for internal partitions, chimneyheads, drains etc. during the eighteenth or nineteenth centuries. The explanation for their decline may have been that the competition of stone was too powerful – who in Scotland would build in brick if stone were to be found? The brickworks may also have found it difficult eventually to withstand the inroads made by English brick from the large industrialised plants that were developing and of the brickmaking activities of the coal companies using the waste materials incidental to their main activity of coal production.

The geological conditions, therefore, have in many localities determined important features such as the type of roof coverings, the pitch of roofs on occasions (heavy stone slates called for shallow pitches) and the type of walls resulting from the material available and techniques required. Colour was usually ordained by the natural properties of materials. Thus good quality sandstone, when available, has enabled masons to produce ashlar-coursed work and fine tooling in the eastern Borders, the central belt, Angus, the north-east and round the Dornoch Firth. Such stone was also suitable for the great variety of squared, coursed and snecked work and the tooling work that accompanied it. In the areas where medium-grained sandstones were widely found, masons also produced coursed work. Where the sandstone split easily to produce flagstone, it has made a unique contribution to character, as may be seen particularly in Orkney and Caithness (**118**).

Whinstone produced fine random rubble work and was found in most counties bordering or within mountainous areas in parts of the counties of Perth, Fife, Kirkcudbright, Stirling, Selkirk, Peebles and Dunbarton. The quality granite counties were Aberdeen, part of Kincardine and Kirkcudbright. Rougher granite was used in the western Highlands. Geology has apparently divided countryside building into recognisable groups in respect of the walls. The different materials have also divided the buildings into further groups where different building methods are adopted to comply with the quality and character of the stone.

Clay was plentiful and was used both as a walling material or, more often for mortar, because local limestone was absent in many parts of the country. Shortage of lime, however, did not ultimately prevent the application of colour wash and harling to walls, especially in those parts in the west of Scotland with direct access to Ireland from where the lime was shipped.

The distribution of slates and tiles over the country has been referred to in Chapter 5. The materials and their locations which have relevance in establishing areas of similar style or character are:

(1)   Slates do not offer so great an opportunity to differentiate regional variations because they were easily transportable and so have become diffused over the whole country. The main point concerning regional variation is that Welsh slates are very common in the Selkirk-Peebles area and north of England slates are common in the south-west. The blue-purple blue slates of Argyll were employed in almost all Scottish counties.

(2)   Stone slates, as has been indicated, have been extracted in the north and are strongly represented in the north of Caithness, in parts of Sutherland and in Orkney. They have also been produced in the Forfar and Arbroath area and in Dumfriesshire.

(3)   Clay roof tiles occur in two parts, both of which readily fit into distinctive areas of character: Fife, Kinross and Clackmannan where many examples of pantiles are found, as well as in the Lothians and part of Angus and Berwickshire which all have examples of pantiled buildings.

Stylistic factors

Over a period of a hundred years and under the influence of former tradition, the countryside was introduced to a new style of building. The buildings to emerge were classical but also Scottish. They were in their parts expertly and inventively proportioned, as explained in Chapter 6, and skilfully put together by the stonemasons, joiners and slaters. Although the new design style developed into a national movement strong enough to have swept aside local preferences, it was sufficiently tolerant in its application to assimilate them and thereby enrich the architecture from both the national and regional point of view.

The urge to create balance and order was the intellectual motivator of the age, but two approaches were discernible. In the first, stylistic control was acknowledged but only lightly applied. Asymmetry was not excluded and an easy-going attitude to design resulted in a manner of building which appeared more relaxed. Evidence of this approach may be seen in East Lothian and in central and northern Ross-shire, as well as in other northern counties. The second approach was towards a more pronounced stylishness which can be observed in some of the southern counties such as Roxburgh, Peebles and Kirkcudbright where the windows are taller with average mean angles of 60° or more. This lends greater elegance to the facade than that which is found further north. In Caithness, the windows are not so elongated and the mean angle is reduced to $58\frac{1}{3}°$ – not much less but sufficient to give the facades a more subdued appearance. Similarly, in Ross-shire the mean angle is $58\frac{1}{2}°$ and in Nairn nearly 59°.

The other generators of style may be found in the details of buildings. For example, a local designer could select from a number of methods in giving form to elevations or to part of a building. For most people this usually signals a particular style which they read as the character typical of one area. Countryside buildings, when submitted to this test, show that preferences were made on grounds of taste and that local character was not entirely shaped by the nature of materials, the conditions of climate or the amount of financial resources available.

One of the most important differences in detailed treatment is at the jambs of doors and windows. In some areas plain margins are favoured, and these predominate in the south-west in the counties of Dumfries, Kirkcudbright, Wigtown as well as in Inverness. Windows and doors in the east of the country are more commonly finished in rybats, with the exception of the coastal strip from Nairn north to eastern Sutherland. In other areas there tends to be less marked distinctions. The finishing of jambs in rybats is less strong in the three areas of Inverness, central Perthshire and Angus. Ross and Cromarty and Caithness tend to have jambs which are either painted over or have indefinite demarcation by rybats. Fife and the Borders, on the other hand, go to the other extreme and definitely emphasise the jambs with rybats sometimes painted in contrasting colours.

The divide of a window may have been selected by the availability of sizes of glass or nowadays by later changes in renewing sashes. Allowing for these factors, however, the choice has contrived to bestow on different areas different patterns of window divides. The subdividing into four vertical panes similar in shape to the whole window has been recorded as a frequently-used method and it was widely adopted in most areas. Sometimes the sashes were made without astragals or they have been removed. Equal divides of windows with two equal sashes are found mostly in the Borders and to a small extent in the counties of Dumfries, Kirkcudbright, Wigtown, Fife, Kinross and Clackmannan. The twelve-pane classical window still survives, especially in Fife and Midlothian. Horizontal panes are not usual but are seen in Lanarkshire and the west of Scotland.

The treatment of chimneyheads is a significant pointer to character and design. Designers paid particular attention to the various ways open to them to finish the top, and one of the most frequently selected finishes consists of the blocking course on top of the string or necking course. It occurs all over the country but is more entrenched in some areas than in others. Plain chimney copes belong to the counties of Moray, Nairn and Banff, Inverness, Aberdeen and Kincardine and the Islands. Moulded chimney copes are not so common in the countryside. Fife, Kinross and Clackmannan have a moderate number and they also appear in the counties of Lanark and Stirling, Ross and Cromarty, and Sutherland. The splayed cope, much favoured by the Gothic designers, is occasionally found but is probably most used in Ayrshire and Renfrewshire.

Porches of many descriptions are encountered in every county and, as previously indicated, some have been designed with the building and are attractive. Others have been added to accord with the original design, but sadly there are many which have failed to match the care which the first builders had for proportion and balance and so the buildings have been disfigured.

The arrangement at the finish to the top of the gables varies across the country. Plain skews are most typical, particularly on the east coast from Kincardine north to the eastern part of Sutherland. Berwickshire, East and Midlothian and Fife also adopted skews. These are the counties where the local close-grain sandstone permitted the use of such skews. They were also introduced in the south-west, in Ayrshire and in the far north in Wester Ross and the Islands.

Open verges are less common in Scotland. Certain areas, however, possess a relatively significant number. They occur frequently in the counties of Selkirk, Peebles, Angus, and from Moray north to east Sutherland, as well as in central Scotland, Argyll, Inverness-shire and central Perthshire.

Nineteenth-century ideas in some areas modified the basic styles formed during the preceding century, but the process was confined in most cases to merely a romantic Gothic overlay. This process of remodelling was most active in the west and in the central area where the forces of social change exerted their most powerful influence.

Another important influence on building character was observed where the preferences of individuals and organisations with a wide authority established over larger areas distinct styles of architecture, including ideas and mannerisms introduced to the countryside through the establishment of planned villages. The influence of estate architecture, planned villages and the design of manses for local clergy was more fully discussed in Chapter 2, pages 28 and 29.

Lastly, practical considerations of technology and economics have affected the form of building, notably on farms. Large herds called for new cattle courts, arable units needed large granaries and northern farms needed drying kilns. Mills were originally powered by water, then by wind or horse gangs and later by coal fired boilers with tall chimneys. Dovecots produced fresh meat for winter in eighteenth-century Scotland and earlier. The very large holdings introduced belfries and clock towers to regulate the hours of the farm servants on distant fields but no doubt also to serve as a grand gesture to impress the surrounding countryside (d.11,o). In contrast, the small and less productive holdings were confined to modest buildings for man, beast and crops. All these different practical requirements are seen to combine with the previously discussed factors to shape the character zones in the following chapter.

8 The character zones

In *Traditional Buildings of Britain*, Dr. Brunskill has attempted to show the way Great Britain can be divided into areas with distinct regional styles. He does not sweep the difficulties under the carpet and enters the following caveat:

Very few of the features are exclusive to a single region: most are represented in adjacent regions or in the country as a whole. Some plan-types are found in all parts of the country but are expressed differently because of the different building materials which have been used. Some regions, quite small in themselves, include a diversity of building types and provide many building materials.

Dr. Brunskill divides Scotland into three main regional areas: the Southern Uplands, the Central Lowlands and the Highlands and Islands. After having stated the difficulties associated with the task, he then goes on to say:

Nevertheless the existence of regional variations has long been recognised and we are rapidly moving towards the time when the regional variations can be precisely defined, when definitive maps to show the distribution of characteristics on a regional basis can be confidently expected and authoritatively prepared.

This study does not claim to have arrived at these authoritative answers, but an attempt has been made to take Dr. Brunskill's hypothesis a step further by going into greater detail as recorded in Map IV (p.156) The results indicate that mainland Scotland can be divided into 12 character zones, the Islands being treated as a separate entity, and this chapter contains short zone profiles derived from a visual assessment of the whole country, which were in turn modified by computer analysis.

The investigation identified the distinctive attributes that belong to the buildings in each character zone and its subdivisions. It does not follow, however, that the typical buildings in any zone display all of these attributes. It was indeed rare to find a building which provided an exact 'identikit' picture corresponding to the image revealed by the analysis. Nevertheless, when a number of buildings in a zone were appraised, it could be seen that the key characteristics of the zone were fairly evenly distributed among them. Thus, the buildings have a family resemblance but are seldom endowed with exactly the same features. Readers will also observe that, although there are buildings in every zone which possess some of the local characteristics, they may display marked individualisms introduced by the style of the designers. The illustrations for the zones convey some of these aspects and demonstrate that variety within limits is one of the delights of country building.

Zone 1 The Lothians and Berwickshire
The following account is by necessity broad-brush and students of this zone will find much detailed information in *The Buildings of Scotland: Lothian except Edinburgh* by Colin McWilliam.

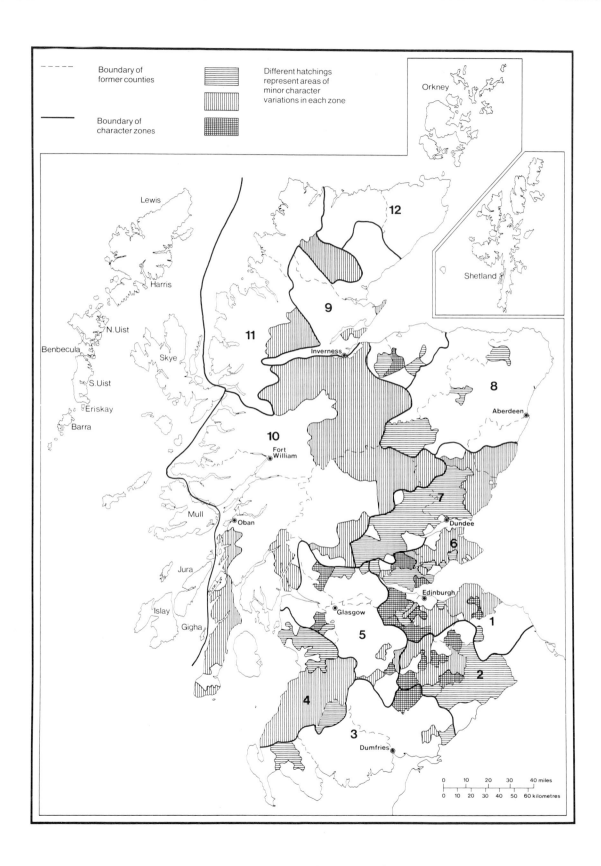

Lewis

Harris

N.Uist

Benbecula

S.Uist

Eriskay

Barra

Skye

Mull

Jura

Islay

Gigha

12

9

11

10

8

7

6

1

2

3

5

4

Inverness

Fort William

Oban

Glasgow

Edinburgh

Dundee

Aberdeen

Dumfries

Boundary of former counties

Boundary of character zones

Different hatchings represent areas of minor character variations in each zone

0   10   20   30   40 miles

0   10   20   30   40   50   60 kilometres

The eighteenth-century agricultural renaissance of Scotland began in the Lothians. As productivity rose, demand increased for new steadings and houses for both farmers and servants. The new buildings were often located on the sites of former steadings, in the open country, or in small towns and many lovely villages which are typical of the zone. Examples of new villages from this time are Gifford, Ormiston and Carlops. Buildings were thus grouped together. Even the cottages were usually built in rows, and farms and offices were planned as combined units round one or two cattle courts (d.8, types G, H and J). Unlike much of the country in Scotland this zone had a high proportion of two-storey building from the outset. Medium scale prevailed but with a tendency towards a larger scale in late nineteenth-century examples in West Lothian.

Local stone was readily available and quarries were worked in many parishes yielding sandstone, whinstone, limestone for mortar, greywacke and rough granite usually for road works. These materials offered varied colours and textures and called for different techniques, masons producing walling which ranged from finely executed coursed work to unrestricted rugged rubble. Notable is the fine droving on the tails of margins in Midlothian which recalls the milling on a coin. The zone had no slate quarries and pantiles were used from, at least, the early nineteenth century. Slates were brought in from Wales, England and North-West Scotland.

Panelled doors with fanlights survive but flush doors in relatively high proportions have been imposed on the zone, especially in Midlothian and West Lothian. In the same way some eighteenth-century Georgian 12-paned windows remain but two- and four-paned types now predominate. There is a higher incidence of modern windows having replaced the originals in the Lothians than in Berwickshire. The milder climate of the zone has not demanded the deep ingoes which are more common in the west and the north. For the same reason builders have seldom provided porches.

Builders have preferred plain chimneycans set on copes of the necking-and-blocking course variety, but there are also examples of splayed and plain copes. In Berwickshire, the chimneyheads on stone buildings were frequently either built or rebuilt in facing brick. In response to the milder weather, builders have erected the chimneyheads slightly higher than those in the west and the north. Skews were normally built to surmount the stone gables, tending to be of medium width and not rising high above the roof surface. The general aspects of character as briefly described above have been combined in various ways to produce the four variations which make up the zone as follows.

The zone can be divided into two major sub-areas, one comprising most of East and Midlothian. It is shown in vertical hatching and has all the characteristics which are mostly associated with this part of Scotland (IV,p.156). First there are the fine villages such as East Saltoun (31) and Dirleton (19, 65). Then the stone-built farms which have houses roofed in slate, pantiled barns, and sheds with the arched cart 'eyes' as the Begbie Farm (15) in East Lothian. Horse gang mills with octagonal pantiled roofs are common and the unused brick chimneys from the coal fired engines which replaced them in the nineteenth century sometimes still stand, as at Beanston in East Lothian. Typical farms include Greendykes at Gladsmuir and Athelstaneford Mains in East

Map IV. The character zones

Lothian, and Ratho Mains in Midlothian. Dovecots also feature widely in the area ranging from the early beehive form at Dirleton and the lectern type at Pilmuir to the formal, such as the classical example, at Huntington in East Lothian.

The stone walls have the warm pink stone so well fitted for the red soil of East Lothian especially in the vicinity of the belt formed by North Berwick and Dunbar in the north, Humbie in the south-west and Whittingehame in the east. Warm cream stone is found in the south of Midlothian.

The building techniques include the lively rubble of East Lothian, a carefree mixture of large and small stones rounded or angular lying side by side just as they left the mason's hand with the minimum intervention from chisel and hammer. In Prestonkirk parish, almost every type of this sort of rubble has

73. *Top right* Crumblands, Midlothian

74. *Above right* Earlston, Berwickshire

been provided. The gnarled, wrinkled surfaces are particularly evident in Aberlady and can be observed in Dirleton. In parts of Midlothian the technique became less exuberant and the coursed rubble beds follow gently undulating lines like the drawing of a freehand draughtsman as at Crumblands (**73**). The orange and terracotta pantiles of East Saltoun give way to the redder colours as one moves further east in the zone. The gentle toned green tiles of Stenton, first shown by the author in 1942 in one of a series of drawings recording towns and villages in East Lothian established where such roof tiles survived at that time. Where slates are used, blue, purple and some grey varieties were introduced. The pitches are shallow as befits pantiled roofs in a mild climate and the chimneyheads are tall.

Begbie Farm in East Lothian (**13**) shows the early introduction of the style of the area. Crumblands in Midlothian (**73**) demonstrates the other approach of squared rubble and contrasting dressed rybats. This building has the characteristic feature of a low stone wall fronting it at the heel of the pavement. East Saltoun (**31**) is a nineteenth-century extension of the local style with splayed chimney copes and slate skirts, and the same basic qualities continued in Dirleton (**65**) well into late Victorian times. The understanding of harmonious proportion has produced large numbers of well designed frontages despite the eccentricities found in some elevations peculiar to East Lothian.

The other major sub-area covers most of Berwickshire, unhatched on the map, and it resembles East and Midlothian with much terraced building in the countryside and with high ratios of two-storey sandstone walls in square coursed work with rybats. The shallow to medium roof pitches are similar, as is the use of stone skews. But changes emerge in the greater amount of 1½-storey houses, approaching about the national average. Other characteristics are the frequent use of reddish cream stone, many dormer bay windows, small reddish purple slates, and pantiles, panelled doors and fanlights and the wide use of brick chimneyheads and copes. The photograph from Earlston (**74**) shows a 2½-storey building with slated roof and bay dormers, a harled brick chimney, contrasting rybats, well dressed margins, rubble walls, and panelled door with fanlight. The buildings of Coldstream (**5** and **12**) display similar characteristics. The cottage in Lennel (**75**) illustrates a pantiled single-storey building typical of the area with harled brick chimneyheads. The dressed stone margins and margin drafts are finished with carefully controlled tooling on the tails.

Then there are two sets of further small areas with some characteristics in common. The sub-areas shown in horizontal hatching present features found in about seven other isolated areas in Scotland. In such areas the buildings often belong to the later periods, the majority are terraced, and the average height is two storeys. The stone walls are generally harled and coloured white. Panelled doors with fanlights are common, although flush doors have been substituted frequently and margins take precedence over rybats at doors and windows. Bay windows are also found in the later buildings. These sub-areas also embrace some older eighteenth-century houses which provide evidence of harling with pantiles having been established at an early date. The old village of Inveresk in Midlothian has early terraced houses where the golden wash of orpiment to the rendered walls produced a soft finish like a ripe peach, a

fruit long cultivated on the south facing walls in nearby East Lothian.

The sub-areas shown in crossed hatching (most of West Lothian, small parts of Midlothian, and Whittingehame and Morham parishes in East Lothian) have a preponderance of the later styles of building slightly imbued with Victorian Gothic similar to that found in the west of Zone 5. Thus there has been less consistent application of traditional proportions. The features shown at Old Philipstoun (**76**) are typical with sandstone coursers, starts and tails at the windows, tooled margins at the door, moulded chimney cope, bay window and panelled door with fanlight.

In the rest of the zone where the farmers of 200 years ago led the world in agricultural improvement, the builders succeeded in meeting the great demand for buildings with an instinct for appropriateness in form. It was an

75. *Top right* Lennel, Berwickshire

76. *Above right* Old Philipstoun, West Lothian

auspicious beginning for Scotland because contemporary planners demonstrated to the rest of the country that when sound practical aims were founded on respect for the land and inspired by faith in the future, life would be triumphantly refreshed. Nearly all the rest of the country at the turn of the eighteenth century followed this lead.

Zone 2   The Borders

Nowhere has the mixture of topography, geology and climate been more potent in determining the evolution of building character. The buildings have become comfortably absorbed among the valleys in the midst of land-locked hills. Only hard intractable whinstone was to be had in parts of the north of the zone, but out of this want sprang an abundance of excellent buildings. While the older eighteenth-century building had offered uncertain defence to weather the assured skill of the new builders left work which has seen nearly 200 winters and emerged unscathed. From the limited reserves of local slate the builders turned to the south and, on the new railways, they brought the purple slate of the Welsh mountains to the roofs among the green Border hills.

The farms, often sheltering among trees, are simple in the uplands. In the lower levels to the south, however, they are complex and more impressive as may be seen at Barns Farm in a six-bay cart shed or as at Pinnacle Farm, in an imposing arched entrance. The Peebles and Selkirk farms are unique in adopting hipped roofs, painted walls and dressed corners at window and door margins (**77**). Fine examples of types C, G and H (d.8) are found at Kaimes, Whitehaugh, Drochil Castle, Stobo Home Farm and Netherurd. The zone is delightfully rural. Outwith the larger county towns, only 22 per cent of the buildings are in the smaller towns, including Innerleithen and Melrose. The rest are located in villages or in small groups in the countryside.

The stylishness of the architecture is in part governed by tall windows (diagonals averaging over 60°) and in part by disciplined proportioning of elevational treatment. Despite the 'High Romance of the Borders', about 12 per cent of the buildings are styled in restrained High Gothic, about 25 per cent

77. Barns, Peebleshire

are merely touched with Gothic feeling and the rest address themselves to the rational language of classicism.

There are three main sub-areas in the zone. The first is shown in horizontal hatching and it consists of terraced development in the villages and towns and semi-detached or detached in about equal proportions. Most villages are of old foundations, except settlements such as Ednam which was planned after the mid-eighteenth century. Building heights of two and 1½-storeys take precedence to the extent that there is no other part of the country where one-storey houses are less common. The scale of building is medium with the familiar cottages situated behind a front garden enclosed by a fence, or more often a hedge. The sandstone or whin walls, with dressed rybats were chiefly constructed in snecked rubble – squared and random rubble performing a secondary role. Colours range from reddish, through cream, to muted cream, and some walls are harled. Largely purple slate, ungraded and finished with zinc or lead ridges, covers nearly all the mainly medium pitched roofs (39°–45°) and open verges are more usual than skews. Some thatch still survives in Denholm. Brick chimneyheads occur as in neighbouring Berwickshire. 40 per cent of those built in stone have splayed or moulded copes surmounted with plain cans. The doors, either framed-and-lined or panelled, normally have fanlights and a single leaf.

Most of these characteristics are shown in the illustration from Melrose (**78**), being a two-storey harled eighteenth-century house, and from Gattonside (**79**),

showing beautifully executed whin walls and sandstone dressings and an unexpectedly colonnaded classical portico delicately constructed in wood. The house from Newstead (**81**) is built in snecked rubble, and the street scene from Melrose (**80**) shows features such as the eighteenth-century way of terminating a gable with a circled convex end, a house preserving the older tradition of building with the gable end facing the street, and the sudden leap into a much larger scale of the Scottish Baronial bank at the head of the street.

The second sub-area is shown in vertical hatching where there are fewer buildings erected in terraces. The most significant attribute governing local character is the random rubble whin and sandstone dressings including various shades of grey which merge into a spectrum of creams. Harled walls seldom occur but white painting has been introduced to Peeblesshire. Large ungraded and purple slates still remain as the principal roof covering. Nowhere else in the country are open verges seen so frequently, possibly because of the scarcity

78. *Opposite top left* Melrose, Roxburghshire

79. *Opposite top right* Gattonside, Roxburghshire

80. *Opposite bottom* Melrose, Roxburghshire

81. *Above right* Newstead, Roxburghshire

of suitable local sandstone, but decorative barge boards were seldom introduced. Moulded or splayed chimney copes outnumber the plainer designs, and some octagonal cans occur in Peeblesshire. Both framed-and-lined and panelled doors, often with fanlights, are found in either single or double leaves. It is of interest that bay windows are more common here than in any other zone. Because this area lies at a higher elevation among the Border hills it is natural that there should be a high incidence of porches. Not as large a proportion of houses as in the sub-area described above are provided with front gardens. The Victorian cottage at Boleside in Selkirkshire (55) conveys the fine quality of whin rubble and ashlar dressings.

The third sub-area, shown in crossed hatching, belongs to the transitional areas of character and style which emerge between neighbouring areas of differing characteristics, principally found between zones on the east and west of the country. Here it is relatively restricted in extent and like elsewhere it displays an even distribution of materials and techniques rather than markedly high or low ratios. The incidence of harling, for example, is only slightly above the national average. However, grey whin is still used in above average ratios and the technique of squared coursed and random rubble is maintained in the construction of the many detached buildings of one or $1\frac{1}{2}$-storeys. This sub-area, along with that described above, shares a greater proportion of $2\frac{1}{2}$-storey houses than any other part of rural Scotland. The roofs, with medium sized or small slates (purple or grey in colour), are seldom provided with stone skews. The doors, many in two leaves, are infrequently furnished with fanlights. As in the preceding sub-area, porches are commonly encountered. Bay windows are favoured and stone, or timber and slate dormers, have a more prominent position than in the rest of the zone.

Barns Farm in Peeblesshire (77), with the typical hipped roof of this part of Scotland, shows the white painted harled walls. However, the impressive frontage of three tall arches and ogee slated central tower remains in the traditional whin rubble finish with dressed sandstone dressings. As in most zones, minor sub-areas have been recorded with character equivalent in materials and techniques to those shown in horizontal hatching in Zone 1. The older town of Yetholm, with further examples of thatch roofing, and the newer village of Morebattle lie within these areas, as well as Innerleithen in Peeblesshire, a textile town which was planned as a spa in the early nineteenth century.

It is well known that the countrymen of the Borders for centuries had forced an existence out of impermanent houses which, the English soldiery had observed, were stubbornly rebuilt as soon as they had been set alight and destroyed. Even in later times their thatched roofs had still to be renewed almost every year. In the rebuilding of the eighteenth and nineteenth centuries the Borderers seized the chance to build well and permanently.

The Borders then followed an ideal approach in producing at intervals over a short period, well-proportioned individual buildings which convincingly combined with one another without requiring the builders to submit to overall street plans and elevations. (Such as were adopted, understandably, in the Georgian city terraces and streets.) Looked at separately the buildings possess a quality of modest good taste. The styles are fairly consistent ranging from the eighteenth century Georgian, to the early Victorian, which are often a

82. Union Place, Moffat, Dumfriesshire

derivative of Georgian, and later Victorian romantic architecture which still is not extreme in its general arrangements of details. The success of this achievement provides a significant lesson for future builders.

Zone 3   Dumfriesshire, Kirkcudbrightshire and Wigtownshire

This zone comprises the counties of Dumfries, Wigtown and Kirkcudbright excluding the parish of Carsphairn. Slight shifts in character brought out in the survey in the north of Wigtown and Dumfries and minor departures in the south of Dumfries have been disregarded in the interests of brevity.

Although there are examples of excellent small town architecture in this zone, four-fifths of the population live in the country or in villages as opposed to the smaller burghs and towns. A dozen new villages and towns were established in the eighteenth and nineteenth centuries, but the countryside was comparatively unaffected by the thrust of nineteenth-century industrialism and the local communities have enjoyed continued tranquility.

This area is less sheltered than the east coast, but not as severely exposed as the west coast further north and therefore does not need extreme measures to protect its buildings against wind or rain. A typical result may be observed in Gatehouse of Fleet (**22**) which is outstanding as a small country town, being of an equal but different quality to Stromness at the other end of Scotland. The villages and towns adopted terraced housing while the open country favoured the numerous detached cottages. Single-storey building, a strong feature of Dumfriesshire as at Union Place in Moffat (**82**), gives way to more $1\frac{1}{2}$-storeys in Kirkcudbright and two-storeys in Wigtown (**56**), but all areas have a fair mixture of different storey heights.

The farms vary from small in the hills to big near the coast, and dairy farms with the house and byres joined are a notable feature of the landscape. Types C, G and H (d.8) are commonly found in the zone. Grennan in Dumfriesshire, built of red sandstone from Locharbriggs with lapped skews on gables and dormers, and the hilltop steadings at Shortrigg and at Mouswald Grange (**50**) are typical Dumfriesshire farms with tower windmills. Horse-mills, mostly circular with slate roofs, are found in the west – while the hexagonal plan belongs to Dumfriesshire. Large mill buildings are attached only to large farms as at Auchenskeroch Castle Farm in Kirkcudbrightshire. Most steadings are plain, whitewashed and very solid in appearance. Other features include stone

83. Ecclefechan, Dumfriesshire

and slate roofed pigsties, stone cheesepresses at the dairy farms and the tapered drystane dykes.

The mixture of painted and unpainted stone walls reflects contrasting attitudes to surface and finish in the same zone. The delight of stone springs from the bond between country and building where Nature contrives by gradual weathering to absorb the material back into its natural character. Painting the walls arrests the gentle process of time and the encroaching lichen whereby each freshening coat preserves the opposites of natural and built environment.

In the counties of Wigtown and Dumfries stone is built in coursed rubble, except where greywacke and whin are used and random rubble substituted, as in Cairnryan (**58**). Aberdeen bond is reserved for the granite walls in Newton Stewart, close to the sources in the area of Creetown and Minnigaff. Brick rybats and flat arches vary the technique for dressing in some whin walls in Wigtownshire as at Cairnryan.

Painted walls are the hallmark of the dairy farms in Wigtownshire where a variety of colours extends over farmhouses, steadings and cottages. In the Mull of Galloway the colour of the farmhouse may be ochre, although as a rule the steadings in the zone rarely depart from white. The lush land with its longer season of growth, later frosts and clear maritime air makes light colouring or white walls singularly apt so that they have become predominantly the local traditional style of both farm and domestic building. Margins round windows and doors, being dominant features, are also frequently painted in various colours particularly in Wigtown. The fashion in colouring changes because at one time the whin walls in Dumfriesshire were painted 'battleship grey'. Now white and light colouring has become more common. In Wigtownshire, dairy farmers before electricity came to the country, conjured a golden tan by one of those tricks of rural alchemy where carbide from the acetylene lamps was mixed in the lime wash, just as the farmers in southern England made pink washes by mixing lime with water in which manure from the cowshed had been soaked. If the walls are not rendered, the texture of the rough stone still shows through the coatings of paint to give a surface like a crumpled piece of cloth as at Ecclefechan in Dumfriesshire (**83**).

Stone and natural or clay slates were used during the eighteenth and nineteenth centuries with stone ridges. The dark and purple greys are prominent in the east and the light to dark greys in the west. The roof pitches usually lie between 39° and 44°. The zone gives an excellent opportunity to observe the stylishness of graded slating, as at Rothwell in Dumfriesshire and at Port William in Wigtownshire (**33**).

The doors generally have a single leaf, frequently with upper glazing or fanlights, and they may be either panelled or framed-and-lined. Two- and four-paned windows prevail with only about one quarter in the 12-paned Georgian style. Simple small pediment dormer windows, as at Port William in Wigtownshire, may be seen on most 1½-storey buildings. Porches are found in below average numbers broadly spread over the zone.

The stone or brick chimneyheads normally have blocking-and-necking course copes, topped with tapered cans and cowls and octagonal cans, except that parts of Dumfriesshire have mainly plain cans. Splayed or moulded copes

appear on less than one third of the buildings surveyed. Skews are medium to wide in Dumfriesshire and narrower in the rest of the zone. They lie close to the slates, which are sometimes fitted into a groove or laid completely under the skews.

The classical pedigree of building in the zone can be seen in the early houses in Ecclefechan (**83**) or in the Burgh building of 1735 in Sanquhar (**53**), both in Dumfriesshire. In Kirkcudbrightshire the Holme (**46**) illustrates one of the many decorative gatehouses and Billies (**84**) pleasingly mixes domestic and ecclesiastical styles.

Zone 4   Ayrshire

The zone comprises the county of Ayr, including the parish of Carsphairn in the north of Kirkcudbright. It lies outside the industrial belt and has maintained its rural character despite the coalfields in the north. The large scale depletion of rural population experienced in other parts of the country in the wake of the agricultural revolution was avoided, and about 70 per cent of houses in the zone are located in small villages with less than 1,000 population or in the open country. The houses in the villages, generally without front gardens, are strung out along the roads – even when curved and on rising

84. *Top* Billies, Kirkcudbrightshire

85. *Above left* Dalrymple, Ayrshire

86. *Above right* Fenwick, Ayrshire

ground as at Ochiltree. Large trees in back gardens, rising above the roofs into view at the front, are a common feature. However, the clean neat aspect of buildings and settings are also strikingly evident.

The farms of the zone display the local tradition of a well brushed, polished appearance unlike the thousands of farms over the country where straw, mire, tin containers, old implements and wooden boxes lie strewn about the steadings apparently unnoticed. The layouts are compact but not comparable to the grand farms in the east of the country. The buildings often range round three sides of a court with the house centrally positioned within easy reach for tending the cattle, types C and F (d.8) being common.

There are two sub-divisions within the zone which display certain attributes that call for each to be examined separately. The first sub-area is shown in vertical hatching, excluding Carsphairn parish, and it has the strongest rural character. Buildings are found lying obliquely to the road, houses are frequently built in pairs and the mixture of storey heights is near to the national average.

The common walling material is stone in snecked or squared-course work with a few examples of Aberdeen bond as at Dalrymple (**85**), but the surface finish in harl or rendering, painted white with dark margins, is more promi-

87. Cairnwhin Farm, Ayrshire

nent than anywhere else in Scotland. Purple or purple-blue slates cover the roofs of shallow pitch, finished with metal ridges, the slates being ungraded and of small or of medium size.

Former framed-and-lined or panelled doors have now been substituted with modern or flush types in some areas. There is a fair proportion of double doors with fanlights. Windows with four panes, equal and unequal, were found in over one-third of the buildings surveyed. Two panes were less often encountered, and the 12-paned Georgian style occurred in about one-sixth of the sample. The incidence of bay windows is below the national average, as is also the case with bay dormers. In respect of the latter, however, the simple rectangular types with pitched roof and finished in slate are found on most $1\frac{1}{2}$-storey houses. Despite the windy and moist weather the custom of adding porches is not a typical feature of the zone, but where they occur the designs are good.

Chimney copes are seldom elaborate, necking-and-blocking copes or plain forms are preferred and there are few of the moulded type. The pots conform to this simplicity and only about one-fifth of the sample was octagonal in shape. About one-quarter of the chimneyheads are built in facing brick. Plain and broad or medium wide skews, lying close to the slates, have prevailed with a few variations such as horizontal skew putts (common in Zone 8) or the curved end skews as at Ochiltree.

The balanced grouping of Nethershield Farm at Sorn (**45**) illustrates the characteristic contrast of a stone-fronted Georgian house and the painted wings and gables of the offices, although marred by the badly sited services pole. The more modest Cairnwhin (**87**) in Barr parish to the south of the zone stands gable end to the road and is painted overall with narrow contrasting window

88. Skeoch Farm, Tarbolton, Ayrshire

margins. At the Stair Inn (9) in the centre of the area the margins project and are painted in contrasting colour except for the corners of the building. Dalrymple (85) in the south-west is finished with Aberdeen bond, but with white painted margins and with a moulded sandstone plinth under the eaves and plain margined corners.

The second sub-area, shown in horizontal hatching, has more terraced houses. The use of harling is more common and panelled doors have survived to a greater extent than in the other sub-area. Bay dormers are used more often, and just under half of the chimney copes are plain as is a high proportion of the pots. The simpler style of building with smooth rendered or harled walls, painted, is aptly illustrated by Fenwick (86) in the north-east of the area. Skeoch Farm (88) in Tarbolton in the south shows the painted harling projection beyond the face of the stone window margins, an old Scottish practice which modern building technologists regard as doomed to failure. The porch, despite the modern infill, is typical of good Scottish Georgian design.

The proportions of the elevational treatment are not particularly well controlled and in this respect the architecture of the zone is less disciplined than in many other parts of the country. The motivation of local builders seems to have leaned more towards decent building than towards perfect proportioning, producing quality through tidiness and restraint. The style of the zone is placid rather than exhibitionist because the builders were clearly not bent on the expression of their own personalities. The value of the style is consistency. For nearly two centuries walls and margins have been carefully repainted by owners to give an ageless appearance as fresh as 'new paint'. It can live on if maintenance is continued in the same neat and good mannered way as in the past.

Zone 5   Renfrewshire, Lanarkshire, Stirlingshire and part of Dunbartonshire

This zone is made up of the counties of Renfrew, Lanark, Stirling and Dunbarton, except the four parishes west of Loch Lomond. The transformation of its countryside during Georgian times only occupied the minds of rural reformers for a short period. Already men with other objectives were at work because chemists, engineers and inventors were enquiring into the source and application of power and entrepreneurs were eager to exploit their discoveries to multiply industrial production and create wealth. The result was inevitable, because such single-minded application could not be bound by the intellectual discipline of which balance was an essential part. The hold of eighteenth-century ideas was loosened and the new leaders were in the grip of the industrial revolution. Nowhere else in Scotland were the forces of this new drive more energetically applied, and the effects on countryside architecture brought both advantage and disadvantage. The centres of Glasgow and the Clyde thrust with explosive energy into the countryside, absorbing several rural parishes in a system of railways, coal and iron mines, factories and tenement dwellings. In seven parishes around Glasgow, the arable land was completely swamped in this process. Similar small side incursions were experienced at other centres in the counties of Stirling, Lanark, Dunbarton and Renfrew. Some well planned areas resulted such as at Greenock, Johnston and Helensburgh which grew into fair sized urban centres. At present, close to half the rural population in

Stirlingshire live in settlements of between 1,000 and 2,000 people. In Lanarkshire the proportion is just under 40 per cent and only Renfrew can still be said to retain a pattern of truly rural settlements.

While the traditional countryside was disappearing the new industrial regime brought powerful influences to bear on architectural style. The new better-off townsmen came to live in new semi-detached and terraced houses in the suburbs and in small towns, escaping from the foul vapours which congregated above works and houses alike, to further parts of the zone where the air more sweetly recommended itself. The zone has thus acquired an unusually high proportion of Romantic and Gothic buildings designed with a conscious aim towards architectural effect by the use of crowsteps, decorative gables and chimneys, bay windows, stone mouldings and mullions, moulded gutters and unequally divided windows. Such displays of lofty elegance and impressive portals combined aptly to frame the emergence of their owners from the tip of their patent leather boots to the top of their silk hats. The country buildings, even at some distance from the industrial cores, became shabby and tired looking from soot and grime. However, although the outward thrust from the urban centres, like the expanding universe, is still with us, some areas further beyond keep fresh the restrained architecture of the earlier more civilised period.

Villages, mostly semi-industrial in origin, are a major element in the zone, with a fair proportion of terraced housing. Many of the later houses have front gardens with hedges. Large scale building is more common here than in most other zones and two-storey buildings exceed the national average of 22 per cent, except in the north-west.

The farms vary across the zone. The dairy farms needed to meet the demand of rapid population growth were small at first, the form being linear at the outset but later developing into courtyard arrangements. The two types may be observed side by side at Auchincarroch Farm in Kilmarnock. In Renfrewshire the dairy farms closely resemble those in Zone 4 with plan types C and F (d.8). The Lanark farms include small units along the River Clyde as well

89. New Mains, Lanarkshire

as large steadings as at New Mains, Lanarkshire (**89**). The simple early examples in Stirling, as at Auchentroig north-east of Drymen, may be compared with the many intensive large farmhouses in the eastern part of the zone as at Claddens, New Monklands, where the house stands apart from the steading. South Bellsdyke Farm, near Larbert in Stirlingshire, employs pantiles for the steading, including the polygonal horse-gang mill. Timber lintels over the cartshed openings and outside stairs in the granary are characteristic of Stirlingshire farms.

Good supplies of workable sandstone ensured that tooled faces and edgings take a commanding position in the zone compared with most others. Polished and broached ashlar and snecked and coursed work were principal choices of masons, random rubble being confined to the whin areas of East Dunbarton-

90. Biggar, Lanarkshire

91. *Top* Bowling,
Dunbartonshire

92. *Above right*
Thorntonhall,
Lanarkshire

93. *Right* Bankfoot,
Renfrewshire

shire and some parts of Lanarkshire. Rendered and white painted wall finishes provide contrasts, particularly in the north of the zone, in parts of west and central Lanarkshire and in the extreme south. Rybats are more usual at windows than margins, but the zone has a rich collection of all the forms of stone masonry and detailing so fervently exploited during the second half of the nineteenth century. A strong feature of the zone is the stone surfaces with droving in fine or broad textures done in long lengths down the side of crow-steps, or in short lengths on individual stones and in random directions in narrow short patches to give an overall texture like trampled grass. Stonework ranges from red to cream in colour, red being strong in the west and cream being predominant in the north of the zone and grey to nearly black in the whinstone area.

Slates in all sizes were preferred for roofing, sometimes graded and occasionally cut into decorative shapes such as 'diamonds' and 'fishscales'. Blue-purple and dark grey colours extend over the whole zone, with purple being well established in the south, and some areas in north central Lanarkshire having a greater emphasis on blue.

Double panelled doors, well constructed and fitted with fanlights, take precedence over lined doors but modern flush doors are becoming common. Moulded architraves in stone were sometimes introduced into the larger Victorian houses. In respect of windows, eighteenth-century buildings have 12-paned windows as at Biggar (**90**) and at Eaglesham in Renfrewshire (**40**), at Bowling in Dunbartonshire (**91**) and at Bankfoot in Renfrewshire (**93**). Tall and unequally divided sashes are fairly prevalent, as at Thorntonhall in Lanarkshire (**92**). However, the equally divided four-paned pattern occurs most frequently, as at New Mains in Douglas parish in Lanarkshire. Horizontal astragals are also seen in many parts of the zone, as at Carbrook Mains at St. Ninians, Stirlingshire, and the late type of unequal sashes with astragals on the upper sashes is found at Candiehead (**94**), also in St. Ninians. Bay

94. Candiehead, Stirlingshire

windows were widely used for their grand effect, demonstrated superbly at Thorntonhall, and at Wemyss Bay in Renfrewshire (**95**). Circled rooflights are a feature of Stirlingshire, as at Candiehead. Dormer windows follow the rich Gothic style, with projecting eaves and being heavily bracketted and decorated with cusps and shaped finials, as at Candiehead. Bay dormers and slate-and-timber types with gables provide the basic styles, but some stone flush dormers have also been used, as at Carbrook Mains. The moderate weather does not give cause for a great many porches, but decorative examples do exist in classical and Gothic styles such as at Thorntonhall and at Candiehead.

The telling feature in chimneyhead design is seen at the copes. Local masons seem to have adopted the policy that if a cope has to be produced it has to be moulded. An eighteenth-century example in Biggar (d.15,a) shows the early Scottish flat splayed-and-moulded style typical of the period. The necking courses at Bowling (**91**) and at Candiehead (**94**) are treated like simple classical cornices. A neat cornice acts for the separate stone shafts of the original chimney at Wemyss Bay (**95**), and Carbrook Mains has a heavy cope with a cavetto moulding below. Octagonal chimney cans and plain cans together accounted for over half the sample surveyed, and nearly 20 per cent have a more ornamental treatment as at Thorntonhall (**92**). Skews are usually medium and less frequently narrow in width. However, open verges provide the finish to many roofs and they are sometimes fitted with a lead edge flashing, as at Candiehead (**94**) and Wemyss Bay (**95**).

Zone 6   Fife, Kinross-shire and Clackmannanshire

The zone includes the counties of Fife, Kinross and Clackmannan, and is characterised by its small burghs, fishing towns and coal mining communities. The prominence of the small burghs is evidenced by such noted examples as Culross, Falkland, St. Monance, Elie, Crail, Pittenweem – all with populations of around 1,500 or less. Charlestown, a little-altered planned village has rows

95. Wemyss Bay, Renfrewshire

of twin gabled cottages cottages with internal valley gutters in the pitched roofs. The custom of building in terraces in towns has been adopted in the countryside where rows of farm workers' cottages are normal. Two- and one-storey buildings prevail and dormer-windowed houses consequently do not feature strongly.

The farms lying on the south-facing slopes looking towards the Forth correspond to their counterparts on the opposite shores – Types G and J (d.8) with big but somewhat less imposing steadings. The building scale is small to average with a majority of single-storey buildings, especially in Fife, but there is a significant proportion of two-storey examples in Kinross.

Walls in natural stone adorn much of the zone for white paint has been applied with restraint, except in some of the burghs. The plentiful supply of local stone embraced many shades of colour, grey in the east, reds prominent

96. Pittenweem, Fife

in the north and south-east and the cream colours through the centre and the
west. The roofing material, like those in Zone 1, consists of slates which were
used predominantly in the counties of Clackmannan and Kinross and over
much of Fife, although pantiles are found in almost all parishes in the zone,
especially in southern Clackmannanshire and in the east of Fife.

Both panelled and framed-and-lined doors were commonly employed, but
modern and flush doors have replaced many of these in Kinross. Georgian
12-paned windows are retained notably in Fife, but the four-paned types are
more usual. A high proportion with two-panes in Kinross-shire has acquired
modern casements. Both plain margins and rybats occur in the surrounds to
doors and windows. Dormers and porches feature relatively rarely in the zone.
Narrow to medium skews and crowsteps are characteristic, along with plain
chimney cans, with blocking-and-necking course copes to the chimneyheads.
However, moulded copes are also common. Carefully composed elevations
may be seen throughout the zone with windows of diagonals on average over
60°.

The zone divides into three sub-areas worthy of special mention. The first

97. *Above* St. Monance,
Fife

98. *Opposite* Pittenweem,
Fife

99. *Top right* Rummond, Fife

100. *Above right* Grahamstone, Kinross-shire

is shown in horizontal hatching and extends along parts of the landward area of the northern shore of the Forth. Here are found many buildings which share characteristics in common with those in Zone 1. The view from Pittenweem (**96**) shows two-storey houses with two flats, the upper being reached by the outside stair and platt. Other features are stone walls with margins, moulded and blocking-and-necking course chimney copes, plain cans and eighteenth-century crowsteps and pantile roofs. The asymmetrical arrangements of the elevations strongly contrast with the regular facade of buildings in other areas of the zone. These very attractive details are repeated in the corner view of the same burgh (**16**), as well as Georgian 12-paned windows and the wide low doors without fanlights. A tympan with gable rises in the background.

The harbour scene at St. Monance (**97**), all stone houses, but where natural stone is little evident, is a good example of burgh architecture which has received the modern 'vernacular' treatment of light painted walls – not the author's favourite style of decoration.

Pittenweem (**98**) shows the handsome 3½-storey type of early tenement house with a 'Dutch' tympan gable, the margins round the replacement Georgian-type windows being unusually prominent. Spencerfield Farm is built round a cattle court. It has a tall brick chimney and the dark rubble walls set off with light rybats characteristic of the zone. These arrangements have close affinity with similar farms in the Lothians.

The second sub-area is shown in vertical hatching (**IV**, p. 156). It is like the area of corresponding hatching in Zone 1 and is typified by Rummond near St. Andrews (**99**). It shows a two-storey house built of roughly squared-

101. Elie, Fife

coursed and tooled masonry, the rybats being set in the Scottish fashion, with the top inband immediately below the lintels of the windows which have flush sills and Georgian divided panes. The pantiled roof, narrow skews and plain chimney cans over a simple splayed cope are characteristic. The stone may have been recovered from an older building. Grahamstone in Kinross-shire (**100**) belongs to the handsome series of symmetrically balanced buildings found in the west of the area. This type of impressive stone chimney is also found in Westhaven Farm in Fife. The slightly Tudor style is as close as most buildings in the zone get to being Gothic. Brucefield is a larger version of the Clackmannanshire farms, where hipped roofs become more popular than in most parts of Scotland, other than some localities in Zone 2. However, the farm at Dairsie in Fife (**29**), with its polygonal horse-mill, also has hipped roofs as the main theme of its style. Typical towns in the area are Ceres, Elie, Strathmiglo and particularly Auchtermuchty where excellent thatch from the reed beds of the Tay still cover the roofs of some houses. Carved stones decorate houses in some of the burghs such as Elie (**101**).

The third sub-area, shown in crossed hatching, is similar to parts of Zone 1 and it also shares characteristics found in neighbouring Zone 5 to the west. The style is more studied and formal and large in scale. The masonry is regularly coursed in snecked rubble in Kinross-shire, and coursers in most parts of Clackmannanshire have tooled finishes. However, random rubble can also be seen. The finish at the windows and doors consists of tooled margins. Slates, small blue or blue-purple, are normally employed for roofs, while pantiles play a secondary role in the smaller buildings. There are many fine panelled doors and fanlights. The picture from Aberdour in Fife (**30**) shows a good local example, with lapped skews and dressed bands at the plinth, below the eaves, at the corners and along the base. The snecked rubble is of good quality. Later versions of this approach, with more elaborate stonework, occur in Clackmannanshire as at Dollar where bay windows, another feature of the area, are employed.

The eighteenth-century style of building took such a firm hold in the zone that, apart from some mild examples of Gothic style, the fine tradition of classical proportioning was still closely followed into the second half of the nineteenth century. To sum up, the essence of character is typified by the balanced elevations of Kinross and by the smaller burgh houses, the latter being asymmetrical with squat wide doors, margins and some walls now harled and painted. The setting is typified by the blackened harbour walls of vertical masonry in the foreground, the slate and tile roofs rising in the background. In the open countryside there are the excellent cottages, houses and farm buildings. Clackmannanshire produced the orderly and symmetrical compositions with tall upright chimneys, models of rectitude. In contrast the slightly tipsy arrangements of doors, windows and projections of the Fife fishing burghs must have seemed to their Clackmannanshire neighbours as bordering on wanton laxity.

Zone 7   Angus, Perthshire and south Kincardineshire

The zone sub-divides into two main parts. The northernmost is shown in vertical hatching, comprising parts of Angus and Kincardineshire (**IV**, p.156). This produced survey values indicating characteristics almost identical with those in parts of Berwickshire in Zone 1. However, the Kincardineshire buildings are on average about 300mm (1ft) shorter and slightly lower. The window shapes vary on average in that in Kincardineshire the average diagonal is 60° against the Berwickshire angle of 59¼°. Another minor local difference is the greater presence in this zone of Aberdeen bond, being influenced by the proximity of Zone 8 to the north. A small area to the north-west also has similarities to parts of Zone 2, chiefly because of the use of whinstone.

The rural quality in this zone is very noticeable in Angus where all the buildings outwith the towns are situated in open country or in small villages of under 1,000 persons. The Kincardineshire area has similar characteristics and only the Perthshire part has a fair proportion of the buildings, about 20 per cent, in villages and towns of between 1,000 and 2,000 persons.

The zone is adjacent to the North-East (zone 8) where the art of village planning developed from the middle of the eighteenth century. The influence spread south to Zone 7 where we now have examples such as Laurencekirk, Auchenblae and Friockheim. Further west, there is Edzell, Letham and Newtyle (a railway and weaving town) in Angus and New Scone and many more which were not completed in Perthshire.

In the second sub-area, shown in horizontal hatching, there are about equal numbers of one- and two-storey buildings. They mostly stand detached, while semi-detached and terraced buildings occur in equal proportions. A garden and hedge fronting the house are frequently provided.

The farms in Angus and south Kincardine take the form of the large types G and J (d.8) with pink sandstone rubble walls and sometimes stone slate roofs. The houses are placed separately like the Snabs at Longforgan in Perthshire where the pigeon loft is provided with a few holes in the gable of the steading, or as at Wardmill Farm in Angus north of Forfar, which demonstrates the marked separation of the house contrasting with the close attachment of house

102. Letham, Angus

and steading in areas of dairy farming. Fine farm buildings, some with horse-gang mills, dovecots and cart 'eyes' may be seen in many areas. Fingask Farm in Kilspindie parish in Perthshire introduced steam power and a large chimney. The numerous cart bays emphasise the importance of arable farming. Inchmartine House Farm represents the more monumental approach with tower and dome above a pedimented archway and the fine mains farms at Edzell, with ten cart bays, and Glamis emphasise the richness of the farming.

The geology of the zone has produced soft pink stone which has strongly influenced local character and invited masons to exercise their skills to the full.

103. *Top* Tannadice, Angus

104. *Above* Johnshaven, Kincardineshire

Walls are built in snecked-and-squared coursed work, having been executed with an accomplished repertoire of dressing techniques such as polished margins, margin drafts, chamfers, stippled surface work and mouldings. There is an example at Letham in Angus (**102**), dated 1864, and still in superb condition after 120 years. The walling styles change over the area: dressed coursers in south Angus, and flagstone and rubble in central and northern parts. Pink and red stone in the south, especially in Angus, gradually gives way to the greyer tints in the north and west. Some white painting has occurred in south Perthshire and even in Angus, c.f. Tannadice (**103**). Where stone slates are not used, blue Scots slates are mostly found. Ridges are either mainly in zinc or lead, in some parts being in stone or clay tile in about equal proportion. Graded slating in shallow to medium pitches (under 45°) is usual with some slopes between 33°–39°. About twice as many doors are lined as are panelled, and the upper parts have often been glazed. Single leaf doors are usual, but the proportion of fanlights is low. The local masons have produced tooled or polished margins in most surroundings.

Generally, windows are not deeply recessed. There are more than the national average of casement windows, but four-paned sash-and-case windows predominate such as at Wardmill Farm in Angus. There are also many of the 12-paned Georgian style as at Mains of Arthurstone in Perthshire (**105**), near Coupar Angus. Bay windows appear less frequently than in most zones, and dormer windows are not very common. Porches are well designed and include both classical styles as at Ballendrick House and decorative timber as at Mains of Arthurstone.

The chimneyheads are finished with blocking-and-necking course copes or less often with moulded designs, see Letham (**102**). Brick examples take the place of stone in the south less frequently than in the north of the zone. Octagonal cans are common. The absence of stone skews, sometimes attributed to

105. Mains of Arthurstone, Perthshire

the belief that the local stone was too loosely grained to meet the need, has established open verges as a primary characteristic. However, decorative barge boards are not a local feature.

The farms in the area of vertical hatching follow types B, C, D and E in style and plan (d.8). There are many 1½-storey houses, often with bay dormers. The walls resemble those in the zone to the north and have a greater incidence of Aberdeen bond and whin with sandstone dressings. Pantile roofs are a noticeable aspect of the fishing villages such as at Johnshaven in Kincardineshire (104) and purple slates are more significant in the north than in the south of the zone.

The doors are often panelled and surmounted with fanlights. Bay windows occur only in small numbers, and porches are not a typical feature. However, brick chimneyheads are conspicuous. Stone skews are also typical with horizontal skew-putts, probably influenced by the adjacent zone to the north.

The variety in building is repeated in the field walls or dykes. Typical of the central area of the zone is the use of flat stone slabs, inserted below the stone-on-edge cope stones, and oversailing both faces for the protection from rain of the wall beneath. In other parts the stone-on-edge copes oversail without the slab below. The finely dressed half round copes in the field walls near Edzell are laid flush above the dressed stone tapering wall. As a further refinement the masons made long tapering gate posts extending from below the cope and sunk into the ground for stability. This type of wall excels all others.

If proof is required of the professional skill of the local masons, evidence is produced in the loving care which a forgotten craftsman bestowed on a humble cheese press built into a wall at Greystone on Carmylie Farm in Angus where the massive stone block is delicately dressed and droved with pride of workmanship normally reserved for a monument.

Lastly contrasts of planning may be observed between the straight lines of Laurencekirk or Edzell and the formality and informality of Johnshaven where, only 30 years after the new extension had been promoted, a critic observed of the older part that 'the great mass of buildings in this place is a congeries of mean cottages huddled all through one another.' The contrasts in the extremes of planning and non-planning could not be better presented.

Zone 8   Aberdeenshire, north Kincardineshire and Banffshire

The zone consists of eight parishes in the north of Kincardineshire and the counties of Aberdeen and Banff. Its characteristics are fairly consistent throughout, the only exception being three separate sub-areas shown in horizontal hatching, which have closer relationships in character to neighbouring Zone 9 (IV, p.156). The other non-conforming areas are small and have only a minor affect on the overall character. There is further reading about local building tradition in *Royal Valley: the Story of the Aberdeenshire Dee* by Fenton Wyness, and in *Farm Buildings in the Grampian Region* by Bruce Walker.

The Agricultural Survey of 1811 made two points about this zone. Referring to granite, it recorded that it was used for most local building and had also been exported to a considerable annual amount chiefly for paving the streets of London. It also emphasised its financial value and, as noted earlier declared it had 'brought gold into Aberdeen'. It was favoured in new buildings for its lustrous appearance and durability. Over one and a half centuries later the buildings are still there to show how material and the techniques associated with it have produced regional character. The choice of shades of grey colour permitted builders to contrast walls with rybats. The large square stones were frequently built with the small square stones between in 'Aberdeen Bond' (d.9,c). In the north, however, as in the New Byth and Cuminestown area, red sandstone is prominent.

In the greater part of the zone to the south, nearly 90 per cent of the houses are situated in the small villages or open country. The proportion in the north is about 71 per cent because of the greater development of the small burghs with a population of between 1,000 and 1,700. This has resulted in most buildings being detached or semi-detached, only about 11 per cent being terraced. Numerous houses with planted front gardens and parapet front walls stand at right angles to the adjoining roads.

Farms consist mainly of small steadings with the houses lying close to the offices, being of types B, C, D and E (d.8). They are built of granite or random rubble with slate roofs. Auchallater near Braemar (1) illustrates the smallest of the types. Barn Yards at Echt excmplifies a typical layout while Delgaty Castle Home Farm (1768) near Turriff (28) in Aberdeenshire represents one of the imposing large scale farms. The farms follow the solid appearance of local tradition and, when raised on a ridge, look like small fortresses with the upper window openings shuttered and the large expanses of granite walls ranging along their great lengths. However, there is room for ornamentation as at Meldrum Mains or Invermarkie with its belfry over the tall arched entrance. At Hatton Home Farm, near Turriff, the 4·2m (16′6″) high entrance, like a Roman triumphal arch, supports a great classical entablature over which an octagonal tower is completed by a dome 12·5m (49′3″) high and capped by a weather vane. In contrast to the ponderous farms, three small graceful doocots with pinnacle roofs or spirelets, stand fastidiously aside from the muscular architecture of Inverquhomery Farm near Longside in Aberdeenshire (49). At Ballindalloch in Speyside (48), the farmers kept their doves in a four-square dovecot built on the lines of a military blockhouse. Cart shed arches are rare, but the one at Nether Mains near Monymusk, is excellent.

Slate was supplied during the nineteenth century by local quarries, at Garioch in Aberdeenshire and in many parts of Banffshire, the central and southern areas providing grey and blue varieties – heavier and larger than Easdale in Argyll. These were generally laid in medium sizes and sometimes graded. Most roofs have purple or blue colours and are finished with tile ridges. The roof slopes tend to be steeper than normal to accommodate the dormer windows. Corrugated asbestos and iron roof coverings are found in some of the farm roofs.

Single leaf doors, mostly deeply panelled and sometimes partly glazed, are usually provided with a fanlight. Modern flush doors have been widely introduced into the zone, as at Insch (57). Four-paned windows are normal, but the Georgian 12-paned design has retained a good presence in the counties of Aberdeen and Kincardine. Driving rain is not a major difficulty in this area and ingoes have not been made deep. The zone excels in the beautiful oriel dormer windows prominent at Stuartfield in Aberdeenshire. No zone has a higher proportion of bay dormers set midway between eaves and ridge. Porches are not typical.

The horizontal skew-putts of Aberdeenshire (St. Combs (d.16,h)) cut in the hard granite, sometimes with a cavetto moulding as at Insch, established a strong hold in the zone. In both Aberdeenshire and Kincardineshire some of the skews have a cut back on the inner face of the skews at the end (d.16,j). In keeping with the spareness of the local style, chimney copes are plain and sharply cut. Plain chimney pots are confined mainly to the counties of Kincardine and Banff, and octagonal designs prevail in Aberdeenshire and are also employed in Banffshire.

It is worthy of note that Findochty (**21**) has unique wall colouring. In Aberdeenshire one may see the contrasts between the contrived architecture of an estate village like Monymusk (**26**) and the natural tradition of the less common older village in Scotland as at Tarves, Fintry and Udny Green.

The solid looking buildings in the zone are clear cut and the general absence of fussy projections results in knife-edge architectural geometry as sharp as the frost of an Aberdeenshire winter. The local approach to design has provided the specific basis for the shapes which relate to either the half of the vertical windows or 45° in nearly 25 per cent of the examples tested, i.e. the controlling angles are commonly about 51° to 52° rather than the window angles of $58\frac{1}{2}°$ to $59\frac{1}{2}°$. This squarer shape relates to the blocks of granite used for the walls.

The modern architectural purists would approve of the style. It adheres to the essentials of fine material, good proportion and scale, having nothing needlessly added. Because the walling material belongs to the zone, local character gains in strength. Those who wish to propagate a creed of 'fitness for purpose', combined with conservation of character, should regard the fine buildings of the zone as sermons in stone.

Zone 9   Moray, Nairn and parts of Easter Ross and of Sutherland

The zone is chiefly comprised of the counties of Moray and Nairn, and parts of Easter Ross and Sutherland. It also extends west in a fringe along the boundary with Inverness-shire to near the west end of Loch Morar (**IV**, p.156). It is the counterpart of Zone 8, the best buildings being erected in sandstone rather than granite. This material was derived from the Old Red Sandstone which also produced good soil – an auspicious conjunction for human habitation to prosper. The characteristics of the zone are fairly consistent with only some minor deviations in sub-areas shown in different hatching on the map.

In the eighteenth century, landowners here began the promotion of new villages and towns like Fochabers (**II**,p.40) and Grantown-on-Spey. These owners stipulated the layouts, distances between buildings, and their maximum heights and materials for walls and roofs. Otherwise builders determined the detailed appearance and so contributed to the essential character of the buildings, each individual consenting to conformity but not regimentation. The zest applied by the landowners in stimulating growth by town building placed a demanding obligation on quarrymen, masons, joiners and others which was met with credit and skill. The buildings they made were polished and endowed with the solid qualities which they still retain.

Although over 40 per cent of the buildings in the countryside are situated in the open country in Nairn, towns, villages and agricultural communities like crofting townships are prominent in the rest of the zone. Most buildings are detached or semi-detached, and terraced building represents only about 15 per cent of the total. Outside the villages, a front area with planting has been adopted and these areas are often protected with low stone walls. Like Zone 8, there is a high proportion of 1½-storey buildings, only about one-quarter being built to a single storey and even less to two storeys.

Because of the differences in types of agricultural land, farms change from the large and sometimes formal layout in Moray (Types C and G) (d.8), to the medium-sized steadings in Sutherland, Ross-shire and the County of Nairn with some crofting land further north as at Dornoch and Birichin (Types B, C and D) (d.8). Altyre House Farm in the north-west of Moray (**106**) shows part of an outstanding steading with an 'art nouveau' theme, an extravaganza in local terms. A more traditional approach in the courtyard farms of single storey height was to introduce a two-storey feature with pigeon loft over the arched entrance as seen at Invergordon Mains in Ross-shire. The walls were constructed of large squared stones, sometimes of granite, and they have frequently been half harled over the joints, leaving the face of the masonry half exposed. The improvement in farming introduced the local drystane dykes just over one metre high (3ft 4in) and under one metre (3ft) wide at the foot and less than ½ metre at the top (1ft 6in) and these sometimes also enclose the garden ground at the steadings.

Walls are produced in a variety of ways such as sandstone in squared-and-coursed rubble, squared coursed work, snecked rubble, random rubble, and harling (particularly in Sutherland and Ross-shire), granite in Aberdeen bond and whinstone. Colours appear in shades of grey, warm cream, and painted white. Some clay walls still survive. The masons made clean cut rybats and employed fine flat tooling techniques to produce margins and less frequently

106. Altyre House Farm, Moray

margin drafts, chamfers and ornamental work. In this area one may see a full repertoire of Scots masonry. Although the joints are generally fine and in keeping with the masonry, Cromarty contains examples of cherry-cocking (or caulking) where the stone beds and the protruding sharp points of embedded slates look like the knotted lines in the fishing nets.

Slates cover most roofs, they are small or medium in size, mostly ungraded and set to a middle or steep pitch as befits an area where dormers prevail. The shades of colour include purple, purple-blue and dark grey with only a small distribution of light grey. Clay or metal forms the ridges and some corrugated iron and diamond asbestos-cement slates have been used.

This zone has more double doors than any other. Panelling or lining has been used for their construction and a high proportion is part glazed. Fanlights are only of secondary importance. The windows are set with deeper ingoes than further south, although most are under 150mm (6in). Tooled or plain stone margins form the surrounds and four equal paned sash-and-case windows are normal. Twelve-panes rarely occur and mostly in the south and some two-paned types are found in the north. Windows tend to be larger in the south, bays being rather uncommon.

The art of designing dormer windows was particularly cultivated in this zone, as in neighbouring Banffshire. There are examples at Dallas (d.24,a) in Moray, at Rosemarkie (d.23,e) and at Hilton of Cadboll and Evanton in Ross-shire (d.22,f). Others can be found at Rheeves (**107**) and Hopeman (**39**) in Moray and at Marybank (**70**), Cromarty (**2**) and Milton (**24**) in Ross-shire. Most varieties of dormers were introduced and the stone type, as at Rheeves and Hopeman, are numerous.

107. Rheeves, Moray

The weather is drier and mild compared with zones to the north and west so that porches serve a more decorative than protective purpose as at Whitemire in Moray (d.20,d).

Stone skews are used in nearly 75 per cent of the roofs, sometimes with cavetto brackets, consoles, or carved Gothic designs at the skew putts. The older traditions in Cromarty show the authentic crowsteps (2) and narrow skews with scroll skew putts. The stone chimneyheads are surmounted by plain copes in Sutherland and Moray, some moulded types in Moray and Nairn, and splayed or blocking-and-necking types in Sutherland and Ross-shire. Plain chimney pots form the basic patterns and only in Nairn, Ross-shire and some areas of Moray were octagonal styles introduced.

The Victorian spa town of Strathpeffer (51) has one of the finest collections of Victorian houses to be found in a typical Scottish setting. Examples of Scottish-style country and suburban building introduced by emigrants during the 19th century are found in various countries, especially Canada and New Zealand. Here at Strathpeffer the process has been reversed by a returning Scot adopting a style influenced by colonial building in New Zealand for his home in the Highlands. Cromarty (114) is in an entirely different category. It has its eighteenth-century frontages, fine Victorian shop fronts and well laid out streets of which the principal one, following an ancient Scottish tradition, slightly curves and closes in upon itself to prevent the too noticeable gaps at the ends and to reduce the length of the space to apparently more appropriate limits. The value of the architecture of this zone lies in its variety and fine details. Some of it belongs to the period of Victorian romanticism, when in similar circumstances in English small towns, a strong mixture of coloured brick and wild Gothic detail was concocted to stimulate the senses at some expense of good taste.

Zone 10   Bute, Argyll, Inverness-shire and part of Dunbartonshire

The zone includes the Counties of Bute, Argyll, parishes in western Dunbarton-shire, parts of Inverness-shire, several parishes in western Perthshire and Angus. It extends from south of Ross-shire to the western seaboard of the Mull of Kintyre, nearly half the length of Scotland, and it reaches across the country to Banffshire and Aberdeenshire, including two of the largest crofting counties (IV,p.156). However, most of the land is mountainous with vast areas of rugged terrain, offering not the procreant Old Red Sandstone but the barren hard metamorphic rock.

The two major areas within this zone sub-divide it almost equally between west and east. The differences between these sub-areas are of degree rather than kind. Compared with the eastern part (vertical hatching), the western part (unhatched) to the north-west has greater ratios of thatch, large and dark grey slates for roofing, more windows with deep ingoes, shallow to medium pitched roofs, more single-storey buildings, a greater incidence of white and coloured washed walls, margins to the windows and doors and blocking-and-necking chimney copes. The eastern part has more dormers, a mixture of grey whin walls and red and yellow and yellow-green sandstone walls. The masonry is tooled, there is planting round most buildings with garden frontages, more moulded chimney copes and windows with horizontal panes.

The dispersed pattern of settlement is evident from the large number of build-ings surveyed which are situated in open country, and in the small villages and townships of about 300 houses or less, the latter representing 80–90 per cent of the sample. The small towns are few in relation to the amount of land contained within the zone and many are concentrated in the counties of Bute and Inverness. Eight new villages and towns were planned in the eighteenth and nineteenth centuries such as Aviemore and Fort Augustus in Inverness-shire, Kerrycroy in Bute and Kilmartin in Argyll, but they were all over-shadowed by Inveraray in Argyll.

Although the western part has less front gardens, either planted or left rough, more use is made of drystane or masonry walls or hedges to mark frontage boundaries. Buildings are mostly detached or semi-detached, with a slightly greater proportion of terraced groups than in the eastern part. About 20 per cent are built obliquely to the road. One and 1½-storey buildings in equal pro-

108. *Top right* Kinlochmoidart, Inverness-shire

109. *Above right* Rednock House Farm, Perthshire

portions represented about 80 per cent of the total sample surveyed.

Most farms in the western part are small, being of types A and B (d.8). Argyll farms are more stylised and usually stand among shrubs and trees, being as well attuned to the landscape of mountain and glen as may be found anywhere in Scotland. The older communal ferme touns have long been deserted, but Auchindrain in Argyll (6) has miraculously escaped total destruction and is in course of conservation. The smallest whitewashed farms in Argyll are most attractive because of their simplicity. The larger courtyard farms in Inverchaolain still retain the same hand-made qualities. Glachavoil (43) in the parish of Inverchaolain in Argyll, typifies the smaller units Kinlochmoidart Farm at Arisaig and Moidart in Inverness-shire (106) has a decorative but simple frontage of three single-storcy gables joined by walls with typical slit ventilators.

While Aberfoyle farms such as Renagour, east of Loch Ard, bear the characteristics of the western farms in the zone, the style of Rednock House Farm (109) north of the Lake of Menteith comes closer to the eastern farms with its arched entrance under a pediment and surmounted by an octagonal dome and weather vane. At Ederline Farm in Glassary, with balanced facades and archways, the loss of some degree of character is compensated for by classical qualities. A stupendous circular steading at Maam (1790) represents the pinnacle of classical folly. The half portion built produced 'five star' accommodation for cows conceived at the time when struggling tenant farmers were living in their humble buildings at the ferme toun of Auchindrain nearby (6). The second half, to provide stables, remained unbuilt so it seems that after all the horses fared worst.

The majority of stone walls in the western part are mostly painted white, either directly on stone, on harling or on rendering. The remainder have a natural finish of granite, whin or sandstone in grey or warm cream colours. Squared-and-coursed masonry, snecked and random rubble broadly represent the varied building techniques. In the south-west, such as in Bute, coloured or harled walls are built in rubble, usually being without rybats or margins. In Argyll the walls have the softened and hesitant edges dictated by the rough

110. Catlelochan, Perthshire

stones. The boundary walling techniques also include small stone rubble in Arran, the craggy heavier rubble in Bute and slabby stone with bands of vertical stone in western Argyll. In Glassary, the stone reverts to the long forms used in Dunbartonshire.

The zone was endowed with one material advantage in that the finest slates in Scotland were produced at the famous quarries at Ballachulish and Easdale. The slates were small to medium and were frequently laid in graded sizes as at Catlelochan in the vicinity of Loch Tay (110). The dark purplish-blue slates appear strongly in the north-west and in the south-west while the bluish-purple slates belong especially to the north and north-west. Dark grey are most evident in the central part of the zone and towards the north. Some light grey slate may be seen, as well as a few examples of thatch, corrugated iron, as at Glachavoil (43) or asbestos and asbestos slates. Metal ridges are widely used. Shallow to middle pitched slopes form three-quarters of the roofs. Despite the high winds, however, nearly half the roofs have projecting eaves – presumably to comply with the styles of the times when they were built.

The doors, mostly framed-and-lined and single leaved, are seldom part glazed or provided with fanlights. Some are panelled or have been replaced with flush doors. Local builders have preferred plain margins to rybats for the surrounds, and the omission of any differentiation with the walling is a recurrent theme as at Glachavoil in Argyll. About one-third of the ingoes to the windows are over 150mm (6in) deep, being a response to the more severe weather conditions. There is a mixture of four-paned windows and the Georgian 12-paned type, as well as the horizontally paned type and the fixed type. The incidence of bay windows, although few in numbers, occurs in proportions above the national average. Dormer windows are simple, generally positioned partially below the eaves, being formed in stone as at Catlelochan. Porches are common, being of interesting designs such as at Meikle Grerach in Bute (d.19,e). The stone chimneyheads, many painted or rendered, are sturdily built. They are short and finished with plain stone copes or with blocking-and-necking courses, and in many cases moulded or splayed copes are provided. Plain chimney pots are most common, supplemented in Dunbartonshire and Inverness-shire with octagonal patterns. The strong feature of the zone, open verges with purlin or barge board ends, appears throughout and the normal style of stone skew is found less than in most other zones in the country.

The eastern sub-division of the zone incorporates the transitional approach between the more stylish forms further east or in the southern parts of the west. However, some significant differences should be noted. There is a higher ratio of detached buildings, more 1½-storey examples, and it is more common for buildings to be set obliquely to the road. Painted stone and rendering give way to exposed warm cream stone which is built in squared-and-coursed or, more frequently, random rubble. The roofing consists more often of medium sized slates in purple colours.

Panelled doors with fanlights and plain margins take greater precedence and horizontal panes contribute to variety in the windows which are set less deeply in their stone surrounds. The dormers, sometimes bays, are seldom set below the eaves. The porches in the area are well composed as at Cortachy in Angus (d.20,b), at Drumguish in Inverness-shire (d.19,c) or at Highfields in Luss in Dunbartonshire (**69**).

Stone chimneyheads, left natural, have fewer moulded or splayed copes. The open skews are in many cases fitted with raised metal flashings. Farms in West Dunbartonshire, many of which are of one storey with dormered upper storeys, sometimes have margins painted in contrast to the wall colouring as at High-fields in Luss. Burn of Cambus in Perthshire (**7**) represents Scottish farms at their grandest. Bridgend to the east of Kintyre (**67**), shows the typical decorated barge boards, the metal flashings at the open skews, a diamond slate pattern on the roof and horizontal window panes. Birnam in Perthshire possesses some of the most ornamental examples of carved wooden barge boards in the zone.

It is apparent that in the remoter parts of the zone the lives of farmer and crofter moved at their own slow pace. For long they managed without change and improvement and the execution of their building was subjected to the limitations of intractable boulders, slabby stone, whin and tough granite unfit for dressing. However, these restrictions did not prevent local builders from exercising their natural aptitude for making out of such unpromising material well proportioned elevations of character. The appearance of secondary rectangles such as the $51\frac{1}{3}°$ shape, recurs to the extent that might have been more expected in the ancient buildings which preceded classical Greece than in the small cottages of this zone. Arnisdale in Inverness-shire (d.30,i) and Ardnamurchan (d.30,h) in Argyll illustrate this interesting quality.

Zone 11   Wester Ross, Cromarty and part of Sutherland

The new ideas towards the land and agriculture of the eighteenth and nineteenth centuries were in this part of the country more revolutionary than evolutionary. The well known resistance shown by the crofters was applied with the same rugged determination in their attitude to building. Many of the small houses and steadings built following this sad but heroic period were the product of their owners' own mental and physical application. As a result there is nowhere in Scotland that one may find a truer reflection of the spirit of a region.

111. Big Sand, Ross and Cromarty

Throughout most of the nineteenth century this zone remained closer to its origins that any of the others. The small crofts and fishing villages have survived despite intervention of tourism and sport in a land of mountains, straths and unspoiled colourful seashores. The planned villages of Plockton and Ullapool (**23**) also retain their original attractive settings. However, the buildings which provided humble shelter for the eighteenth-century farmers have all but disappeared. The earlier houses of the previous centuries had wattle walls finished with mud and turf and rough timber roofs supported on crucks and covered with turf, heather, straw or ferns. Of windows there were none and a door so low that a contemporary visitor observed that a man had almost to crouch on his hands and feet to enter.

When the Highlander was forced out of home to start anew, his resolve not to jeopardise his independent way of life led him to retain the form of his older dwellings while accepting new material in stone walls and coupled roofs. In 1830 the one door was still employed for both household and cattle 'the bipeds to the possession of one end of the house and quadrupeds of the other.' These 'black houses' were common in the first half of the nineteenth century. The improved 'white' cottages with fully built chimneys and windows followed in the later nineteenth century. These later houses have the thick rubble walls of massive stones with small windows and thatched roofs, but their numbers have declined in this century and the process continues. A good example can be seen at Big Sand in Ross-shire, near Gairloch (**111**). The subsequent phase of building produced long rectangular buildings with steepish roofs covered with medium or small sized blue slates, often graded and supported on thick rough rubble walls. The houses, crofts, farms and steadings are seldom terraced and mostly built with a ground floor and attic. The small windows and low lined doors retain the earlier style of large areas of walls as found at Kinnahaird in Ross-shire, near Contin (**112**).

The zone can be sub-divided into two areas in a similar fashion to Zone 10. The western part, left unhatched on the map, contains the highest ratios of buildings which are detached and confined to 1½ storeys, and the lowest ratios of two storeys. Drystone boundary walls and gardens left wild round the houses conform to the natural scenery. This is indeed crofting land, farms being of

112. Kinnahaird, Ross and Cromarty

113. *Right* Laide, Sutherland

114. *Below* Cromarty, Ross and Cromarty

types A and B (d.8). The holdings in the west consist on average of ten tenants, as may be seen around Plockton and Poolewe in Ross-shire where the common grazing lies outwith the units. In other parts the steadings are spaced at considerable distances to take advantage of the best available land, and they are not located in the manner of regularly laid-out villages. In Sutherland the crofts are set out on either side of the road as at Oldshorebeg in Eddrahillis. The traditional long narrow form of houses and buildings, illustrated at Big Sand in Ross-shire (**111**), is repeated in the later house at Laide in Durness in Sutherland (**113**). Some large farms have less simple plans. Achfary Farm in Eddrahillis extends to a two-storey steading with arched cart bays and decorative mono-pitched roof ventilators. Balchreick in Eddrahillis in Sutherland shows how these modest buildings suited the rough bare countryside. At Kirkton of Lochalsh in Ross-shire, a drystone rubble barn has the top triangular gable filled in with wattle, a traditional method of obtaining ventilation.

Over half of the walling, being built with large roughly squared stones in

115. *Top right* Balchreick, Sutherland

116. *Above right* Clashmore, Sutherland

the interior and south, has been coated with harling or rendered. Nearly half of all buildings are painted white – indeed to a greater extent than nearly anywhere else in the Scottish countryside. Medium sized dark grey slates cover the pitched roofs which tend to be steeper than elsewhere in the country. Blue Scotch slates contribute to the local character which is also marked by a high proportion of thatched and corrugated iron roofs as at Big Sand. Metal ridges are normal.

Framed-and-lined single leaf doors, with and without fanlights, are common. Some part-glazed doors have been introduced. In most instances the surrounds to doors and windows are plain, rybats and margins being unusual. Deep ingoes to the doors and windows have evidently been regarded as advisable because of the fierce exposure. Nowhere else in Scotland are there so few examples of bay windows. The windows are relatively small and the majority are divided into four equal panes, some having horizontal panes. But as in all zones, some noticeable variants occur as at Clashmore near Eddrahillis in Sutherland (116) with the later style of mullioned windows with divided upper sashes and margin surrounds. Dormer windows as at Plockton in Lochalsh (d.22,c) and at Lower Diabaig at Applecross in Ross-shire (d.23,g), set at or below the eaves, are very common compared with other zones and there is much use of rooflights. Porches are understandably a common adjunct as at Clashmore.

Stone skews were chosen by local builders in the past to protect the slates against gales as at Laide (113), at Big Sand and at Balchreick (115). Open verges are not found except in some of the later building as at Clashmore. The low heavy chimneyheads are surmounted with plain copes or blocking-and-necking styles, some examples having very thin necking courses as at Big Sand. The splayed and moulded cope, with corner margins and richly decorated pots as at Clashmore (d.13,i), form a novel contrast. Inchnadamph at Assynt in Sutherland (d.13,n) features an interesting chimney can.

The eastern part, shown in vertical hatching, has many similarities to the corresponding sub-area of Zone 10 where the influences of east and west coalesce. Compared with the western area, there are here more two-storey buildings, fewer harled walls, more random rubble, more natural stone finish in warm cream tones and a noticeable reduction in white painted walls. Thatching has seldom survived, corrugated iron appears in fewer examples and purple slates are found on roofs which mostly tend to be average in slope.

Double leaf varieties of doors with panelling make a slight variation to the predominant single leaf framed-and-lined type as at Gorstan near Contin in Ross-shire (117). The incidence of fanlights is close to the national average and rybats at both door and window openings represent a feature of the eastern part. Deep window ingoes are not so much of a requirement, and there are some bay windows, but frequent porches testify to the severity of the climate. Chimney copes are similar to those further west. Open verges supersede the plain stone skews and some barge board finishes are found. Kinnahaird in Ross-shire (112) illustrates the changes that typify the intermediate area within the zone.

The attributes described above and the 'unprofessional' look of their construction speak its own unmistakable language as much as precision building and finesse give the regional accent to the buildings in Zone 8 or 9. Whether by the lochside at Ullapool in Ross-shire (23) or against the background of

the mountains, these white buildings caught in the sunlight with sparkling slate roofs after a spring shower, and with perhaps a column of blue smoke rising from a peat fire, have an irresistible appeal.

Zone 12   Caithness and part of Sutherland

In this zone building in the open country is solid geometry, bare of even the merest architectural superimposition. For centuries the buildings, like the inhabitants, experienced hard frontier conditions far from the prosperous south. With short summers and poor climate the available economic resources had to be directed to maintaining only the essential needs. When building had achieved the standard to resist boisterous winds and long winters then practical owners did or could not ask for more. In the eighteenth and nineteenth centuries some extensions and new villages introduced the more formalised grouping of buildings. At least five new villages were then established, and Wick and Thurso were given planned extensions. However, about a quarter of the houses are located in the open countryside away from villages or towns, and this dispersed pattern has influenced the character throughout the zone.

Buildings are often seen lying angled to the road, like the examples found at Sordale Farm, north-east of Halkirk (**61**), or at Huna at Canisbay in Caithness (**118**). They are fronted by flagstone paving, rough open ground, and bordered with fences formed by vertical flagstones, drystone dykes, or post-and-wire fences. Because of the few formal villages and towns, terraced buildings are untypical. About half of the buildings consist of one-storey houses and barns, less than one-third are of $1\frac{1}{2}$-storeys, and the rest are two-storeys.

Crofts and the small farms belong to types A and B, but some larger units in Sutherland and Caithness are planned on the C or D types (d.8). Farms and croft buildings follow the style of other Highland zones, with long low single-storey houses and barns, some one-storey parts surviving where two-storey extensions have later been introduced as at Strathy Point in Sutherland (**3**). However, some tall two-storey barns can be seen as at Upper Dounreay (**119**), at Huna (**118**), and at Old Hall near Canisbay in Caithness. These agricultural buildings rank among the best, their strength of character being derived from the ease with which they recline in their settings, the unity of flagstone walls and roofs, and the fascinating texture of flagstone masonry that

117. Gorstan, Ross and Cromarty

118. *Top* Huna, Caithness

119. *Centre* Upper Dounreay, Caithness

120. *Right* Reay, Caithness

is sparingly interrupted by a few neat windows and doors. Although mostly stripped of all inessentials, some buildings do have adornments such as crow-stepped gables, a dovecot in the oldest beehive shape as at Freswick near Canisbay (**47**), a built-in cheese press as at Reay in Caithness (**120**), or a mill water-wheel as at Westerdale, south of Halkirk in Caithness. Viewing the vermiculated surface finish of the walls in a steading at Langwell in Caithness, is a unique experience for those looking for the unusual in architecture. The flagstone walls, grey with slightly yellowish or rusty red tints, are built with long stones, some being spidery and slim, others thick and solid – even around the corners and at openings as at Sordale in Caithness (**61**). Rybats are also employed in some cases as at Upper Dounreay (**119**) and at Huna in Caithness (**118**). Painting has been applied in about one-tenth of the buildings as shown at Reay in Caithness (**120**) and at Strathy Point in Sutherland (**3**). Likewise, about one-tenth of the buildings are harled.

Nearly half of the roofs are covered with medium or large sized flagstone slabs, fitted with tile or stone ridges and graded from large to small. The stone slabs lend particular distinction to parts of Caithness as at Mid Clyth and Tor-rovaich (**27**). Thatch still survives as at Strathy Point and there are cases where a large flagstone has been inserted in the thatch to permit a rooflight to be fitted into it. As is customary in the farthest parts of the north, corrugated sheeting and diamond asbestos slates have been resorted to as an alternative to thatch. Slates were imported through the small harbours round the coasts and were used in these localities, as at Castletown, where diamond shaped roof patterning with ornamental ridge tiles may be seen. Roof pitches are generally average to steep.

Framed-and-lined doors with a single leaf are common, but fanlights have been omitted. A large number of surrounds are finished with rybats and nearly

121. Watten, Caithness

as many are left without any distinction between wall and opening. The windows are generally not deep-set and tend to be small, being on average about 85mm (2ft 9¼in) wide and 1·45m (4ft 9in) high. Four equal panes are most common, with a few Georgian 12-paned windows surviving as at Castletown and Scrabster. Horizontal panes have been introduced in various parts of the zone, as at Watten in Caithness (**121**) where the unlikely plaster surrounds are equivalent to the more exuberant rococo ornamentation of Austria. Bay windows are seldom seen. Dormer windows follow the traditional stone designs but with barge board verges as at Swiney (d.23,f) and Dunbeath (d.24,f) in Caithness. Lybster has ornamental timber examples (d.22,g) and Bower tall gables (d.22,e). Bay dormers are unusual, but porches are common, being mostly simple in form. Some fine specimens occur, like that at Castletown (d.20,f).

The stone chimneys are easily recognisable, being built in flagstone with slender necking courses (d.14,g). Plain chimney cans are sometimes substituted with octagonal or ornamental varieties (d.13,l). Over half of the buildings have broad to medium width skew stones. Some open verge finishes are found, and some barge board gables appear in later buildings.

As if to compensate for the unadorned architecture of the zone, some interesting stone carving and ironwork has been produced in Castletown (d.11,c,e) and at Bower in Caithness (d.25,d). However, the uncomplicated style of buildings holds sway and it might be thought that from such simple foundations the builders would not be able to produce very well organised designs. Yet, the elevations have been composed into such sound proportioning that buildings compare favourably with those in most other parts of the country. The elevations are shaped to conform to the window rectangles, with square shapes overlying the fundamental arrangements of frontages, where expanses of stone walling are more significant because of the smaller windows. It is plain that the old builders of between two and three centuries ago may have been poor crofters but they were rich in their natural instinct for geometric proportion in design.

The Islands

One must expect the Islands to display variations in materials, form and techniques because of their differences in geology and climate. Furthermore, 675km (420 miles) as the crow flies, separate the north of Unst in Shetland from the south of Islay. This is equal to about the distance from Edinburgh to Lands End. Climate also varies over the islands. In Orkney, not the most weather beaten of the Islands, wind speeds average over 18 m.p.h. during 40 per cent of the year bringing damaging salt spray to the vegetation. In the Western Isles the climate is milder and more favourable for the growth of vegetation. Such variations in nature change building character gradually, from the rugged and tightly enclosed in the north, to the gentler and more open form in the south.

In the following text Shetland, Orkney and Lewis are discussed together. Although each displays features which are distinctly its own, the study revealed that their building traditions share common characteristics. Readers with a particular interest in Shetland and Orkney will find much of relevance in *The*

Northern Isles by Alexander Fenton. Similarly, detail in his booklet *The Island Black House*, is closely related to what follows.

Shetland, Orkney and Lewis

These Islands have few small towns or burghs, although Orkney adopts in urban terms, the same rich idiom as is found in its isolated farms. Stromness (**4**) in particular has retained its individuality perfectly and its form compares with the best in Scotland. Two-thirds of the country population live in scattered farms and separate houses and in Shetland all the countryside buildings are in small groups, villages of less than 1,000 people or isolated farms and houses set apart in the open country. In Lewis similar conditions apply. These Islands have more single-storey and detached buildings than elsewhere in the country and comparatively few dormered houses. About one-fifth of the buildings are of two storeys. Half of them have not been built parallel to a road, few have a planted garden, and any enclosure is confined to a drystone wall or post-and-wire fence. The absence of hedges in the Islands is plainly evident.

The small farms generally of type A and B (d.8), have low eaves heights, especially in the case of Shetland. At Hoswick, for example, there is the 'long-house' type of steading with thatched roof and timber chimneys. At Huxter, also in Shetland, the alternative type may be seen with the outhouses at right angles to the house. Black-houses were erected in Lewis up to the end of last century and retained as habitations until the middle of the twentieth century. The hipped roofs suited thatch and the rounded corners were slightly modified

122. South Ronaldsay, Orkney

in the newer 'white-houses' which had the massive stone chimneys built off the wallhead with angled corners. Leurbost and Crossbost in Lewis, have examples of the exposed wallheads although the set-back corrugated iron has now replaced thatch. The older beehive buildings of Lewis have been left standing at Lower Barvas. Another primitive type of farm, also in Lewis, comprises a cluster of three separately roofed but inter-communicating buildings of house, byre etc. However, anyone wishing to appreciate building in this area should focus attention on the Orkney farms as at South Ronaldsay (122). They stand in a foreground of stubble and rough grazing and a background of fields with low horizons in the wide clear light of the northern skies. There is nothing to shadow or shelter them but the low stone dykes at the front and at the ends. Stripped down to the bare elements they register on the mind like lonely statues on Easter Island.

Other kinds of buildings with local significance include the fine mills in Orkney, the horizontal water-wheel mills by the fast flowing streams and the round-ended corn drying kilns of Shetland. The flagstone walls of Orkney have the same characteristics as those in Zone 12 and are supplemented by harled rubble and painted walls. The flagstone is cut with the familiar split face and the rest of the stone is in rubble, sometimes built dry. Grey and white walls extend over most of the area in this group relieved occasionally by the warmer tan colours. The corners are normally finished plain or, less often, provided with rybats. In the older buildings in Lewis the walls may be as thick as 1·8m (6ft 0in) and stand out from the thatched roofs which rest near the inner face. The drystone walls, with round corners to deflect the wind, have large central cavities filled with turf or similar material. The top of the walls are bedded with thick turf. This cavity insulation far out-performed the modern equivalent. The builders also knew that the point where the eaves meets the outside wall is the most vulnerable part of a structure in a gale. So they wisely set back the thatched roofs for protection. The surrounding ledge at roof level served as a platform for repairs and rethatching. Inside in a wild night the crofters did not need to have fear of the furious winter's rages. They neither felt the wind nor heard it.

The light grey stone slates of medium or large size, graded and set on shallow to medium pitched roofs, have assumed an important position in the building style of Orkney and Shetland. In Lewis some slates have been imported but corrugated or felt sheeting and asbestos or felt tiles have been extensively substituted for thatch which has declined as a roofing material.

The single leaf lined doors of the area, mostly without fanlights or glazed panels are not provided with surrounds to the wall openings other than the rubble or harling. The window openings are similarly treated but, like the doors, have a greater proportion of deep ingoes than any other part of Scotland. Some fixed or casement windows have been used in place of the predominant sash and case varieties, the numbers of which, in consequence, are proportionately the lowest in Scotland. The simplicity of style has prevented the wide introduction of bay windows as at Manig in Lewis. A small portion of the windows in Orkney have 12 panes as at Stromness and on South Ronaldsay (122). The rest of the area favours four panes, suitable for the smaller scale of the fenestration imposed by the severe climate as illustrated at Lusbay in

Eday in Orkney, although a few horizontally divided examples do appear in some places. In Shetland the windows are small to the extent that to view the outside from within is like looking through the wrong end of a telescope.

The few dormers to be observed, as at Brettabister in Shetland (d.23,b), are strongly constructed and usually of stone positioned below or at the eaves. Porches are found here in higher ratios than elsewhere, and they usually have a solid protective appearance as at Clett on Whalsay in Shetland (d.19,g) and at Carloway near Uig in Lewis. However, modern types have been erected and can be seen at Lythes, South Ronaldsay in Orkney (d.20,h), and at Scalloway in Shetland.

Chimneyheads vary from stone to rendered finish and painted white, and the plain copes of Shetland and Lewis contrast with blocking-and-necking forms in Orkney and some moulded examples in Lewis. The cans are plain in Orkney and Shetland and tapered models with cowls are common in Lewis. The strong winds have led to the choice of stone skews, medium to broad at the gables with some rough crowstep finishes in Orkney.

From Harris to Barra
The next Island group which possesses common characteristics is comprised of the rest of the Outer Hebrides and Skye. The main features conform closely with those which apply in the western part of Ross-shire, the unhatched sub-area in Zone 11. The vegetation now becomes less sparse. Hedges are grown and the land round buildings is often left growing wild. There are more instances of buildings set parallel to the road and a far higher representation of two-storey and, especially, 1½-storey buildings. The flagstone of Orkney and the slabby stone of Shetland give way to igneous stone, and white

123. Dunganachy, Benbecula

painted walls become more common. Stone roofing slabs are not present and dark grey or purple-blue slates with steeper pitches and metal ridges take their place.

The doors are similar and only vary by a slight increase in the number of the two-leaved type. There are more examples of part glazing and fanlights, as well as stone framed dormer windows, as at Bailivanish in South Uist (d.22,d). The use of porches is less frequent and a greater application of harling and painting is observed in the stone chimneyheads.

124. *Right* Leamish, Barra

125. *Below* Ullinish, Skye

In Harris the older drystone random rubble walls employ stones from small 'pins' to specimens approaching in the extreme, nearly 0·5 tons as at Oban (**54**). Even in the town houses at Tarbet, the stones are comparatively large. The builders of Skye were able to draw on greater stone resources in the form of granite, marble, freestone, whin and greywacke. The colouring is more diverse, white painting contrasting with cream, and pinkish masonry. Ullinish (**125**) in Skye illustrates the still simple style, but set in less barren surroundings. Larger farm units occur among the crofts, such as two-storeyed Dunvegan with twin arched entrances and courtyard.

The very early form of construction is illustrated at Dunganachy (**123**) in Benbecula. The one-storey house with attic rooms, large and squared stonework with asbestos tiled toof and porch, indicates the dramatic effect of placing an island croft on raised ground in Leamish on Barra (**124**). Readers will find further information related to what is discussed at the end of this chapter in *Housing Improvement Surveys in Barra* by Peter Whyman. His work was concerned with the effects of housing improvements upon the integrity of local building tradition in the Islands, particularly on Barra.

From Mull to Islay

The third Island group presents even greater diversity of characteristics, Jura and Gigha having more affinity with the previous group. The climate changes for the better and with it the natural background, which is transformed from lonely and stunted leaning trees with exposed roots clinging tenaciously to the thin soil as if out of Wuthering Heights, to the tall upright trees of Mull. These influences manifest themselves in the immediate surroundings of buildings where hedges and trees are generally grown and buildings on average increase in height because of the higher ratios of two storeys. Sandstone walls are built more regularly because the stone is easier to work. In this situation cases of harled walls with stone dressings are less common. The softening of character to the south is reflected in Jura and in the architecture set in a richer vegetation as at Achamore on Gigha (**14**).

Smaller and less heavy slates, being lighter grey in colour and laid on shallow roofs with open verges and metal ridges, demonstrate the extent of change from the Islands further north. This emphasis on slate has resulted in fewer roofs being covered with thatch, corrugated sheeting or diamond shaped asbestos.

Double and panelled doors, sometimes with fanlights, become more common in this southern part, and the surrounds are occasionally distinguished from the wall face by margins. The number of deep ingoes represents a smaller proportion of the total and windows are now much larger than those in the Northern Isles. More bay windows make an appearance as do bay dormers. The dormer windows at Dervaig in Mull (d.23,d) have decorative barge boards. The less violent climate causes more people to dispense with porches. The chimneyheads are more frequently left in natural stone and some splayed and moulded copes have been used.

The individual Islands as indicated display the following very varied use of materials and techniques. Mull's freestone walls and blue Easdale slates are combined with some open verges with fretted barge boards and, although white

126. *Opposite top*
Kilchiaran, Islay

127. *Opposite bottom*
Dervaig, Mull

walls take precedence over much of these Islands, the walls left in natural stone are warmer in tone, sometimes in the pink range, so that buildings become more stylish but possess less character. The romantic style of Torosay Castle in Mull shows how a richer architecture is nurtured by a more fertile soil. Dervaig (**127**) in its pleasant setting illustrates how the southern and northern influences operate in adjacent buildings.

In Islay, further south, finishes alter again with white walls, some painted margins to the dressed stone, local and imported slate and some larger farms, in particular Kilchiaran (**126**) with a courtyard contained within a curved steading. A very decorative scheme of plaster work has been applied to a house in Ballygrant (**128**) and Bridgend contributes a uniquely designed window (d.21,n). Planned villages were established on Islay at Bowmore (**131**), Port Charlotte and Port Ellen. Ardilistry (**130**) shows the further development of stylish design, the architectural features of which have been sadly smothered in white paint. The softened environment of Bridge House (**129**) contrasts with the starkness of the landscape in the Northern Isles and reveals how buildings in the south adopt a crisp unfaltering form compared with the rough hesitancy of building in the grim surroundings of Shetland. Even in Toberonochy on Luing Island (**37**), the rough textured and painted walls and the smoother and plainly slated roofs, assume a gentler expression. Tiree, not included in this survey, is worthy of a brief mention because it contains the liveliest painted buildings in the Islands.

The appearance of the earliest buildings in the Islands, in an architectural

128. *Opposite top* Ballygrant, Islay

129. *Opposite bottom* Bridge House, Islay

130. *Above* Ardilistry, Islay

sense, was uncontrived and it might at one time have earned little respect. However, the strength of its character now disarms criticism. There are some occasions when the artistic language of a previous age has special meaning for a later generation. Many today have ceased to find anything intelligible in the high technology which has come to dominate so much of modern building. The return to 'historicism' and the decorative apparatus of styles of former times has signified that some architects, who may have formerly adopted design in advanced building technology as an end in itself, are themselves aware of the inadequacy of this approach. Yet, their alternative solutions may not carry much conviction because they have not produced reasons why a style selected from one period should have more significance than one from any other period. The indigenous houses of the Islands occupy a special position because they seem to respond to much of what is being sought for in an architecture of local character. The old houses with robust walls, rounded corners, thick chimneys and roofs set back from the face of the walls, having outlines like modern inflatables, speak in a direct vocabulary that, for Scots who are sensitive to their environment, has a special meaning.

A first sight of these houses leaves a potent image in the mind which will not be eradicated because they are suddenly new in experience and modern in the way the solution to a need was produced: logical, adequate and built to meet individual requirements. The Islands need buildings in the future which take their point of departure from the form of those buildings in the past. Buildings of the late nineteenth century did follow the scale and plan of the older buildings with some degree of success but selected harder outlines. The older buildings should now be re-appraised, and the new buildings related more to them in design so as to retrieve a measure of original character in their composition. In these older buildings the modern eye recognises that their techniques lie completely outside the technology to which by blanket legislation twentieth-century Scottish buildings have to subscribe. Yet, thoughtful modern minds must wonder whether buildings could again portray these finer shades of local quality which make them respond so well to place and use. Therein from now lies the central problem of building in the Scottish countryside.

131. Bowmore, Islay

Glossary

Apron – a length of metal, usually lead, fixed into a groove (raggle) in masonry to cover and protect a joint with a roof.

Arris (Arres) – the external corner formed where two plain surfaces meet.

Ashlar – stone shaped in rectangular blocks with fine beds and joints usually polished or finely tooled (broached) on the face.

Astragal – a sash bar for sub-dividing a window sash into smaller panes.

Barge board – timber plate, often carved, scalloped or pierced, fitted down end of open verge roof at gable to cover ends of purlins (American 'Gingerbread') (d.17,a).

Beaded – having a small projecting moulding usually rounded in section (also cockbeaded).

Bed – horizontal joint of mortar in masonry.

Beehive Dovecot (Scots 'doocot') – a dovecote circular on plan and built in stone and shaped like a beehive. Usually built with horizontal projecting rings at intervals to guard against entry of vermin (47).

Bellcast – the slight flattening of the pitch of a roof at the eaves by the insertion of a short tapered piece of timber below the slates or tiles to give a graceful finish, like the rim of a bell (38).

Blocking – the square finishing course above a cornice, or cope (d.15,f).

Bolection moulding – a joinery moulding on door or wall panel which projects beyond the face of the frame.

Boule or Bool – rounded stone used with clay for wall building. (Scottish 'bool' for Bowl or boy's marble.)

Brace – the diagonal member at the back of a framed-and-lined door to stiffen the framing and prevent sagging (d.18,c).

Broaching – the facing of stone – usually of ashlar finished with a mason's pointed chisel to give a lined finish (diagonal or horizontal).

Byre – a cow-shed or farm building for keeping cattle.

Can (Chimney Pot) – the fireclay or metal terminal on top of chimney stack at end of a flue (d.13).

Chamfer – a bevel, usually at 45° cut at a corner (d.10,c).

Cheek – the side (also called haffit). Usually the external side of a dormer window.

Cherry-Cocking or Cherrycaulking – small stone or slate filling in the beds and joints of masonry.

Chimneyhead, Chimneystack or Chimneyshaft – the part of the chimney projecting beyond a roof or gable.

Clinkstone – hard form of felspar which rings when struck.

Cockle Shells – shells of edible sea mollusc used as cheap way of producing lime by burning.

Conglomerate – rock composed of rounded fragments in a cement of hardened clay or sand.

Cope or Coping – top course of masonry on wall or chimneyhead.

Cottar – farm labourer in the eighteenth and nineteenth centuries who held a house and a portion of land which was tilled by the farmer.

Couple Rafter – e.g. coupled roof – a roof supported by pairs of rafters.

Coursers – squared stones, usually with roughly dressed faces laid in courses (d.9,b).

Crowstep or Corbiestep – stepped ends on top of stone gable taking the place of a sloping cope on a skew. (d.16,a,b).

Cruck – a timber roof support consisting of a short upright post continued on top with a sloping rafter (or steeple): sometimes in one piece as cut from a tree or elaborately jointed and fixed with wooden pegs. The ends of the cruck in Scotland were usually set upon stone ledges in the wall about 300mm (1ft) above floor level. The crucks were set at about 1·80–3·0m (6ft–10ft) centres supporting rough purlins above.

Dormer – a window partly or wholly fitted in sloping roof giving light to rooms formed partly or wholly in roof space.

Double-gauge Lap – laying of slate whereby at each nail hole there are three layers of slate and elsewhere two layers. Normal practice in roofs of houses and public buildings as compared with byres where single lap open slating was often employed.

Dovecote or Doocot – pigeon house or loft either in a separate building or incorporated in the roof or gable of a building.

Drip – a projecting member on wall of stone or timber designed to throw surface water clear of wall or joint below.

Drove – to dress the face of stone by forming incised scores or lines either horizontally or diagonally.

Drystone or Drystane – masonry wall built without mortar.

Dyke – a stone wall built without mortar, e.g. drystane dyke.

Ferme toun or Farm town – farm managed by joint tenants, 8–12 families each provided with a house, kail-yard (vegetable patch), barn or byre, communally managed arable land and hill summer pastures (Sheilings) cf. Auchindrain.

Feu – a perpetual ground lease for which an annual feu-duty was paid to the landowner (superior) by the tenant.

Feuar – a tenant or leaseholder of land.

Feu-ferme – cash transaction for land holding sometimes embodying a large initial down payment or 'grassum' along with an annual payment of feu duty.

Fielded Panel – a panel with a sunk edge cut round the perimeter so that the centre of the panel projects. The sunk edge may slope slightly and form a mitre at each corner.

Fillet – a small flat section used as part of a large moulding or as a cover piece of joint, e.g. a triangular fillet being a triangular flashing of cement and lime and sand.

Finial – the ornament at the apex of a gable in stone (d.11,a), timber (d.24,f) or iron (d.25,c).

Flagstone – sandstone capable of splitting into hard flat stone slabs, found principally in Caithness, Angus and Orkney.

Flashing – a metal cover (lead or zinc) formed as in an apron. A triangular fillet of cement, lime and sand formed over a joint between masonry and slates or tiles.

Forestair – the external stair usually at the front of a house leading to a separate flat at the upper floor, being common in the Lothians and Fife (16).

Framed-and-Lined Door – a door faced with lining boards and framed round the top and sides and sometimes the bottom with timber rails and stile (d.18,c).

Freestone – stone without pronounced laminations.

Furze – gorse or whin (bot.).

Gable – the end wall of a building.

Glebe – arable land, about five acres, attached or near to a parish minister's manse (house) given to him as a supplement to his stipend (annual salary).

Granite – hard igneous rock of crystalline texture capable of a high polish.

Graywacke or Greywacke – grey gritty hard sandstone.

Grieve – a farm overseer or steward. A tenant of a small farm acting also as manager of the landowner's farm, i.e. the 'home' or 'mains' farm.

Harle, Harl or Roughcast – to cover the external face of a stone wall with two or three coats of lime, or lime and cement, mixed with sand and small aggregate, the final coat being cast or thrown on.

Hipped – a sloping end to a gable to provide a pyramid-shaped end instead of a pointed gable. Seldom prominent in Scotland before 1914 (**29**).

Ice-house – an underground store for preserving winter ice and snow for use in preserving food in summer, especially fish.

Inband – the short header stone in rybats (d.10,1).

Ingo – the side face of the wall at a door or window opening.

Jamb – the side of an opening (as in ingo) or of a fireplace.

Joint – in masonry walls, the vertical joints between the stone or bricks.

Kerb or Curb – the edge stone on a pavement or round a planting plot of ground. Made of stone, whin, granite or concrete.

Kneeler – part of a skew or gable coping usually situated about half way up the slope and bonded into the masonry of the gable for strength to prevent slipping of the skew stones.

Laird – landowner with tenanted houses and farms.

Lectern – applied to dovecots. The late form of freestanding dovecot rectangular on plan and with a one-way sloping roof and thus shaped like a lectern.

Limestone – rock with a carbonate of lime constituent, not plentiful in Scotland and usually exploited for extracting lime for farming or mortar and not for limestone building.

Lintel – the beam over a door or window opening, usually of stone in Scotland prior to 1914, but in early country building timber lintels were also employed especially on the inner side of an opening.

Lock-rail – a middle horizontal rail on a panelled or lined door set at a height convenient to the placing of the lock and door knob (d.18,1).

Marble – metamorphosed limestone capable of high polish – rare in Scotland and used only for highly decorative interior work.

Margin – flat border round a door or window or at the corner of a building mostly worked on the stone, sometimes slightly projecting over the face of the wall. Usually finished in polished ashlar face or with tooled finish. Not moulded (d.10,e,n).

Margin Draft – finish of surface at edge of stone corner, tooled or polished in contrast to rest of face. Usually narrow, about 1in–1½in (25–37mm) (d.10,g).

Mason's Mitre – 45° angle formed by the meeting of a splay or moulding at a corner cut on the stone and not formed by a joint as in a Joiner's mitre (d.10,c).

Meeting rail – the part of a sash-and-case window where the top of the bottom sash meets the bottom of the upper sash. Diagonally checked to prevent draughts.

Mid-rail – similar to lock rail but may be more than one on panelled door (d.18,i).

Mort-house – a cemetery building holding the hand vehicle (or hearse) on which the coffin was placed for funerals.

Muntin – central vertical frame on a panelled door (d.18,1).

Necking – the projecting moulding separating a column from the capital. A projecting moulding separating the chimney stack from the cope or blocking course (d.15,f).

Nib – a small projection on a wall. The small projection on the back of a roof tile which lies over the top of the tiling batten to prevent slippage.

Ogee – a moulding in stone, joinery or plaster consisting of two reverse curves like the letter S.

Ogival – shaped like an ogee moulding as in a roof to a turret.

Oriel – a projecting bay window on an upper floor (d.23,e).

Orpiment or Orpanent – gold coloured pigment used in lime washing of walls; prominent in seventeenth and eighteenth centuries in mid-Scotland and Northern England and made from sulphide of arsenic.

Outband – the face of a rybat or quoin which is long as compared with the return on the adjacent face inband (d.10,1).

Parish – the name given to the sub-division of a county. Formerly used as the statistical basis of population enumeration etc.

Piend – the joint between the faces of a hipped roof.

Platt – landing on a staircase or the flat area at a front door formed by a square stone flag. The landing at the top of an outside stair leading to an upper floor house or flat – hence 'platties', the name given to such flats in Dundee.

Polished (Ashlar) – the stone surface tooled to a fine smooth finish in close grained stone.

Porphyry – a rock consisting of feldspar crystals embedded in a compact groundmass, of dark red or purple and found in some Highland areas.

Pots – chimney cans (d.13).

Purlins – timber members used in carpentry spanning horizontally across the roof couples or trusses to carry the roof boarding.

Putts or Clubstones – a skewputt, the lowest stone at the foot of a skew built into the wall below for strength. Sometimes moulded or decorated (d.16,f).

Rail – the horizontal framing on a panelled or framed-and-lined door or on window sashes, as well as ledges on lined doors.

Reveal – the return face of an opening (ingo) at a window or door.

Roll – a moulding circular in section such as the roll finish on a ridge tile (d.13,r); the roll formed by a joint on metal roofing.

Roup – a sale by auction.

Rubble – rough undressed or partially dressed stonework.

Rybat – a quoin stone, a dressed stone used in forming corners at openings or at the corner of a building (d.10,1).

Sandstone – sedimentary rock composed chiefly of fine grains of sand of a quartz variety. Where it is formed in laminations, it must be built with those laminations in their natural position, i.e. horizontally or 'on bed' to prevent the stone from splitting. Where this precaution has been omitted the stone is said to be built 'on cant' and splitting of the face usually follows.

Sarking – the rough timber sheeting or boarding laid over rafters on which the roof covering is fixed. Scottish from 'sark' – a shirt.

Sash-and-case – vertically sliding sash window with side cases in which the balancing weights are suspended from ropes or chains.

Scallop – edge decoration especially on barge boards, but in a series of circular segments, as on a scallop shell.

Schist – a fissile rock of igneous origin.

Scribe – to cut a finishing timber to fit over a moulding instead of mitring such as at astragal joints.

Seating – a dressed top on masonry prepared for building above as at the end of a sill when it is built into the wall.

Sheiling (Sheilin) – periodically occupied shelter for shepherds used at summer grazings.

Sill – the stone finishing to the foot of a window. The bottom member of a timber sash-and-case or casement window.

Skew – the raking top of a gable projecting above the roof surface. See Putts (d.16,c).

Skirt – in roofing, the lower courses of slates laid along the eaves and exposed prior to the commencement of the first row of pantiles (31).

Sneck – a small stone built into a rubble masonry wall to fill a gap and achieve a level bed to receive the next course above (d.9,e).

Soaker – a lead piece fitted across a piend at the same intervals as the slates and fixed under the slates to prevent water penetration at the mitres. Also used on rare occasions where slates in a lower roof abut the gable of a higher roof.

Square necked or Squared-and-snecked rubble – rubble masonry built with header stones through the wall, stretchers on the surface and snecks to allow frequent breaking of the horizontal beds (d.9,e).

Start – a tall vertical stone, sometimes built in cant (see sandstone), employed at the sides of door and window openings usually in late Victorian building in conjunction with tails or tie stones (d.10,h).

Steading – the farm buildings such as barns, byres, cart houses, stables etc. and sometimes including the farm house.

Stile or Style – the vertical member of a panelled or framed door or window sash or window case.

Stop – the plate placed on door stiles and lintels against which a door is closed.

Stop-chamfer – the splayed finish at the end of a chamfer in masonry (d.10,d).

Strap – a long flat timber piece such as that used for fixing pantiles on a roof or for fixing lead on a flashing or in producing a level surface for lath in a plaster wall (a brander).

Tail – a single rybat at a stone door or window opening used in conjunction with a start to provide a bond with the adjacent masonry (d.10,h).

Tenon – a thin projection at the end of a timber frame cut to fit a mortice on a second frame to provide a traditional timber joint.

Tifting – the pointed ends of the slates, sometimes with small pieces of slate inserted, at an open verge, designed to tilt the slates up to prevent rain water running down the gable.

Timpan – gable built above wallhead at front of building to support chimney and increase attic floor space (98).

Torch – to point with mortar the vertical joints of pantiles, mostly from the underside, to prevent ingress of rain or snow.

Trap – a hard igneous rock.

Tuber Basket – a wicker basket.

Turnpike – circular staircase with central stone newel.

Upstand – an element rising vertically above a horizontal flat area such as a roof.

V-jointed – the jointing on lining boards where the vertical edges of each board are chamfered to provide a v-shaped groove at each joint. Such boards are normally jointed using a tongue in one side and a groove in the other on each board so that the tongues fit into the grooves.

Verge – a projecting plate at the foot of a door designed to cast rain water running down the face of a door away from the foot and the threshold step.

Verge – the top of a gable wall without a skew, i.e. the roof covering extending over the wallhead to its outside surface.

Wallhead – the top of the wall on which the roof rests.

Wattle – partition built of vertical timber poles with tree branches or similar material woven through. Sometimes covered with clay and known also as 'rice'.

Whin or Whinstone – various types of stone, usually diorite, noted for their hard impervious composition and difficulty for working. Also known as greenstone.

Bibliography

O. C. Bailey and M. C. Tindall, *Dovecotes of East Lothian*, in Transactions of Ancient Monuments Society, New Series Vol XI, 1963.

Lord Belhaven, *The Countryman's Rudiments*, 1699.

Board of Agriculture, *General View of the Agriculture of the County of –, by various authors, 1794–1814*.

R. W. Brunskill, *Illustrated Handbook of Vernacular Architecture*, 1971

R. W. Brunskill, *Traditional Buildings of Britain*, 1981.

R. Callander, *Drystane Dyking in Deeside*, 1982.

R. H. Campbell and A. S. Skinner (Ed), *The Origins and Nature of the Scottish Enlightenment*, 1982.

J. D. Dunbar, *The Historic Architecture of Scotland*, 1966.

A. Fenton and B. Walker, *The Rural Architecture of Scotland*, 1981.

A. Fenton, *Scottish Country Life*, 1976.

A. Fenton, *The Northern Isles: Orkney and Shetland*, 1978.

A. Fenton, *Clay Building and Clay Thatch in Scotland*, 1970.

A. Fenton, *The Island Black House*, 1978.

D. Fraser, *Discovering East Scotland*, 1974.

S. Hackett and N. Livingston, *Scottish Parliamentary Churches and their Munses*, Studies in Scottish Antiquity, 1984

Inspector of Mines, *List of Quarries*, 1895 onwards.

Lord Kames, *The Gentleman Farmer*, 1776.

M. Lindsay, *Lowland Scottish Villages*, 1980.

D. G. Lockhart, *Scottish Village Plans: A Preliminary Analysis*, in Scottish Geographical Magazine, Vol 96 No 3, December 1980.

G. Meiklejohn, *The Settlements and Roads of Scotland*, 1927.

P. McNeill and R. Nicholson (Ed), *An Historical Atlas of Scotland, (c. 400–1600)*, 1975.

C. McWilliam, *The Buildings of Scotland: Lothian except Edinburgh*, 1978.

C. McWilliam, *Scottish Townscape*, 1975.

W. H. Murray, *The Islands of Western Scotland*, 1973.

H. Petzsch, *Architecture in Scotland*, 1971.

N. T. Phillipson and R. Mitchison (Ed), *Scotland in the Age of Improvement*, 1970, (Chapter by T. C. Smout on Landowners and Planned Villages in Scotland).

G. L. Pride, *Glossary of Scottish Building*, 1975.

J. M. Robinson, *Georgian Model Farms: A Study of Decorative and Model Farms in the Age of Improvement*, 1983.

R. Scott Morton, *Traditional Farm Architecture in Scotland*, 1976.

T. C. Smout, *A History of the Scottish People 1560–1830*, 1969.

First Statistical Account of Scotland, *c.* 1790.

Second Statistical Account of Scotland, *c.* 1845.

J. Stirling-Maxwell, *Shrines and Homes of Scotland*, 1937.

N. Tranter, *The Fortified House in Scotland*, Vols I–V, 1962–70 (New Edition 1977).

B. Walker, *Clay Buildings in North-East Scotland*, Scottish Vernacular Building Working Group, 1977.

B. Walker, *Farm Buildings in the Grampian Region*, 1979.

T. W. West, *A History of Architecture in Scotland*, 1969.

P. Whyman, *Housing Improvement Surveys in Barra*, 1974.

I. Whyte, *Rural Housing in Lowland Scotland in the 17th Century*, Scottish Studies, 1975.

R. Wittkower, *Architectural Principles in the Age of Humanism*, 1949.

S. Wood and J. Patrick, *History in the Grampian Landscape*, 1982.

F. Wyness, *Royal Valley: The Story of the Aberdeenshire Dee*, 1968.

Index

Maps and drawings are set in italic type

Photographic illustrations are in bold type, and indexed under plate number: not page number